Turkey and Europe

Turkey and Europe

Edited by
Canan Balkır and Allan M. Williams

Pinter Publishers Ltd
London and New York

Distributed exclusively in the USA and Canada by **St. Martin's Press**

Pinter Publishers Ltd
25 Floral Street, Covent Garden, London, WC2E 9DS, United Kingdom

First published in 1993

Distributed Exclusively in the USA and Canada by St. Martin's Press, Inc., Room 400, 175 Fifth Avenue, New York, NY10010, USA

British Library Cataloguing in Publication Data
A CIP record for this book is available from the British Library

ISBN 1 85567 012 7

Library of Congress Cataloging-in-Publication Data
Turkey and Europe / edited by Canan Balkır and Allan M. Williams.
    p.   cm.
    Includes bibliographical references and index.
    ISBN 1–85567–012–7
    1. Turkey—Relations—Europe. 2. Europe—Relations—Turkey.
  3. Turkey—Foreign economic relations—Europe. 4. Europe—Foreign economic relations—Turkey. I. Balkır, Canan. II. Williams, Allan M.
D1065.T8T87 1993
303.48′256104—dc20   92–41816
                                                              CIP

Typeset by Florencetype Ltd, Kewstoke, Avon
Printed and bound in Great Britain by Biddles Ltd of Guildford and King's Lynn

Contents

List of contributors

Feride Acar — Department of Public Administration, Middle East Technical University, Ankara, Turkey

Türkkaya Ataöv — Department of International Relations, Ankara University, Ankara, Turkey

Canan Balkır — European Community and International Economic Relations Research Centre, Dokuz Eylül University, Izmir, Turkey

Atila Eralp — Department of International Relations, Middle East Technical University, Ankara, Turkey

Şükrü S. Gürel — Faculty of Political Science, Ankara University, Ankara, Turkey

Ayşe Kadioğlu — Department of Political Science and Public Administration, Bilkent University, Ankara, Turkey

Gülten Kazgan — Department of Economics, University of Istanbul, Istanbul, Turkey

Allan M. Williams — Centre for European Studies, University of Exeter, UK

Part One
Introduction

1
Introduction: Turkey and Europe

Canan Balkır and Allan M. Williams

Reassessing relationships

Turkey's relationships with Europe are long-rooted whether looked at in terms of trade, military power, culture or diplomacy. These have not always been easy relationships, but they have been critical in shaping the evolutions of Europe and European states, as well as of Turkey itself. Neither symmetry nor constancy has characterised these ties, and the alliance between Turkey and Europe has taken many unexpected turns even in the mid-and late-twentieth century. Moreover, events in the late 1980s and the early 1990s have, once again, made it necessary to reassess these relationships. Turkey's position in the world economic and political order has been changing at the same time as Europe has been radically reconstructed. Turkey's economic growth, its application for full membership of the European Community, the Gulf Crisis, the break-up of the Soviet Union, the 'new Balkans crisis', developments in Cyprus and the recharting of political and economic spaces in Western Europe have all been instrumental in reshaping the Turkey–Europe relationship as well as exposing it to greater popular scrutiny in Europe.

Turkey's remarkable economic growth, averaging 4.7 per cent per annum in the 1980s, has made this one of the more dynamic economies in the region. Increased openness in trade and investment (including privatisation) has exposed it to greater tensions in external economic relationships. This was highlighted by the 1987 Turkish application for full membership of the European Community, a decision on which was deferred until at least 1992 following a discouraging preliminary assessment by the Commission of the EC. Nevertheless, Turkey's economic links with the Community are and will be subject to change irrespective of the eventual outcome of the application for membership. Turkey is already committed to completing a customs union by 1996, thereby fulfilling one stage in a process of economic integration which was initiated by the 1963 Ankara agreement. Moreover, the creation of the European Economic Space between the EC and EFTA will probably lead to a reorientation of European trade. The precise implications for Turkey are not known, but it is significant that the EFTA countries have agreed to contribute to a compensation fund for the Mediterranean member states; non-member states, such as Turkey, are excluded from this programme.

Other events have also necessitated a reassessment of Turkey's relationships with Europe. The Gulf crisis underlined the extent of American military hegemony, while it also emphasised the key role of Turkey in the Middle East. Turkey, for so long conceptualised by military strategists as a bulwark of Western defence against the military power of the Soviet Union, is now being reassessed as a critical hinge in relationships between Europe and what is seen as a volatile Middle East. At the same time, the disintegration of the Soviet empire and, latterly of the Commonwealth of Independent States, has created an economic and military vacuum in the southern part of the old Soviet Union. This cannot be filled by Russia alone, while several of the central and southern Asian republics are suspicious of such alliances with the historic imperial power. A number of countries — including Iran and Saudi Arabia — are vying to establish their influence among these newly independent states. Turkey is at the forefront in creating these new networks of international relationships and has been seeking to establish a pivotal role in relation to the Turkic republics. It has also been the prime mover behind the Black Sea Economic Co-operation Region agreement. Elsewhere in Eastern and Central Europe, ethnic and cultural divides are leading to increasing tensions and instability within the region. This is epitomised most dramatically by the violent break-up of Yugoslavia, but it is not the only point of political flux. Turkey, in contrast, is increasingly seen to be a zone of territorial stability in the midst of these crises, despite the unresolved Kurdish question.

Western Europe is also being reconstructed. The prime focus is the European Community where there has been a major economic reorganisation following the Single Market programme. The Maastricht agreement has also pointed the way to greater political and social integration, as well as monetary and economic union, although the eventual outcome of this is uncertain. These actual and potential institutional changes have released centripetal forces, drawing a number of applications for membership from the EFTA countries in the early 1990s. The eventual membership of some of the former Eastern-bloc countries is also being contemplated, with Hungary, Poland and Czechoslovakia having been offered a special association agreement in December 1991. This has given rise to a discussion of whether — and if so how — EC institutions can be remodelled to meet these new demands. This is often dichotomised — somewhat simplistically — as the 'widening versus deepening' debate. The result is that the very nature of the Community, which Turkey has formally applied to join, is changing, as well as the rules of membership.

The aims of this book are to reassess Turkey's relationships with Europe in the context of the evolving new world and macro-regional orders. In order to place this in perspective, it is necessary to examine the evolution of these relationships during the post-1945 period. This is the objective of the following section. To simplify what are necessarily complex series of events, we have adopted a threefold periodisation: 1945–74, 1974 to the late 1980s, and the late 1980s through early 1990s. Within each of these periods we have identified what we consider to be the salient features of economic and political changes at three different levels: the global, the European, and the Turkish. The underlying themes are the changing internal–external balance of the Turkish economy and the mutual defence needs of Turkey, the United States and Europe. However, there is no claim that political and economic changes at these disparate levels all fit comfortably into the simple threefold periodisation. Indeed, it is the lack of synchronisation between these different processes of change at different levels which is the key to understanding the relationship between Turkey and Europe.

Economic and political isolation at a time of global expansion and integration

In the 1930s the Atatürk government formulated a new economic strategy that gave the state a dominant role in Turkey's economic development. This was based on two five-year industrial plans, establishing new state banks charged with leading investment roles, and the nationalisation (with compensation) of foreign interests. The latter brought the mines, transport and other principal forms of infrastructure into public ownership. Celasun and Rodrik (1989, p. 619) consider that 'Turkey's government-led industrial drive in the 1930s was quite successful in resource mobilization, and generated growth and considerable structural change in output'. It was certainly true that major investment projects were implemented within the framework of the first industrial plan, 1934–8, but the attempt to implement a second plan, 1938–44, was severely disrupted by the Second World War. Even more fundamental was the fact that state intervention was limited to industrialisation, but even in this sector, 'it could not account for all factors of production' (Barkey 1990, p. 48).

Agriculture was initially ignored because 'the application of Etatism was ad hoc, concentrating solely on creation of an industrial base' (Barkey 1990 p. 48). In the 1950s agriculture was to gain in importance under the Democratic Party (DP), not least because the latter's main support was essentially rural. The DP's agricultural policies included a large-scale mechanisation programme, the elimination of agricultural taxes, high minimum prices offered by state buying agencies and extensive rural road construction in order to improve marketing opportunities. As a result there was a steep rise in agricultural output in the early 1950s (up to the disastrous harvest of 1954) which contributed to the rapid expansion of the economy (Celasun and Rodrik 1989, p. 620).

Although there was an upward trend in growth from the 1930s, it was 1946 which proved to be a major turning point in Turkey's modern political and economic development. This was the year in which Turkey decisively entered the Western camp, as part of a strategic alliance against communism and national liberation struggles in the Middle East (see Keyder 1987 for a discussion of this period). It was also the year in which the Democratic Party broke away from the Republican People's Party. This was the position of Turkey at the start of the first of the three periods considered here.

In the first period, American hegemony was undoubtedly the dominant force at the global level. The stability provided by American influence, and the new framework provided by the Bretton Woods international monetary system, allowed for rapid growth in output. Trade increased even more rapidly than production, underlining the increasing internationalisation of economic activity. Trade expanded at a rate of more than 7 per cent per annum in 1958–63 and by more than 8 per cent in 1963–8. Foreign direct-investment growth rates also outstripped those of output, approximately doubling during the 1960s (Julius 1990). While the United States was the dominant economic power at this time, there was already evidence of economic recovery in Europe, the reconstruction of Japan's industrial strength and the early emergence of the Newly Industrialising Countries. These economic changes provided a potential demand stimulus for Turkish economic growth, although in the 1960s the country was not necessarily best placed to benefit from this. The changes also provided a potential increase in competition in international markets.

The global political scene was largely shaped at this time by the United States and especially by the Cold War. The establishment of NATO as an American–European mutual defence organisation symbolised the lack of independent European options. Defence strategies were conceived of largely in terms of containment. Turkey was soon drawn into the containment strategy. This was facilitated by the financial assistance for economic development and the arms provided by the United States after 1947. More directly, Turkey became an active participant in the Korean War; this underlined its commitment to the Western alliance, which was recognised by the Truman Doctrine (1947). Perhaps of even greater significance was Turkey's membership of NATO after 1952.

While the United States was the leading player in economic and political affairs, Europe's role increased through the 1950s and the 1960s. These were the years of the long economic boom as both investment and consumption levels recovered and then expanded rapidly. By the end of the 1950s, the European trade deficit with the United States had already been reversed. Thanks to the favourable global context, to technological advances, and to the ability of Europe to draw in labour from the Mediterranean basin (including Turkey) and former European colonies, there was unparalleled, sustained economic growth (see Williams 1987, ch. 1).

Economic reorganisation in Europe — based on internationalisation — was symbolised by the creation of the European Economic Community and, to a lesser extent, by the European Free Trade Area. Turkey signed an association agreement with the EC as early as 1963. But the EC and EFTA were only two of the more successful outcomes of a series of attempts to establish integrationist institutions during the 1950s. Among some of the more far-reaching failures were the non-adoption of the proposed European

Defence Community and the European Political Community. As a result, Europe remained very much a supporting player to the United States on the world political stage.

Meanwhile, the Cold War ensured that Eastern and Central Europe were locked economically and politically into dependence on the Soviet Union. While Turkey did have relations with these countries, these were limited. In effect, therefore, a territorial divide emerged between Turkey and northern Europe which geographically distanced it from the centre of European capitalist development, even if also increasing Turkey's strategic importance.

Turkey's development in the period after 1945 has been alluded to previously. At that date it had already experienced two decades of growth which had resulted in a marked increase in development levels. For example, between 1938 and 1948 the number of schools more than doubled, bank deposits increased threefold, and the labour force doubled. However, between 1940 and 1945 'Turkey could not escape the devastating economic effects of the external environment and faced severe commodity shortages, black markets, and high inflation' (Celasun and Rodrik 1989, p. 619). The result was a significant income decline in Turkey, reinforcing the country's dependence on the United States. This was formally recognised when Turkey was brought into the Marshall Aid programme in 1948; the specific objective was to increase production to the point where food and raw materials could be supplied to Western Europe. This strategy allocated Turkey a particular role in the international division of labour which was rather similar to that of the European colonies at that time. It is a strategy which also partly explains the policy shift away from the headlong industrialisation of the 1930s and increased emphasis on agriculture.

Turkey's economy had the potential to benefit from the internationalisation of economic activity after 1945. The first three years of Democratic Party rule (1950–3) were characterised by high growth rates, helped by the favourable international trade conditions created by the Korean War. The latter partly stimulated a surge in agricultural production and primary exports. However, there was a disastrous crop failure in 1954, and GNP growth fell to only 4 per cent per annum, half that recorded in 1948–53 (Celasun and Rodrik 1989, p. 620). During the 1950s increasing economic difficulties emerged, notably high inflation, trade deficits and foreign-exchange crises. The International Monetary Fund came to the rescue in 1958 with a package of external financial assistance and debt consolidation, but its assistance was also tied to a programme of structural reforms including reduced public expenditure.

The Menderes (Democratic Party) government had initially set out a programme of economic liberalisation but by the late 1950s had become relatively inward-looking. Trade restrictions, tariff protectionism and encouragement of import-substitution industrialisation were the order of the day (see Celasun and Rodrik 1989). The Industrial Development Bank of Turkey partly encouraged this shift in order to reduce imports in the face of rising consumption levels. However, as Barkey (1990, pp. 53–4) emphasises, 'these efforts at substitution were not the result of the government's clearly thought out and executed policy decisions, but rather a reaction to the changes in the internal economic conditions as well as foreign exchange difficulties experienced after 1953'. The newly elected Democratic Party government in 1950 had also emphasised greater encouragement of the private sector, but in practice this was 'never more than token' (Goodman 1976, p. 17).

In 1960 there was a military takeover, and the new rulers – with the encouragement of the Organisation for Economic Cooperation and Development (OECD) – reinstituted the pre-1945 system of five-year plans which were now extended to the economy as a whole, under the aegis of the State Planning Organisation. These plans were indicative for the private sector but provided a compulsory framework for the public sector. Import-substitution industrialisation (ISI) was the main vehicle for economic development in the 1960s. Barkey (1990) has shown how this was promoted by parts of the manufacturing sector, the military and civilian bureaucracies, and the intelligentsia; the weakness of the export sector and the chronic balance-of-payments' problems of the 1950s also favoured import substitution. These plans 'had a significant impact because they institutionalized ISI as the official development strategy' (p. 66).

Economic recovery, at first, was slow, but it took off after 1963 aided by two successive good agricultural harvests. The GDP per-capita growth rate increased steadily and over the 1960s averaged 3.1 per cent, boosted by a net inflow of foreign capital funds, including the growth of emigrant remittances as Turkish workers responded to labour shortages in the booming economies of Northern Europe.

The Turkish economy in 1973–4, at the time of the first oil crisis, was vastly different from that which had required American aid in 1948. Yet there was still an enormous gap between economic and social conditions in Turkey and other Southern European countries. For example, Turkish GNP per capita in 1973 was only $600, little more than one-half of Portugal's and one-third of that in Greece. Turkey also consistently came bottom of all the rankings of Mediterranean European countries in literacy, health care and consumer goods. Additionally, there was a serious infrastructure deficit which would remain to challenge future governments.

While some economic trends can be observed in Turkey over the 1950–74 period, political life was characterised by sharp discontinuities. The major turning points were the election of the Democratic Party in 1950 and the military interventions of 1960 and 1971. Domestic politics therefore were characterised by acute instability; there were also shifts, if not discontinuities, in Turkey's international relations. Brown (1988, p. 71) argues that 'Early in 1945, the Soviet Union reasserted its historic expansionist aims against Turkey; coupled with the British retreat from the eastern Mediterranean region, this Soviet action gave birth to the alliance between Ankara and Washington, as outlined by the Truman doctrine in 1947'. Even if the Cyprus crisis did lead to some cooling of relations with the United States, Turkey remained closely allied to the West during this period. Indeed, to some extent Turkey's relations with the EC were shaped by the need for an alternative to, sometimes strained, relations with the United

States. Events in the early 1990s demonstrated that the inverse relationship is also to be observed.

In summary, it can be argued that developments in Turkey, while of course influenced by events in Europe and elsewhere, were to some extent not synchronised with these during this period. At a time of unrivalled internationalisation of economic activities in the capitalist world, Turkey's economic policies remained inward looking. At a time of democratic consolidation in northern Europe, Turkey was twice subject to military interventionism. There were of course military or dictatorial governments in power in Portugal, Spain and Greece during all or part of this period. However, whereas the economies of these countries did at least decisively internationalise and industrialise during the 1960s and early 1970s, Turkey's economic as well as its political construction remained differentiated from that of Northern Europe. The economic implications were particularly acute. There were relatively high growth rates in Turkey in both the 1950s and the 1960s, but it remained substantially closed to world trade at the very time that international conditions were most favourable to growth and integration. However, this was also the period in which Turkey's strategic alliance with the West, especially the United States, was forged, born out of the strategic dictates of the Cold War.

Military intervention and internationalisation at a time of global economic crisis

By the late 1960s, at the start of our second period, global economic conditions were already deteriorating as the international monetary system began to break down. There was also the rising challenge of the newly industrialising countries, especially the four Asian tigers, as well as the decisive emergence of Japan as a global industrial power. Dicken (1992, p. 23) writes that 'in 1963 Japan ranked fifth in the world [industrial] league table; by 1987 it had risen to second place on the basis of extremely high annual growth rates . . . By 1987, therefore, Japan's share of world manufacturing production had increased from 5.5 per cent in 1963 to 19.4 per cent.' By the 1980s, it was possible to refer to the world economy as being multi-polar and as being dominated by a 'triad' (Ohmae 1985) of mega economic powers: North America, Western Europe and Japan.

There was already growing economic uncertainty and slow-down even before the 1973–4 oil crisis delivered a severe recessionary and inflationary shock to the global economic system. There was slow recovery from this crisis through the latter 1970s before the second oil price rise in 1979 led to a further recessionary trough. The average growth rate in the OECD group of countries fell precipitously from 3.3 per cent in 1979 to −0.5 per cent in 1982. There were also clear differences in the responses of the major economic powers to the crisis. Growth rates in Japan hardly faltered, while those in Western Europe and the United States fell sharply. However, by the end of 1981 growth rates in the United States were recovering and unemployment was falling. In contrast, sustained economic recovery throughout

Western Europe arguably did not begin until the mid-1980s (Williams 1987, pp. 49–50). By the late 1980s, therefore, there was a return to expansionary global economic conditions; however, conditions were now very different to those pertaining prior to the 1970s. There was a far greater degree of uncertainty, related to the breakdown of the Bretton Woods international monetary system, and there was also growing concern about the long-term structural problems of the American economy and the competitiveness of the Western European economy.

The global political scene continued to be dominated by the Cold War during the 1970s and the first part of the 1980s, but American influence was in decline, especially after its withdrawal from Vietnam. Probably the most important development during this period — at least with respect to Turkey — was a series of linked changes in the Middle East. The oil price rises led to a major shift in economic power in favour of the Middle-Eastern oil producers but they also sharpened the conflict between Western influences and more traditional Islamic values. This was illustrated during the next few years by the Iranian revolution, the Iran–Iraq War, the attempts to build pan-Arab unity and the rise of Islamic fundamentalism. Turkey was exposed in various ways to these vicarious influences: for example, there was some spill-over of Islamic fundamentalism into politics in the 1980s (Sunar and Toprak 1983); there were opportunities for trade with oil-rich neighbours, and there was growing Kurdish unrest both at home and in neighbouring Iran and Iraq.

While Turkey did experience some trade diversion from Europe to the Middle East, especially during the mid-1980s, the former remained its principal trading partner throughout this period. Within Europe the second enlargement of the EC reinforced its economic importance. The 1970s and the early 1980s were, however, difficult years for the Community (Harrop 1989). It was beset by budgetary difficulties, failed to make progress on economic and monetary union, and faced recessionary conditions. The Community itself responded to these difficulties by seeking an ordered restructuring of industries such as steel, while introducing limited protectionism against non-members, most notably with the Multi-Fibre Agreement. Therefore, while the EC continued to be the major market for Turkey's imports and exports, it became more unstable and, for some sectors, more constrained during this period. Politically, these were also difficult years for the EC. As a consequence of the system of unanimous voting, its internal decision-making machinery became clogged up with the minutiae of bargaining. There was some attempt to develop a co-ordinated foreign policy, via the European Political Co-operation framework, but in practice it was difficult to harmonise diverse member states' interests over such issues as relations with the Middle East or South Africa. The most that can be claimed is that there were 'discreet shifts in national foreign policies towards a Euro middle ground' (Lodge 1989, p. 236). On the world political stage, therefore, Europe mainly played a secondary role in relation to a more uncertain United States.

In Turkey inward-looking economic policies were continued during the first part of this period. The industrialisation effort was based on import substitution, but it was handicapped by the high costs of inputs and capital and the limited market for industrial goods. Given the deep-rooted structural problems of the Turkish economy, the oil crisis of 1973–4 and the global recession which followed hit the country very hard (Rosenthal 1982). There were balance-of-payments difficulties and a series of foreign-exchange crises which peaked in 1978–9. A $450 million IMF loan in 1978 only provided temporary relief to the economy. The position was exacerbated by the fall-off in emigration as the economic crisis reduced job opportunities in Northern Europe. Whereas emigrant remittances covered most or all of the trade deficit in the early 1970s, coverage in the late 1970s was only some 20–60 per cent. The economic position was clearly unsustainable and a radical redirection in economic policy was called for. The IMF added its weight to the need for such a change of direction. Kazgan (1989, p. 1) summarises the series of events that led to the new economic orientation:

> Throughout the crisis years of 1978 and 1979, the governments in office failed to adopt and implement effectively the IMF stabilization programs. As negotiations were prolonged, fresh credits could not be obtained and the crisis deepened. Following the advent to power of a new government, a new policy program, known as the January 24, 1980 program, was announced; this program coincided exactly with the policies advocated by the IMF — as well as the restructuring policies of the World Bank.

1980 was to prove a major watershed in the development of the Turkish economy. Import substitution policies were replaced by those of export-led growth. High export growth was pursued via realistic exchange-rate policies (based on the 'crawling peg' system), the removal of restrictions on foreign trade and capital movements, and export credits and incentives. Imports were also successively liberalised during the 1980s: nominal tariffs were cut, direct controls were reduced and bureaucratic formalities were mostly eliminated. Foreign investment was also encouraged by the removal of bureaucratic hindrances. As a result the total amount of Foreign Direct Investment (FDI) increased to $6.22 billion in 1980–90 compared to only $228 million during 1954–80. The success of the 1980 programme is illustrated by the growth in exports from $2.9 billion in 1980 to $12.9 billion in 1990. The 1980 economic reform programme also aimed to reduce state intervention and liberalise goods and financial markets. One of the symbols of change during this period was the opening of the Istanbul Stock Exchange in 1986, although the volume of shares traded remained limited even in 1992.

These economic reforms have contributed to a major transformation in the Turkish economy. Between 1980 and 1990, the annual growth rate of GDP was 4.7 per cent (see table 1.1). The most dynamic sector has been industry, the share of which in GDP increased from 25 per cent in 1980 to 29 per cent in 1990, while the relative importance of the agricultural sector declined. The export performance of industry has been even more impressive: industry's share of exports increased from 36 per cent in 1980 to almost

Table 1.1 GDP growth rates 1979–90

	GDP	Agriculture	Industry	Services
1st 5-year Plan* (1963–68)	6.6	3.1	10.6	7.3
2nd 5-year Plan* (1968–73)	7.1	3.5	7.8	7.9
3rd 5-year Plan* (1973–78)	5.9	3.4	8.8	7.3
1979	−0.4	2.8	−5.6	0.2
1980	−1.1	1.7	−5.5	−0.2
1981	4.1	0.1	7.2	4.8
1982	4.6	6.4	4.6	3.3
1983	3.3	−0.1	8.0	3.9
1984	5.9	3.5	10.1	5.3
1985	5.1	2.5	6.3	4.0
1986	8.1	7.9	8.7	6.4
1987	7.4	2.1	9.6	6.8
1988	3.6	8.0	3.1	4.1
1980–4*	3.4	2.3	4.9	3.4
1984–90*	5.8	3.4	6.8	5.3
1980–90*	4.7	2.9	5.9	4.4

Source: State Planning Organization

* Period annual average growth rate

80 per cent in 1990. In general terms, there has been an increase in the competitiveness required to survive, as state protectionism has receded. The external factors which contributed to this export boom were the Iranian revolution which cut off Iran from one of its major suppliers (hence creating opportunities for Turkey) and the Iran–Iraq war which increased the demand for Turkish goods from both countries. The internal factors which were important in the spectacular growth of exports were depressed domestic demand, increased export incentives, the flexible exchange-rate policy, and the government's strong commitment to exports (Balkır 1991). Celasun (1989) also argues that the Turkish economy benefited from the existence of a military regime until November 1983 and, thereafter, a restricted constitutional order. This meant that open social conflict over the adverse distributional effects of the programme with respect to agriculture and labour were avoided. Whereas there were 220 strikes involving 84,800 workers in 1980, there were none in 1981–3 inclusively and only twenty-one strikes as late as 1986. Yet, in that period, agricultural incomes declined relative to non-agricultural ones, and real wages were depressed.

There have, however, been areas of economic difficulties: these include a growing current account deficit (until 1987, but reversed in 1988, 1989 and 1991), rising foreign debts, continuing high inflation rates (see Table 1.2), high real interest rates and only limited success in the liberalisation of the economy. The economy has also become more susceptible to cyclical fluctuations. Kazgan (1989, pp. 11–12) writes that: 'Starting from the dip of 1979–80, deep crises have buffeted the economy in 1983 as well as in 1988 and 1989 . . . the dizzying fluctuations have gone hand in hand with abrupt policy reversals'. As a result there has been a shift in domestic private investment into property, trade and financial services where the economic

Table 1.2 Wholesale Price Inflation 1973–90

Year	Per cent
1973	20.5
1974	29.9
1975	10.1
1976	15.6
1977	24.1
1978	52.6
1979	63.9
1980	107.2
1981	36.8
1982	27.0
1983	30.5
1984	50.3
1985	43.2
1986	29.6
1987	32.0
1988	68.3
1989	69.6
1990	53.0

Source: State Planning Organization

risks are considered to be fewer. Therefore, while export orientation has led to greater industrial output, there are concerns that Turkish industry has failed to modernise in terms of technology. Agriculture also tended to stagnate during the 1980s following successful commercialisation, modernisation and expansion in the 1970s. The agricultural slow-down is related in part to the withdrawal of government support, but it is also influenced by reversals in domestic and international demand for agricultural products. While there were serious structural weaknesses in the Turkish economy in the 1980s, there was also unparalleled dynamism, as evidenced by some of the highest growth rates in the world, outside of the Asian NICs. It should also be emphasised that Turkey's achievements were recorded at a time of global economic recession and uncertainty.

In Turkish politics 1980 was also the decisive year. A military coup ousted the Demirel government, at a time of deepening economic crisis and a rising tide of violence and political unrest. The story of the 1980s was that of the gradual restoration of democratic institutions. Parliamentary elections were held in 1983, but these were heavily circumscribed in terms of the parties and the individuals allowed to participate. In the following year, less restricted local government elections were held, but it was the 1987 parliamentary elections which truly marked the restoration of previous democratic procedures. The 1980s, politically, were dominated by Ozal and the Motherland Party, and this pattern was not broken until the 1991 assembly elections. The 1980s were also marked by a rise in support for Islamic fundamentalism and for an Islamic political party, the Welfare Party (Sunar and Toprak 1983; Tapper 1991), partly because this had been one of the few channels for legitimate opposition to the 1980s' coup. The Welfare

Party also benefited from the sense of displacement and marginalisation that many social groups have experienced amid the rapid growth of recent decades. Toprak (1988, p. 129) eloquently describes its appeal: 'The vision is simple yet powerful. It promises prosperity and wealth without the all-too-familiar pains of rapid industrialization: an industrial country where a sense of community, of belongingness, mutual help and love of brothers reigns.'

One of the most significant events of the period was the 1987 Turkish application for full EC membership. To some extent, this has to be seen in the context of Turkey's long journey towards modernisation during the twentieth century. However, in many ways this was the logical outcome of developments during the 1980s. Given the outward orientation of the economy and the importance of the EC as a trading partner, full membership of the EC would provide a means of giving Turkey a share in the decision-making which profoundly influenced its development trajectory. Membership of the Community could also be seen as a way of guaranteeing the fragile return to democracy; similar arguments and sentiments had been used to back the Iberian applications for membership, a decade earlier. However, the outcome for Turkey was to be quite different than that for Spain and Portugal.

In this second period Turkey moved, somewhat unsteadily, towards closer economic integration with the West and especially with Europe. The logic behind this was the necessity for foreign investment and for trade and technology transfer, once the limitations of the import substitution programme of the 1970s had been exposed. At the same time, while the Gorbachev–Reagan strategic arms limitations talks began to signal a thaw in the Cold War, events in the Middle East indicated that Turkey could acquire a new geopolitical importance. Therefore, economic logic moved Turkey towards closer ties with Europe, but the political framework was less favourable. While it was true that Turkey retained geostrategic importance for the West, this factor had a greater impact on relationships with the United States than with Europe. Instead, relationships with the EC were coloured by events in Turkey — the 1980 military coup and its aftermath — and by developments in the Community itself, including both institutional difficulties and the Mediterranean enlargements.

Defining a new role in an era of uncertainty

Turning to the third of our time periods, the late 1980s and early 1990s, the main feature has been the rapidity and the unpredictability of events. Politically, the dominant event has been the demise of the Soviet Union and the turmoil which has followed both within the former Union and in Eastern Europe. The collapse of Soviet power has meant that American military power is unchallenged at the global scale. This was most dramatically illustrated by the Gulf crisis and American-led military intervention in Kuwait. To a lesser extent, the renewed American self-confidence as a global power is also seen in the increased pressure it has exerted on Libya, Israel and other Mediterranean and Middle-Eastern countries. Turkey, more than most other countries, has been exposed to these global political reconstructions. Its close proximity to the Balkans, its common border with Armenia and other former Soviet republics, and its involvement in the Gulf crisis all have grave economic and political repercussions for the country. On a political level, these events have given Turkey an increased international role as a potential regional power.

On an economic level, the Gulf Crisis led to a sharp reverse in growth in 1991 (0.3 per cent), while the break-up of the Soviet Union poses short-term economic difficulties given the loss of markets. In addition, there are also economic uncertainties surrounding the outcome of the Uruguay round of GATT negotiations. Liberalisation of agricultural trade may potentially benefit Turkey, but the liberalisation of trade in financial services and the pressure to sign agreements on intellectual property rights could damage the economy.

Events in Europe have been equally momentous and uncertain during recent years. The dominant role of the EC within Europe has been underlined by the creation of the European Economic Space and by the applications of most EFTA countries for full membership. There is also strong pressure for deeper levels of integration within the European Community. The Single Market Programme will certainly reshape economic relations within the Community. The Maastricht conference also promises to reshape political union, monetary union and social rights, although the eventual outcome of this agreement is still in doubt. However, the recent 'deepening' of the EC has significantly raised the 'price' of new membership by adding substantially to the *acquis communautaire*. The political transformation in Central and Eastern Europe has also increased the competition for Turkey in terms of securing EC assistance (once the Fourth Protocol is unfrozen) and full membership.

This leads us, finally, to consider the position of Turkey in the early 1990s, when it appears to have reached one of the major crossroads in its twentieth-century development. There was high and sustained economic growth in GDP during the 1980s (see Table 1.1). There were, however, signs of stagnation after 1988, particularly as exports stalled at a level of approximately $11–$12 billion. Expansion recovered in 1990 with GDP growth rates peaking at 9.2 per cent. However, the Gulf Crisis led to sharply reduced growth in 1991 (an estimated 0.3 per cent). The impact of the Gulf Crisis was extensive: exports to Iraq, Turkey's second largest market, were disrupted; the bill for higher oil prices exceeded $900 million; more than a billion dollars was lost from oil pipeline revenue; Iraq ceased to service substantial credits that had been advanced by Turkey; and tourism, which had generated $3.3 billion in receipts in 1990, was severely disrupted. More rapid growth was resumed in 1992.

Growth has, however, been accompanied by structural difficulties. The most spectacular of these has been inflation; according to official estimates — based on wholesale prices — annual inflation rates never dropped below 25 per cent during the 1980s and, in fact, crept upwards during the late 1980s to reach 70 per cent in 1991 (see Table 1.2). High interest rates resulted, with nominal levels topping 70 per cent for many investors by the 1990s. This was partly fuelled by the large public-sector borrowing requirement, significant elements of which were due to the enormous costs of the GAP (Güneydoğu Anadolu Projesi — Southeastern Anatolian Project) project in south-east Turkey and deficit financing of state economic enterprises. Furthermore, by the late 1980s it was no longer possible to depress domestic demand as the labour unions began to reassert their power in the more democratic environment and as general elections loomed. High real interest rates also attracted 'hot' money, especially from emigrants, and this added to inflationary pressures. Finally, despite the high growth rates, the economy could not generate sufficient employment opportunities, especially given the high rate of population increase; by 1991 the average unemployment rate was over 12 per cent. Among the other structural weaknesses of the economy are the level of state indebtedness and a substantial budget deficit.

Ever since the introduction of the 1980 reform programme, one of the aims of economic policy has been the reduction of the size of the state sector, which is estimated to account for 45 per cent of fixed investment, half a million jobs, and one-quarter of manufacturing output. Privatisation is one important element of the state strategy in this field. In addition to reducing the burden of the state economic enterprises deficits on the domestic budget, there is also the objective of using privatisation to make Turkish industry more internationally competitive. Between 1986 and 1991 a proportion of the equities held by the state in fifteen companies have been privatised via stock-market flotations (Economic Report on Turkey–EC Integration 1991). There are two principal criticisms of the programme: that it has been extremely limited, and that it has allowed foreign purchasers easy opportunities to acquire some of the key enterprises in the Turkish economy. If privatisation is to be pursued more vigorously, then there are difficult decisions ahead. Many of the state-owned companies are not competitive at present and will require major restructuring (involving large-scale redundancies) if they are to become so.

Turkey's economy has considerable potential for sustained economic growth, not least because there are large reserves of underutilised productive capacity in all sectors as well as a young, rapidly expanding labour force. There are, however, barriers to developments: many sectors of industry require modernisation and may not survive without protection, while agricultural holdings are still small and fragmented (60 per cent are of less than five hectares). The future course of economic development will depend on global events but, above all, on the European economy, on which there is so much dependence.

Turkish politics also face a number of questions in the late 1990s. The Demirel government has launched a series of important political reforms, seeking to restrict police powers and strengthen constitutional rights. It remains to be seen whether these can be successfully implemented. The Demirel government has also come to power at a time when Turkey has the potential to construct a new regional role for itself in relation to the newly independent former Soviet republics, especially the Turkic ones. However, this will not obviate the need for Turkey to reconstruct its relations with

Europe, with which it has such strong political and economic ties. Indeed, one of the tasks of any government during the 1990s will be to redefine relationships with the EC, which, after 1992, is due to reconsider the question of full Turkish membership.

Another major issue in Turkish politics is the Kurdish question, which has implications for both domestic politics and for Turkey's international relations. There are an estimated eight to twelve million Kurds in Turkey. While originally concentrated in the south-eastern region, large-scale migrations in recent decades mean that they are now widely distributed among the larger cities of Marmara, the Aegean, and Central Anatolia. Kurdish unrest in south-eastern Turkey is not a new development. There have been periodic uprisings since the early nineteenth century, and a more sustained movement in the early twentieth century. Yalçın-Heckmann (1991, p. 103) writes that 'looking at analyses of various Kurdish uprisings around the time of the First World War and the early years of the Republic, one sees a curious mixture of religious and nationalist motivations'. What is clear is that the Lausanne Treaty simply ignored the Kurdish claims for minority rights, so that this remained a dormant issue, one which again erupted in violence in the 1980s.

The governments of Ozal and Demirel have approached the issue in three ways. First, through much of the late 1980s the police and military were given, in effect, a free hand to stem the rising tide of Kurdish Workers' Party (PKK) orchestrated violence; their heavy handed methods were, in fact, often politically counter-productive. Second, the Motherland Party government and later the Demirel government has been seeking short- and medium-term political solutions via offering language and cultural concessions to the Kurds. However, the scope for negotiation is limited by the strong opposition among the Turkish population and the military to any such concessions. The Turkish government is also aware that there are other minorities within its borders, such as Armenians who were given minority rights according to the Lausanne Treaty (see Gürel, this volume) and some Arab communities living in a few provinces near the Syrian border (Robins 1991). The third arm of government strategy has been to foster the economic development of the south-eastern regions, in the belief that an improvement in living standards will diffuse separatist ambitions. The GAP project is the showpiece of this programme, but there is also a lower-key programme to improve basic infrastructure throughout the region. The Kurdish issue is one of the most potent in Turkish politics, but its resolution will depend also on developments in neighbouring Iran and Iraq (where there are also large Kurdish minorities) and on external pressures from the United States and the EC. Turkish politics, in common with many other aspects of life in Turkey, are increasingly open to external influence.

Geopolitical events in this third period have underlined the mutual interests of Turkey and the West in a strategic alliance; the demise of the Soviet threat has been replaced by new international uncertainties in both the Middle East and in Central and Eastern Europe. This has brought a warmer relationship between Turkey and the United States. However, the EC's relationships with Turkey are dictated less by geopolitics and more by

economic logic and domestic politics. From the Turkish viewpoint, international political and economic changes have done nothing but strengthen
the argument for closer institutional ties with Europe, even though there are
intriguing new regional opportunities opening up in relation to the former
Soviet republics (see Ataöv, this volume). But the problems of institutional
reform, and the domestic political situations in the member states, not to
mention global recession, continue to relegate Turkey in the Community's
list of priorities.

Disentangling the relationships: the structure of this volume

The focus of this volume is the relationships between Turkey and Europe.
The European Community is for Turkey, in economic and many political
respects, the most important of the three global superpowers. Investment,
migration and trade flows all serve to underline this important fact. For
example, the EC accounted for 53 per cent of exports and 42 per cent of
imports in 1990 which is more than double the share of any other grouping
(see Table 1.3). However, while the EC figures large in several of the

Table 1.3 Turkey's major trade relationships, 1990 %

	Exports	Imports
EC	53.4	41.9
Eastern Europe and Soviet Union	6.2	8.7
Middle East countries	12.5	12.1
North American countries	5.0	4.2
United States	7.5	10.2
Japan	1.8	5.0
Other	13.6	17.9
Total	100.0	100.0

Source: State Planning Organization, Main Economic Indicators, March 1991

contributions, this is not to be equated with Europe. This statement serves
to open up the difficult questions of the definition of Europe and of
Europeanness.

It is, of course, much easier to state what does not constitute Europe
rather than what does. There are no clear geographical boundaries to
Europe, for it is evident that there is no greater socio-economic or political
significance to the Bosphorous than there is to the Urals as a territorial
limiter. Similarly, Europe can not be defined in terms of market economies;
quite apart from the definitional problems of what constitutes a market
economy, any such definition involves problems of exclusion at the time of
writing (of Bulgaria, Albania etc) as well as of inclusion (of Japan, the
United States and other market economies). A definition of Europe and
Europeanness based on concepts of pluralist democracy can also be
excluded on similar grounds. This leaves culture as one possible definition
of Europeanness, but this is also unsatisfactory. Quite apart from the issue

of exclusion (how are the United States, Australia etc to be treated?), there is the question of inclusion. For example, there are no sharp discontinuities in, say, literary traditions between Germany and Poland or Poland and Russia. Religion is another possible denominator, with a possible claim that European culture is based on Christianity. Quite apart from the fact that Christianity has its own deep cleavages, any such definition would risk defining large segments of the populations of Yugoslavia and Albania as being non-European; there are also substantial first-, second- and third-generation immigrant communities in Northern European countries. The issue of definitions is of more than academic interest in its own right, for it also informs the approach that we have taken in this volume.

The volume is divided into three sections: these provide, respectively, introductory overviews, analyses of economic structure and relationships, and assessments of international relations. Any such division is necessarily arbitrary, for it is no more possible to divide political from economic or cultural issues, than it is to separate domestic, European and global analyses. Nevertheless, these three clusters of chapters do provide differing degrees of emphases which can either be taken as free standing units or, as the book as a whole aims to do, provide a broad introduction to relationships between Turkey and Europe.

In the first section, 'Introduction: Turkey the European context', the central theme of the book is placed in perspective from three different viewpoints. The introduction has examined the lack of synchronisation among developments in Turkey, Europe and the global scene. While Turkey has never been isolated from larger political and economic movements, there have been times when autarkic economic policies have made it difficult to benefit from some of the integrationist tendencies in Europe. Periods of military dictatorship have also estranged Turkey from its potential allies in international affairs. In the 1980s, however, economic and political reforms have brought Turkey closer to the political mainstream in Western Europe. However, there continues to be a lack of synchronisation between Turkish and European world views, and their priorities in terms of international relations.

These themes are taken up and elaborated in the second chapter, 'Turkey and the EC in the changing post-war international order'. Eralp examines in detail the shifting and often difficult relationships between Turkey and the EC. He argues that these are influenced by Turkey's Westernisation project, the concern not to be outflanked by Greece on Western international platforms, and the domestic economic and political situations which have sometimes driven Turkey's leaders to look for new policy alternatives abroad. This backdrop provides the framework for understanding Turkey's application for full membership of the EC.

The third chapter in this section shifts the analytical focus to the Mediterranean region. Williams, in 'Turkey: a Mediterranean perspective', assesses developments in the EC's relationships with the member and non-member states, and considers how these have influenced Turkey's position. The importance of this chapter is that while Turkey can lay claim to membership of several macro regions, it is most often considered as a

Mediterranean region by EC policy analysts, and some of its closest economic competitors also belong to this group. Williams argues that Turkey's relationships with the EC are conditioned by two parallel processes: the Mediterraneanisation and the globalisation of Community interests. The difficulty for Turkey is that, by the 1980s, global concerns were paramount. One of the important sub-themes of this first section, as a whole, is the contrast between the different views of the Turkey–EC relationship that are held by the two sides.

The second section of the book has a largely economic focus. It looks at Turkey's economic structures and its relationships with the EC. The unifying theme here is a concern with convergence and divergence between the Turkish economy and that of the EC. Chapter Four, by Kazgan, looks at 'External pressures and the economic policy outlook'. It traces recent external pressures on the Turkish economy, particularly those emanating from the IMF, and the way that these have impinged on economic policies during the 1980s. It therefore provides an essential assessment of some of the strengths and weaknesses of the Turkish economy in a decade which has witnessed major economic changes. Kazgan's key argument is that the requirements of development, and domestic economic circumstance, clearly shaped the shift in economic policy during the 1960s from import substitution to export-led growth. At the same time, the structural features of the domestic economy mediated the macro-economic impact of external influences.

The other two chapters in this section examine the linkages between Turkey and its principal economic partner, the EC. Balkir, in 'Turkey and the EC: foreign trade and investment in the 1980s', looks at some of the central themes of the book. She analyses the volume, content and influences on the trade and investment flows between Turkey and the EC. These fluctuations are explained by reference to internal developments in Turkey as well as by its relations with other economic blocs. In particular, it is argued that to understand Turkey's trade relations with the EC, and the application for membership, there is a need to analyse Turkey's global trading position, which was changing during the 1980s. It is therefore useful to read these first two economic chapters in close conjunction, for together they provide a comprehensive overview of the Turkish economy and its role in the world economy.

Kadioğlu, in 'The human tie: international labour migration', adds to the analysis of relationships between Turkey and Europe. After a preliminary review of the development of labour migration, which positions Turkey among the principal labour exporters, she provides a detailed review of relationships with Germany, the main recipient country. While her analysis considers the contribution of emigrant remittances to the Turkish economy, she also considers some of the cultural and political implications. This is essential in clarifying the precise nature of Turkish emigration to Germany which is an important issue in the further improvement of relationships with the EC.

The theme of the third section is that of 'International relations: constraints and opportunities'. It is impossible to provide a comprehensive coverage of such a broad canvas. We have therefore selected three themes which have particular significance for relationships with Europe, none of which have been covered in any detail in earlier chapters. First, Gürel looks at interactions with Greece in 'A difficult Aegean relationship'. He traces developments in the disputes over airspace, territorial waters and, above all, Cyprus. This has greater importance than merely as a case study of bilateral relations, for these are carried over and influence Turkey's relationships with the EC as a whole. An example of the economic implications would be the continued blocking of EC Fourth Protocol financial assistance for Turkey.

In the second chapter, Ataöv looks at 'Turkey, Eastern Europe and the USSR'. He examines historical ties, newly emerging ones and the potential for further development of relationships with the Central and Eastern European countries. There is potential for Turkey to play a major role with respect to the Turkic countries with which it has linguistic ties. This has already been recognised in the agreement that Turkey will co-operate with the European Bank for Reconstruction and Development in order to deliver financial assistance to this region. This is where the definition of Europe becomes important. If such countries — in addition to Russia, the Ukraine and others — can be considered European, then Turkey, in locational terms, is far from being peripheral to Europe. The other area of major potential for new relations is with the Balkans, particularly as these countries move to more open, market economies.

In the final chapter in this section, Acar discusses 'Turkey and Islam'. This chapter makes three important contributions to this volume. First, it explains some of the complexities of Islam as a cultural form, thereby helping to correct the widely held but erroneous Western view that this is a homogeneous theological and cultural construction. Second, Acar highlights the way in which Islam impinges on party politics in Turkey and influences the drive to modernisation. And, finally, Islam is a factor which influences the potential and the limits of Turkey's relationships with both the Middle East and other Islamic countries and with the EC itself. This is an appropriate note on which to end the comments on the individual contributions, since it underlines the way in which culture, domestic and international politics and economic development are all interlinked.

This book has been written for a wide readership. We hope that it will be of interest to an audience that includes academics, students and policy-makers in both Turkey and Europe. The relationship between the two is fundamental to Turkey, to the Mediterranean and to the 'Balkans', and is likely to be of increasing importance to the European Community in the new world order. The need for mutual understanding has never been greater and we hope that this book will at least contribute a starting point for this goal.

References

Arıcanli, T. and Rodrik, D. (eds) (1990), *The Political Economy of Turkey: Debt. Adjustment and Sustainability*, London: Macmillan.

Balkır, C. (1991), 'The role of the export sector in the restructuring of industry: Turkish case in the 1980s', Colloque International de Paris, Industrialisation, Communication et Rapports Sociaux en Turquie et en Meditérranée Orientale, Paris.

Ballance, R. and Sinclair, S. (1983), *Collapse and Survival: Industrial Strategies in a Changing World*, London: George, Allen and Unwin.

Barkey, H.J. (1990), *The State and the Industrialization Crises in Turkey*, Boulder: Westview Press.

Boratav, K. (1982), *Turkiyede Devletçilik*, Ankara: Savas Yayıenları.

Brown, J. (1988), 'The politics of transition in Turkey', *Current History*, 87, no. 526, pp. 69–72.

Celasun, M. (1989), 'Income redistribution and employment: aspects of Turkey's post-1980 adjustment', *Middle Eastern Technical University Studies in Development*, 16, pp. 1–31.

Celasun, M. and Rodrik, D. (1989), 'Debt, adjustment and growth: Turkey' in J.D. Sachs and S.M. Collins (eds), *Developing Country Debt and Economic Performance: Volume Three Country Studies, Indonesia, Korea, Philippines and Turkey*, Chicago: Chicago University Press.

Dicken, P. (1992), *Global Shift: The Internationalization of Economic Activity*, second edition, London: Paul Chapman.

Dodd, C.H. (1983), *The Crises of Turkish Democracy*, London: Euthen Press.

Economic Report on Turkey–EC Integration (1991), Ankara: Report prepared for the 34th session of the Turkey–EC Joint Parliamentary Committee.

Goodman, S.S. (1976), 'Turkey', in E.N. Baklanoff (ed.), *Mediterranean Europe and the Common Market*, Birmingham: University of Alabama Press.

Hale, W. (1981), *The Political and Economic Development of Turkey*, New York: St Martin's Press.

Harrop, J. (1989), *The Political Economy of Integration in the European Community*, Aldershot: Edward Elgar.

Heper, M. and Ahmet, E. (eds) (1988), *State, Democracy and Military: Turkey in the 1980s*, New York: Walter de Gruyter.

Hershlag, Z.Y. (1968), *Turkey: the Challenge of Growth*, Leiden: Brill.

Julius, D. (1990), *Global Companies and Public Policy: The Growing Challenge of Foreign Direct Investment*, London: Frances Pinter.

Kazgan, G. (1989), *Turkey's Experience With the Restructuring Program: 1980–90*, Tunis: Seminar on Structural Adjustment Programs, December 1989.

Krueger, A.O. and O.H. Aktan (1982) *Swimming Against the Tide*, California: International Centre for Economic Growth.

Keyder, G. (1987), *State and Class in Turkey*, London: Verso.

Landau, J.M. (1988), 'The fortunes and misfortunes of Pan-Turkism', *Central Asian Survey*, Oxford, VII, pp. 1–5.

Lewis, B. (1979), *The Emergence of Modern Turkey*, New York: Oxford University Press.

Lodge, J. (1989), 'European political co-operation towards the 1990s', in J. Lodge (ed.), *The European Community and the Challenge of the Future*, London: Pinter Publishers.

Ohmae, K. (1985), *Triad Power: The Coming Shape of Global Competition*, New York: Free Press.

Osman, O. (1979), 'Development background of the Turkish economy: 1923–1973', *International Journal of Middle East Studies*, 10, pp. 336–9.

Robins, P. (1991), *Turkey and the Middle East*, London: Royal Institute of International Affairs.

Rosenthal, G.G. (1982), *The Mediterranean Basin: its political economy and changing international relations*, London: Butterworth Scientific.
Singer, M. (1977), *The Economic Advance of Turkey*, Ankara: Turkish Economic Society.
Sunar, I. and Toprak, B. (1983), 'Islam in politics: the case of Turkey', *Government and Opposition*, 18, pp. 421–41.
Tapper, R. (ed.) (1991), *Islam in Modern Turkey: Religion, Politics and Literature in a Secular State*, London: I.B. Tauris.
Toprak, B. (1988), 'The state, politics and religion in Turkey', in M. Heper and E. Ahmet (eds), *State, Democracy and Military: Turkey in the 1980s*, New York: Walter de Gruyter.
Williams, A.M. (1987), *The Western European Economy*, London: Hutchinson.
Yalçın-Heckmann, L. (1991), 'Ethnic Islam and nationalism among the Kurds in Turkey', in R. Tapper (ed.), *Islam in Modern Turkey*, London: I.B. Tauris.

2
Turkey and the European Community in the changing post-war international system

Atila Eralp

Introduction

Turkish foreign policy has for a long time been carried out in staunch alliance with the West. In turn, the West has been perceived as an unitary bloc: the United States and Europe were conceived as the two pillars of what was seen as a progressive and powerful alliance. Turkish foreign policy-makers kept close and balanced relations with both pillars in the bipolar world order established in the post-war era. In effect, it was this order which provided Turkey with the possibility of establishing itself within the Western alliance and thereby forging organic links with the West. Such links were also in line with the declared aim of modernization espoused by the leaders of the Turkish republic since its inception. Modernization, in turn, was defined as Westernization and these projects, it was thought could not be realized unless in cooperation with the United States and Western Europe. Thus, Turkey sought to be included in the international institutions set up in the wake of the Second World War.

Seeking closer relations with the European Community (EC) was a logical extension of this approach to foreign policy. The EC was regarded by the Turkish policy-makers as the economic axis of the Western alliance, supplementing and cementing the political pact. Europeans, for their part, also regarded relations with Turkey mainly in the framework of the Western alliance.

Subsequently, changes in the international system have forced all parties to revise their previous assumptions. As relations between the United States and Europe no longer unfold in terms of an unproblematic cooperation, Turkish policy-makers have found that they cannot count on an undifferentiated Western alliance. Maintaining good relations with Europe is no longer based on the same premises as before. This change became increasingly apparent during the 1980s when cooperation with the United States did not also ensure a smooth relationship with Europe, as it had done previously. Events in Eastern Europe and the Gulf Crisis reinforced this divergence: Turkey became increasingly marginalized in Europe at the same time that ties to the United States were strengthened beyond all expectations.

As in the aftermath of the Second World War, the dramatic changes in the international climate are prompting Turkish policy-makers to develop new options for integration in the emerging international order. Efforts are now directed to the formulation of a new type of strategic importance, one that would emphasize that importance more in relation to Turkey's role in the region rather than in terms of the East–West conflict. This represents a considerable transformation in Turkish policy orientations which, ever since the demise of the Ottoman Empire, have consistently faced West rather than East. I intend to argue in this chapter that Turkey's new regional trajectory has the potential of further distancing her from the European Community.

This chapter will basically show that two traditional concerns have always preoccupied the governing elite of the Turkish republic in their efforts to become part of Europe: Westernization and the so-called 'Greek factor' — Turkey's concern not to be outflanked by Greece on Western-dominated international platforms. I will also suggest that Turkish policy-makers have turned to Europe when economic and political difficulties at home urged them to look for new policy alternatives abroad. The interplay of these factors will be examined in three periods. The first period will cover basically the 1950s and the 1960s, when an association agreement was signed between Turkey and the Community and when relations ran rather smoothly. Then I will look at the 1970s and the controversies arising from the idea of a customs union between Turkey and the Community. I will show how tensions developed between Turkey's Westernization project and her economic development strategy, as economic concerns predominated over political calculations. Finally, I will focus on the 1980s and particularly on Turkey's application for full membership of the EC in 1987. I will argue that Turkey applied to the Community for full membership when the chances of its immediate inclusion were at their lowest. I will try to show why such a paradoxical step was taken and how this step has subsequently shaped the course of relations between the Community and Turkey. The final sections of the chapter will focus on how Turkey's application to the EC triggered a reassessment of Turkey's 'Europeanness' both in Europe and in Turkey and resulted in the marginalization of Turkey in the emerging new Europe.

The post-war international climate and Turkey's moves towards association with the European Community

Ever since its conception, policy-makers in the Turkish republic had followed a policy of Westernization according to which they hoped to reorganize their society and their relations with the outside world (see Ülman and Sander, 1972).[1]

Numerous factors, including the Depression and the war in Europe prevented the forging of mutual relations with the West that would have very much aided this project. The post-war international system, for the first time, offered Turkish policy-makers a fertile ground for instituting organic links with the West. The division of Europe into two rival blocs, and the position of Turkey as a 'front-line state' in the emerging cold-war atmosphere, were among the factors which eased Turkey's entry into the nascent Western alliance. In the cold-war climate, the West was trying to create a united front from which Turkish policy-makers did not wish to be excluded; consequently, Turkey's leaders applied to join almost all the institutions that were created in the process of forging the Western alliance: the Marshall Plan, the OEEC (later OECD), the Council of Europe, NATO (cf. Gönlübol and Ülman, 1987).[2]

Turkish policy-makers were specifically interested in two benefits that they hoped inclusion in the Western alliance would provide. First and foremost came security considerations; they did not believe that Turkey could survive the cold war alone and hoped to enter into larger and more secure alliances. In support of their application to the Western military alliance NATO, Turkish policy-makers emphasized the geo-political importance of their country, a position which coincided with the American cold-war strategy of containment. The second benefit concerned the material resources necessary for Turkey's economic development. Indeed the Marshall Plan, and the economic and military aid received by Turkey after the Second World War, did turn out to be important channels for the flow of credit as well as much needed machinery. In the four years following the end of the war, Turkey began to accede to the different organizations designed to increase economic cooperation between Europe and the United States. Inclusion in the Western military alliance did not come until 1952, after Turkey had demonstrated its allegiance by sending troops to fight in Korea (see Sander, 1979: 74).

According to Turkish policy-makers, membership of the new European Community (EC) was a logical extension of Turkey's inclusion in the other Western organizations, since it was seen as the economic dimension supplementing and cementing the Western alliances.[3] At this time, application to the EC did not conflict with Turkey's efforts to maintain intimate relations with the United States. Turkish policy-makers believed (and perhaps rightly) that the United States strongly supported the creation of a community based on the premise of Western unity. Such a community also suited the needs of Turkish policy-makers. Other interests within Turkey were also committed to the idea of closer ties with Europe. These groups included a small number of entrepreneurs organized as the Istanbul Chamber of Commerce and a few government functionaries working in the Ministry of Foreign Affairs. Both groups stressed not only the trade benefits but also the 'civilizing mission' of association with the West. But, rather than regarding membership of the EC as solving the problem of how to establish relations with Europe, Turkey adopted a holistic approach in which relations with Europe were considered as one strand of the more encompassing issue of relations with the West.

Apart from concern with inclusion in the Western alliance, the so-called 'Greek factor' was another important consideration in Turkey's application for EC membership. Turkey's application to the Community on 31 July 1959 was mainly a response to the similar application made by Greece two months earlier and can be understood in terms of the long-standing conflict between the two countries. Turkish policy-makers, especially those in the Ministry of Foreign Affairs, believed that Turkey had to be present on each and every platform where the Greeks figured. For many policy-makers in Turkey, the EC was an unknown entity, and the implication of Turkey's membership had not been considered in depth. What mattered was the possible damage that Greece could inflict on Turkey in the Western alliance if it were to monopolize the European arena which was thought to be an important prospective site for Turkish–Greek rivalry (Birand, 1985: 56–7).

The severe economic and political difficulties experienced at the time by the Turkish government were among the more conjunctural factors that served to expedite Turkey's application to the EC. The Democrat Party (DP) government, which came to power in 1950, at first followed liberal trade policies and received substantial credit from the United States and traditional institutions. This easy access to foreign funds created a dependence on external finance which, in turn, caused the looming debt problem. As the international terms of trade turned against producers of agricultural commodities after the mid-fifties, balance-of- payments difficulties prompted the government to adopt protectionist policies. Already faltering under these pressures, the DP was also squeezed by rampant inflation caused by its economic strategy of investing in expensive infrastructural projects such as the building of roads. These economic difficulties finally forced the government to agree to an IMF stabilization programme in 1958. As the electoral strength of the Democratic Party had also began to erode, the party experienced increasing competition from its rival, the Republican People's Party. In this climate, the EC was regarded by the DP government not only as a new source of credit and aid, but also as a means of boosting its political morale and credibility at home. Moreover, by the late fifties Turkey's stance in the international arena, especially its relations with the United States, was no longer as unproblematic as it had been at the beginning of the decade. In this context, a successful association with Europe would also have been welcome.

The European Community, for its part, viewed Turkey's inclusion cautiously. European policy-makers believed that Turkey's level of economic development would stand in the way of European economic integration since the latter was premised on advanced levels of industrialization. They thus planned to offer Turkey economic assistance as well as certain trade and tariff concessions (Turan, 1989: 35–6). But, after the EC signed a treaty of association with Greece (the Athens Treaty), such a posture became difficult to maintain. Aware of the competition between Greece and Turkey, European policy-makers were careful to strike a balance in their relations with the two countries. Furthermore, since the European Community was still in its infancy and welcomed the application of new members, there were many in the Community who regarded both Greece and Turkey's membership favourably. The cold war prompted the members of the EC to act with strategic considerations in mind. Turkey and Greece were front-line states and their economic strength, thought to be crucial for political stability in the context of the cold war, needed to be bolstered. Drawing their lessons from the Cuba missiles crisis, NATO leaders began to stress what they called their 'flexible response strategy' which relied on conventional forces — a move which reinforced the strategic position of Turkey and Greece within the alliance. The increased importance of security concerns encouraged the EC to waive economic objections to Turkey's accession.

Turkey and the EC signed the Ankara Agreement regulating Turkey's association with the Community on 12 September 1963, two years after the Athens Treaty set out the terms of Greek association with the EC. The delay in Turkey's association was caused by the prolonged negotiations that took place between the signatories after the 1960 military coup in Turkey which suspended parliamentary politics for about eighteen months. Although the EC has signed association agreements with countries such as Malta and Cyprus, only in the cases of Turkey and Greece were clauses included in the agreements which envisaged the ultimate full membership of the two governments at a future unspecified date. Thus accession to the EC has been seen as a legal right by both Turkey and Greece.

The Ankara agreement encompassed three stages, consisting of a preparatory period followed by transitional and final periods, through which association between Turkey and the EC would have to proceed (see Balkir this volume). The preparatory stage proceeded smoothly enough and Turkey took the necessary steps to initiate the second stage of the association agreement by applying to the Community in May 1967. But the issue of a customs union proved to be thorny, and it was not until July 1970 that a Supplementary Protocol setting a revised timetable was finally agreed on at the EC–Turkey Association Council meeting; this was signed the following November. Ratification of the agreement took even longer and had to weather not only misgivings felt by both parties but also the military intervention in Turkey in March 1971.

Tensions between Westernization and development projects in the 1970s

Previously smooth relations changed in the early 1970s as Turkey increasingly began to see association with Europe in terms of economic development strategies rather than as a matter of foreign policy (Eralp, 1990). The possible negative impact of EC membership on Turkish industrialization was a fear that industrialists also began to voice. Although the latter generally supported the spirit of the Ankara agreement, they were sceptical of the terms and the timing of the customs union stipulated in the Supplementary Protocol. As balance-of-payments difficulties increased, especially after the 1973 oil crisis, industrialists started to complain that the transition period specified by the Protocol was too short to effect the necessary restructuring of Turkish industry. Even in the original pro-Europe institutions, such as the Istanbul Chamber of Industry and the Economic Development Foundation,[4] strong opposition to the idea of a customs union began to be mounted. Industrialists went so far as to ask the government to abandon the idea of the customs union altogether and to seek ways of formulating new forms of association with the EC.

The prioritization of economic issues in relations with the EC was not shared uniformly by all government agencies. The Ministry of Foreign Affairs had, throughout the sixties and much of the seventies, followed their initial assessment of the importance to Turkey of accession to the EC and had argued for the primacy of political rather than economic considerations in shaping Turkey's policy. By contrast, the State Planning Organization, in line with industrialists' demands, emphasized the detrimental effects of a customs union on Turkey's industrialization. It would not be unfair to say that the seventies witnessed the emergence of a tension between two of Turkey's basic national projects, Westernization and development, which had hitherto seemed quite compatible.

The difficulties involved in implementing tariff reductions finally compelled Prime Minister Ecevit, in an effort to gain time, to freeze the terms of the Association Agreement in October 1978. Although Turkey had already put into effect two phases of the tariff-reduction scheme, a third set of cuts envisaged by the agreement to take effect by January 1978 was increasingly putting the squeeze on the Ecevit government, which had just acceded to power. There were also other issues which caused dissatisfaction among Turkish policy-makers. They argued that the value of agricultural preferences given to Turkey by the Association Agreement had been undermined by the extension of similar concessions to other Mediterranean countries as a result of the EC's Global Mediterranean Policy. Moreover, in their view, the level of Community aid extended to Turkey was not adequate for the latter to reach a stage where the implementation of a customs union would be possible. The Ecevit government thus presented a plan to revise the terms of the Association Agreement and asked for a five-year period in which it hoped to honour its tariff-reduction obligations.

A close observer of Turkish relations with the EC argues that rather than trying to finalize Turkey's application, Ecevit's primary concern at the time was to secure for the Turkish economy, ailing under the American-imposed arms embargo, the foreign credit urgently needed for its revitalization. It was with such concerns in mind that Ecevit had approached the IMF as well as the EC (Birand, 1985: 364–87). At a time when the EC was embroiled in economic difficulties, Ecevit's request for an $8 billion aid package could not have met with a favourable response. Turkey's inability to estricate itself from the Cyprus quagmire perhaps provided Europe with a suitable excuse to refuse this request, in spite of its support of a social-democratic government in Turkey. Whatever the cause, Europe finally offered the Ecevit government $600 million under the aegis of a Fourth Financial Protocol already envisaged in the initial Protocol.

While Turkey was trying to cope with its economic troubles by freezing its relations with the EC, Greece applied to the Community for full membership in 1975 after the fall of the military regime. Although Greek Prime Minister Karamanlis shared Ecevit's misgivings over the terms of the Association Agreement, Karamanlis's response, unlike Ecevit's, was to apply to the Community for full membership. This move was based on the assumption that participation in Community decision-making processes was the only way for Greece to improve its position, eroded as a consequence of the EC's Global Mediterranean Policy (Verney, 1987: 258). The primacy of political issues in Greece at that time, as well as the different attitude in Greece towards the problem of industrialization, meant that Karamanlis did not have to face the opposition from industrialists with which Ecevit had to contend.

Greek moves towards the EC served to alarm only a small section of the Turkish policy-makers in spite of the latter's sensitivity towards Greek foreign policy. In order to stem the possible negative effects for Turkey of Greek accession to the EC in January 1981, Hayrettin Erkmen, the Minister of Foreign Affairs in the minority Demirel government (which had succeeded Ecevit in 1979), announced, at an Association Council meeting held on 6 February 1980, Turkey's intention to follow Greece's example. But this last-minute attempt not to be outmanoeuvred by Greece in Europe did not carry much weight, even in the minister's own government.[5] With hindsight many observers have argued that Turkey had missed its historical opportunity to join the EC (see Ceyhan, 1988). It might be argued that the effect of Greek membership on Turkey's chances to follow suit had not received the careful consideration that subsequent events showed to be necessary. Concern with other issues, such as the increasing street violence at home and the urgency of economic problems as well as the Cyprus imbroglio, forced attention to be diverted away from Europe.

Attitudes towards Turkey's association with the EC during the seventies were very much coloured by increasing global economic difficulties. As Turkey continued to regard the EC as an organization that would meet Turkey's economic needs, the Community adopted a luke-warm stance towards Turkey's requests. Moreover, the seventies was also a decade during which concern with political issues acquired increasing weight within the Community. Economic considerations were not completely absent from this shift in emphasis as Europe, in an effort to buttress its economic strength *vis-à-vis* the United States and Japan, began to open up to its southern neighbours. The Global Mediterranean Policy and the Lomé Conventions are important indications of Europe's endeavours to find new markets and investment outlets. As these policies failed to produce the desired impact, Europe gradually began to consider the inclusion of some Mediterranean countries within the structure of the Community. The move towards the south brought in its wake new political attitudes that included the promotion of democracy as a foreign-policy issue. Such considerations were very apparent in the Greek case, as Europe froze all relations with that country as long as the Junta was in power. The belief that membership of the Community would strengthen democratic regimes guided European responses to the Portuguese and Spannish applications as well (see Tsoukalis, 1981). This greater emphasis on political issues outweighed the new economic burdens that inclusion of these countries in the Community would bring (Eralp, 1988).

It was this shift in emphasis in Europe that Greek policy-makers had captured in their decision to forge ahead with their bid for full membership. By contrast, the Turkish leaders emphasis on economic parameters served to create a gulf between the experiences of those southern Mediterranean countries that sought to establish closer links with the EC. The 1980 military intervention in Turkey exacerbated this divergence and further complicated Turkish bids for incorporation in Europe, thus ushering in a new and tense phase in Turkish–EC relations.

Mounting tensions in Turkey–EC relations in the 1980s

While Turkey decided to shift the orientation of its economy from a more inward-looking position to greater integration in world markets, its relations with the EC suffered a serious set-back. This was in spite of the widespread expectation in Turkey that an outward-looking economic policy would also serve to improve its relations with the EC. As it turned out, its greater integration in world markets by-passed Europe, and the volume of Turkey's trade with Europe — which had always retained a significant share of Turkish foreign trade — began to dwindle dramatically. There were increasing problems with the Community concerning restrictions on Turkey's textile exports as well as the Community's increased sensitivity to the immigration of Turkish workers (see Williams, this volume). The decline in trade was accompanied by a similar reduction in the financial assistance Europe provided to Turkey. Moreover, the souring of economic relations was also paralleled by the emergence of a serious rift between Turkey and the EC on political issues. Geopolitical considerations, which had dominated European attitudes to Turkey during the fifties and sixties, gradually lost their importance as Europe began to prioritize democracy and foreign-policy issues. While the military intervention posed the problem of democracy, Turkey's increasing *rapprochement* with the United States created a serious rift in foreign policy between it and a Europe which was trying to distance itself from its powerful ally.

After the events in Afghanistan and Iran, the strategic location of Turkey, once again, served its goal of *rapprochement* with the United States, in the wake of which American funds began to flow back into Turkey. These events also led to a quick resolution of several issues that had soured American–Turkish relations, the most important of which were the conclusion of the American–Turkish Defence and Economic Cooperation Agreement and Turkey's acceptance of the Rogers' Plan, which enabled the return of Greece to NATO's military structure. In this climate, the United States undertook the modernization of airfields in the east of Turkey, and American assistance to Turkey quadrupled between 1978 and 1981, reaching an all time peak in 1985 (see Eralp, 1991: 28–33).

Immediately after the military intervention, the EC adopted a wait-and-see attitude in its relations with Turkey. In the first few months, the Council of Europe, traditionally concerned with the issues of democracy and human rights, emerged as the main institution to oversee Europe's negotiations with Turkey. The Council's Parliamentary Assembly suspended Turkey's membership and refused to invite Turkish parliamentarians to its sessions, but it did not advise the expulsion of Turkey from the Committee of Ministers (Birand, 1985: 434). However, relations with the EC were not completely severed even at a time when the Council of Europe had distanced itself from Turkey, and it was in this early period that the Fourth Financial Protocol was ratified (19 June 1981). The Community's attitude to Turkey began to harden in the autumn of that year following the National Security Council's decree dissolving all political parties (15 October 1981) (Birand, 1985: 422–3). Among the many indications of this hardening of attitudes was the Commission's decision to delay the implementation of the Fourth Financial Protocol. The mission to Turkey in March 1982 by Belgian Foreign Minister Tindemans, as president of the EC Council of Ministers, produced a critical report voicing serious concern regarding human rights in Turkey. Furthermore, the European Parliament passed a resolution on 22 January 1982 suspending the joint Community–Turkey Parliamentary Committee, and the Association Council did not call for another meeting. The 1983 elections did not produce any change in EC attitudes towards Turkey, in spite of the fact that the Council of Europe resumed relations with the Turkish Parliament in the spring of 1984.

European insistence on democracy, publicized by a number of reports attesting to inhuman practices in Turkish courts and jails, were interpreted by the military government and by Prime Minister Özal as unwarranted interference in a sovereign country's internal affairs. This pointed to another serious divergence between Europe and Turkey. While the former regarded democracy as a *sine qua non* for inclusion into Europe, Turkey's leaders considered it to be an internal problem. Furthermore, Turkish leaders saw democracy in relative rather than absolute terms and believed that relations with Europe would resume a smooth course once Turkey was able to announce a timetable of transition to its version of democracy. The inability of Turkish policy-makers to assess correctly the importance placed by Europe on the question of democracy, even in view of the Greek, Spanish and Portuguese examples, served to escalate tensions between Turkey and the EC.

Turkey's application for full membership

The relationship between Europe and Turkey during much of the eighties continued to unfold in terms of competing definitions of democracy. Rather than the 1983 general elections, which the then Turkish government depicted as marking the transition to democratic rule, the European Community regarded the 1984 local elections as constituting the first steps towards the establishment of a parliamentary democracy in Turkey. In was in these local elections that those parties banned from participation in the general elections were first allowed to take part. The Özal government, elected to power in 1983, attempted to normalize relations with the EC, but several issues continued to plague the EC–Turkey dialogue. Among these the question of human rights figured strongly, but other unresolved issues such as the volume of Turkish textile exports to the Community, the resumption of the financial aid blocked in 1981, and the free movement of Turkish workers in Community countries as of December 1986 remained central. Added to these was the obstruction of the Greek lobby, which, as a full member of the Community, became increasingly effective.

In spite of such problems, the EC reversed its earlier stance and started a process of reactivating the Association Agreement, albeit without easing the pressure on the question of democracy. Thus, on 17 February 1986 EC foreign ministers agreed to convene a special meeting of the EC–Turkey Association Council which was eventually held on 16 September 1986 after Turkey's call for reactivation of the agreement. After this meeting, from which Greeks were significantly absent, Turkey was given the green light for the normalization of relations. But reactivation of the Association Agreement and the implementation of the Fourth Financial Protocol took much longer as a result of Greek opposition. One step that facilitated the reactivation of relations was Turkey's agreement in the winter of 1987 to grant the right of individual petition at the Council of Europe to its citizens. The action prompted the five European countries to drop their charges of human rights' violations which they had brought against Turkey at the Council of Europe. Association institutions, however, have begun to function only within the last few years: the joint Turkey–EC Parliamentary Committee met for the first time in January 1989. After several attempts that were pre-empted by Greek efforts to introduce the Cyprus question, the EC–Turkey Association Council has still been unable to convene.

In circumstances under which normalization of Turkish–EC relations were still debated, the decision taken by Prime Minister Özal to apply to the EC for full membership on 14 April 1987 came as a surprise to many observers inside and outside Turkey. The two traditional factors shaping Turkish foreign policy, Westernization and Greek international action, contributed greatly to this decision. The Turkish officials involved in the decision-making process stressed openly the importance they attached to the issue of Westernization. The Minister of Foreign Affairs went as far as declaring that Turkey's membership in all Western institutions prevented its exclusion from the EC (Yilmaz, 1988). Nevertheless, Turkey's commitment to Westernization no longer appears today to be the simple act of will that its founders hoped it would be. Islam has become a political force that has to be contended with and, at least according to one observer, is being transformed into a potent ideology (Mardin, 1989: 177) that is able to contest Turkey's traditional adherence to a goal of Westernization.[6] The ruling party itself, squeezed by demands within the country for the state apparatus to accord greater autonomy for the expression of Islamic identity, had to adopt a pragmatic policy, combining pro-Islamic and pro-Western tendencies. Mardin sees the success of Özal's party as lying in its ability to articulate a society that can accommodate the aspirations of, and create the space needed by, a Turkish 'provincial' and 'bazaar' population bred on Islamic precepts (1989: 177, 183).

These diverse internal pressures increasingly began to impinge on foreign-policy decisions taken by Turkish governments in the 1980s, and closer links were established with Middle-Eastern countries both at governmental level and also at the level of private entrepreneurs. Thus, Turkey began to take a more active role in the Islamic Conference and increased its links with the Islamic world. In 1981 Turkey assumed the chair of a Standing Committee for Economic and Commercial Cooperation, established at the third summit meeting of the organization. The decline in the volume of trade with the EC was accompanied in the early 1980s by an increase in trade with the Middle East, and the government encouraged the prolifer-ation of joint Turkish–Arab banks and trading companies. Prominent Turkish businessmen, including the prime minister's brother, have taken an active part in forging such links, especially with Saudi Arabia. Against such an economic backdrop, Turkey's foreign policy shows the marks of greater cooperation with Arab and other Islamic states. Thus, Turkey adopted what its policy-makers called an attitude of 'active neutrality' with respect to the Iran–Iraq war. Effectively this meant that, unlike the United States, it did not pursue either an overt or a covert anti-Iranian foreign policy. Furthermore, Turkey began to forge closer links with the PLO, and was among the first countries to recognize the newly declared independent Palestine state.

The *rapprochement* between Turkey and the Arab world has been cir-cumscribed by internal and external considerations. First, trade with the Middle East suffered a severe set-back in the mid-eighties, mainly as a result of the decline in oil revenues. In view of this volatility of Middle-Eastern markets, entrepreneurs once again turned to the comparatively more stable and thus reliable European markets. Second, the pro-Arab stance adopted by Turkish foreign policy has increasingly strained its more traditional alliances. Turkey's almost immediate recognition of Palestine served to create grave tensions with the United States, as well as marking the first overtly anti-Israel decision taken by a Turkish government. These tensions with the United States have been exacerbated by Turkey's refusal to follow the American policy of isolating Libya. The policy of forging stronger ties with the Arab world has also met strong opposition within Turkey itself. Economic and political links with Saudi Arabia and other Islamic countries are increasingly greeted with extreme concern by the country's secularist intelligentsia and press who regard Arab and Iranian interest in Turkish Islam with deep suspicion. The revelation that the government had obtained funds from a Saudi organization in order to pay wages to Turkish religious officials in Europe created a scandal that even implicated the president of the republic.

Finally, the changes in the nature of the Western alliance within the last decades complicate Turkish attempts at Westernisation, defined as taking part in institutions created by the Western alliance. The premise of an undifferentiated Western unity, on which Turkish perceptions are based, seems no longer to hold as economic and political rivalries undermine European–American cooperation. As Turkey applies for full membership of the EC, the difficulties of reconciling greater participation in Western institutions with a higher profile in the Islamic world will be matched by those faced in defining a new role for Turkey within the changing Western alliance.

As Turkey's hurried application for full membership shows, the Turkish government seems to have realized belatedly the significance of the 'Greek factor'. That Greece would have an advantage over Turkey in furthering its policies in Cyprus and the Aegean by being inside the Community only became apparent to Turkish policy-makers after the event. These political advantages have been accompanied by the economic gains that accrued to Greece as a result of full membership. Greece not only receives funds through the Community's regional and social policies but is also able to gain a competitive edge over Turkey with whom a similar export portfolio is shared. Turkey's trade difficulties in European markets are exacerbated by the accession of Spain and Portugal since they, too, are mainly exporters of broadly similar agricultural products and textiles (see William's, this volume). The accession of countries that are also premier exporters of textiles severely curtails Turkey's chances of success in having the quotas imposed on its textile exports by the EC reduced. Under such conditions, full membership appears to both policy-makers and industrialists in Turkey as the only way of securing export capability to Europe.

Turkey, drawing on the experiences of Greece, Spain and Portugal, has finally realized that mere association with the EC is no longer meaningful. According to Yılmaz, the Turkish Minister for Foreign Affairs in 1988, Greece had ceased association procedures in favour of full membership on the grounds that association brought heavy economic burdens without providing any compensating advantages. In Yılmaz's estimation, it was the same calculation that had prompted Spain and Portugal to negotiate for full membership directly. In all three cases it was the issue of a customs union that appeared to Yilmaz as the source of gravest concern. The disadvantages brought by customs union could only be out weighed by obtaining access to the financial benefits that membership to the European Community could provide. This view was also shared by Turkey's leading industrialists, whose apprehensions over a customs union had in the past been quite effective in stalling the association agreement (Eczacıbaşçı, 1988; Koç, 1988).

That the above argument captures more than a grain of truth does not suffice to explain the timing of Turkey's application to the EC for full membership. The decline in Turkey's economic profile in recent years also goes a long way towards accounting for this seemingly abrupt decision. After the mid-eighties, the earlier optimism generated by Özal's economic policies disappeared in the face of rising inflation and increasing debt problems. This rather bleak economic picture, reminiscent of the later

Democrat Party years, forced the Özal government to look for new sources of aid and credit. The prime minister seems to rely on longer-term credit than the EC would provide as a way of easing the pressure created by the short-term loans under which the Turkish economy operates. Leading industrialists are sending the same message to the prime minister, arguing that Turkey should be able to use the same funds available to her international competitors. One such industrialist calculates that EC membership would provide an inflow of foreign funds to the value of 6 billion ECU, a sum which would also be useful in curbing inflation (see IKV, 1989).

Becoming part of Europe is also in line with Özal's stated aim of improving Turkey's present standing in the international system. Ever since military intervention (if not before), Turkey's isolation on many international platforms had pushed it towards greater dependence on American political as well as financial backing. The questions raised about the nature of Turkish democracy — both at home and abroad and the uneven performance of Turkey's economy — had significantly contributed to this isolation. It is widely recognized that disputes with Greece, and especially over Turkish policy in Cyprus, have significantly added to this isolation, (see Sezer, 1989: 96). Reversing this situation, and retrieving Turkey's political and economic respectability, had been one of Özal's election planks. In fact, a look at other Mediterranean countries' foreign policies shows that while Greece, Spain and Portugal adopted a multidimensional stance in their policy orientations, the Turkish government in the early 1980s closely supported American policies. The United States administration, for its part, did not after the mid-eighties, maintain its earlier pro-Turkish attitude. The decline in American military assistance to Turkey, as of 1984, as well as the increasing importance of the Cyprus issue in considerations of aid to Turkey attest to this change in American policy (see Sezer, 1989: 91).[7] One wonders whether reactivation of links with the EC is one way of counterbalancing the effects of American policy.

Aftermath of Turkey's application: marginalization in Europe

It took more than two and a half years for the Commission of the European Community to prepare its report on Turkey. Compared with the Greek, Spain and Portugal's applications this seems rather a long period, demonstrating that the Commission had been trying to postpone the declaration of its negative opinion about Turkey's. I think it further indicates that the Turkish application had come at a point when the EC itself was facing important problems of consolidation. The addition of new members in the 1970s and 1980s slowed down the pace of European economic and political integration; larger membership has also made the process of decision-making longer and more complicated. The difficulties of small, independent nations operating in the world economy has finally prompted the Community to take more decisive steps towards reforming its constitution. These attempts, specially aimed at creating a more integrated structure, were crystallized with the adoption of the Single European Act in 1986.

Apart from a number of clauses designed to speed the process of decision-making, the Single Act accepted as a concrete short-term strategy the creation of a Single Market within Europe by the end of 1992. It is fairly obvious that the Community would be rather reluctant to welcome the application of a new country at such a stage (see Williams this volume).

These considerations have, to a large extent, determined the views of the Commission on Turkey's application, delivered on 17 December 1989. The decision amounted to a recommendation that accession negotiations with any country should not start before 1993 at the earliest, except in exceptional circumstances. In addition to such a general assessment, the Commission also stated that the specific analysis of the economic and political situation of Turkey showed that it would be hard for Turkey to cope with the adjustment constraints with which it would be confronted in the medium term if it acceded to the Community. Economic problems, for example the rate of inflation and the level of unemployment, as well as political problems such as the need to expand political pluralism, the ability to sustain the improvement in human rights, the rights of minorities, the persistence of disputes with Greece, and the lack of solution to the Cyprus problem were characterized as some of the factors which would create adjustment constraints for Turkey. The Commission concluded that 'it would not be useful to open accession negotiations with Turkey straight away' (Commission Opinion: 8). Nevertheless, the Commission suggested the reactivation of the Association Agreement which had been dormant for a long time and proposed a set of measures towards increasing interdependence between the Community and Turkey. These proposals included measures in four areas: the completion of the customs union, the resumption and intensification of financial cooperation, the promotion of industrial and technological cooperation, and the strengthening of political and cultural links.

The Commission report resulted in mixed interpretations in Turkey, leading to controversies over whether or not Turkey was still eligible for full membership. The comments by Matutes, the Commissioner for Mediterranean Affairs, implying that Turkey was eligible for membership, and formulation of proposals to increase relations between the Community and Turkey (in the Commission Report), led to the optimistic interpretation that the Commission's proposals could be thought of as part of a more comprehensive programme which would eventually lead Turkey to full membership. However, the fact that no date was specified in the report for the resumption of negotiations created dismay in official circles.

Government functionaries, as well as the representatives of the private sector, wished that the Council of Ministers had been more forthcoming, indicating a date to start negotiations. It did not matter whether this date corresponded to Turkish expectations; the mere announcement of the date was regarded as an important symbolic act. It is fairly clear that the Turkish government was not thinking of reactivating the Association Agreement at this stage but rather of steps leading to full membership.

The Council of Ministers met on 5 February 1990 and adopted the Report of the Commission without making any changes. In the earlier

Greek, Spanish and Portuguese applications, the Council of Ministers had a more favourable attitude and, in some cases, particularly in the Greek one, had overridden the negative opinion of the Commission. Although the trips of Ali Bozer, then vice-prime minister, to several Community capitals did not signal a different attitude, there were still expectations in official circles of a more favourable response from the Council of Ministers. However, it seems that the international climates surrounding the Turkish application and the earlier Greek, Portuguese and Spanish applications were rather different. In addition to the problems related to 'deepening' since the adoption of the Single European Act, the Community was immersed in the dramatic political changes in Eastern Europe during the last months of 1989 and early months of 1990. The uncertain political situation in Eastern Europe probably increased the reservations of the member countries of the Community with regard to accepting a new and a large country. In this respect, the timing of the Turkish application was more problematic for the Community than the earlier applications.

In line with the Commission Report, the Council of Ministers endorsed the reactivation of the Association Agreement and the strengthening of relations between the Community and Turkey and delegated to the Commission the study of a 'package of cooperation' between the Community and Turkey. In the course of negotiations, however, increasingly divergent interpretations of this 'package' were made by Community and Turkish officials. While the Turks emphasized that these proposals should be thought of as part of a comprehensive programme which would eventually lead Turkey to full membership, Community officials viewed them simply as measures to increase cooperation between the Community and Turkey, not committing the EC to Turkish membership. On 6 June the Commission formulated its specific proposals which primarily foresaw the establishment of a customs union for industrial products by the end of 1995. The proposals also included an important section on cooperation between Turkey and the Community in various sectors including industry, agriculture, financial services, transport, energy, the environment, science and technology. The Commission further advocated the promotion of political cooperation and the resumption of financial cooperation with Turkey and proposed that the Council concluded the long-awaited Fourth Financial Protocol which had been initialed in 1981.

This 'package of cooperation' which was conceived to reactivate the Association Agreement, met with Greek resistance in the Council of Ministers; the Greeks used their veto power, particularly with regard to the proposals for resumption of financial cooperation and the conclusion of the Fourth Financial Protocol. Indeed, the Fourth Financial Protocol has become one of the major symbols of Turkey–EC relations. Its history shows how these relations have worsened during the 1980s: the Protocol, which was initialed in 1981, has not yet become effective after more than a decade. As a full member of the Community, Greece was able to use the Community platform to voice her demands and cast her veto whenever cooperation between the Community and Turkey came on to the agenda. Greece's attitude became particularly manifest after the Dublin meeting of the

European Council in which the improvement of Turkey–EC relations was organically linked to the solution of the Cyprus dispute. Greek representatives increasingly began to demonstrate their arguments on the Cyprus dispute by opposing Community proposals which aimed to improve relations with Turkey.

It also shows how Greece's membership in the Community created an imbalance in Community attitudes *vis-à-vis* Greece and Turkey. It seems that the Community became an arena for the Greek–Turkish dispute in the 1980s, a possibility which had alarmed Community policy-makers when Greece applied for full membership in 1975. Because of the competition between Turkey and Greece, Community policy-makers, in general, tried to treat both countries rather equally and had maintained this careful balance over time. When Greece was given associate membership, Turkey followed suit. However with Greece's full membership in 1981, it became rather difficult for the Community to maintain this balance. Greek policy-makers began to utilize their status in the Community to further their political positions on international issues. Thus, it seems that Greek membership in the Community has aggravated rather than alleviated tensions between the two countries. Greek membership, especially her use of veto power on issues related to Turkey, has also led to the greater isolation of Turkey in Europe. It had resulted in more problematic relations between the Community and Turkey.

The examination of the post-war period shows that the European Community was quite functional in alleviating the tensions between two traditional enemies in Europe. France and Germany have improved their relations considerably as they became members of the Community. Bearing this example in mind, the Community might have had a catalytic role in the solution of the Greek–Turkish dispute, if Turkey had acceded to the Community with Greece. With Greece's membership, however, the Community was increasingly drawn into the Greek–Turkish dispute and found itself in a position of having to support Greek moves.

It would appear that the Greek veto power has also been useful for other Community members who have had reservations about Turkey's membership. In particular, Germany became sensitive about the issue of the immigration of Turkish workers and developed important reservations about free movement of Turkish workers in the Community as of December 1986. For newcomers Portugal and Spain, as well as France and Italy, the volume of Turkish textile exports to the Community was a critical issue. For nearly all, as I mentioned before, the question of human rights in Turkey remained central. Rather than pressurizing Greece to change her orientations, other members reinforced the idea that Turkish membership was not feasible because of the Greek veto. In this climate, Greece was able to create the image of being a 'victim', treated unfairly by its Western allies especially in the Cyprus dispute. With their strengthened position in the Community, it would be difficult for the Greek policy-makers to continue with this image. In the event of an improvement of relations between Turkey and other members of the Community, to use its veto power might be self-destructive for Greece. Recently, there has been an increasing realization that the Greek veto is obstructing the normalization of relations between the Community and Turkey.

The 'Greek factor' acquired significance for Community–Turkish relations primarily because of the changes in the international climate which led the Community to give less attention to the issue of Turkey's membership. As the European Community was facing important problems of integration following the adoption of its strategy on the Single European Market, dramatic changes in Eastern Europe and the Soviet Union began to shake the very basis of the post-war international system. The dissolution of the 'socialist regimes' in Eastern Europe and the ending of the cold war and 'divisions' in Europe forced the Community members to focus attention on these historical changes. In particular, Germany, the most powerful member of the Community, was increasingly drawn into immense economic and political problems after the incorporation of the former East Germany. As revealed in the Gulf Crisis, the European Community, faced with such dramatic changes in Europe, has became dangerously introverted. The European Community was unable to exercise an effective role in a region with which it has very close ties and in which it has important stakes.

The Gulf war also revealed how Turkey's relations with the West have changed. It is evident that the global events in Eastern Europe and the Soviet Union have posed a serious problem for the Turkish governing elite since, with the decline of the cold war, Turkey's geo-political significance in the East–West conflict has also declined. For a while it looked as if Turkish policy-makers faced a bleak future with regard to their relations with the West which, in view of the events in the Eastern bloc, would remove all interest in Turkey, leaving it to 'sweat out' its problems alone. Fears about the loss of Turkey's strategic importance, however, were quickly reversed in the Gulf Crisis. Efforts were now directed to the formulation of a new type of strategic importance, one that would relocate that importance more in relation to Turkey's role in the region rather than in terms of the East–West dimension.

The Gulf Crisis represents an important turning point in terms of the way in which Turkey's leaders sought to involve the country in global politics. During the 1980s, Turkish political and military leaders had recognized the divisions that existed among the Western powers regarding their assessment of the role Turkey should play in the international system. The Gulf Crisis finally induced the Turkish leadership to recognize this division and to opt for the United States rather than Europe, a tendency which had already appeared in the late 1970s and early 1980s. For the Turkish governing elite, the 'West' had largely meant Western Europe and the United States, undifferentiated as the Western alliance for a long time. At the end of the 1970s Turkey belatedly realized that the West was no longer an undifferentiated entity.

Turkish policy-makers began to voice the concept of 'strategic cooperation' to emphasize the development of special relations between Turkey and the United States. Based on his closer cooperation with the United States, Özal increasingly pointed out that Turkey provided a model to be emulated by other Middle Eastern countries. According to Özal, the

Turkish example demonstrated how a radical Islam which challenges Western interests could be successfully contained while Islamic values could at the same time be promoted. Wedding Islamic identity and aspirations to Western modernity in this fashion, Özal hoped that the Turkish example might be recognized and therefore supported financially by the West. Özal also thought of exporting his model for social order which seemed successful domestically: the promotion of trade as a way of minimizing political tensions in the region. The basic obstacle to these ambitious plans seemed to be the unwillingness of Arab nations to accept Turkey as a role model and a viable broker in regional affairs.

In effect, Turkish policy-makers had been unable to create an effective role of regional brokerage with regard to the Middle East. But, the Gulf Crisis set Turkey firmly on a regional course, in the wake of which came the proliferation of regional links such as the Black Sea Cooperation Project, improvement of relations with the Balkan countries and with the Turkic Republics of the Soviet Union. This new regional trajectory removed the issue of full membership from the agenda of the governing elite. In the beginning, there were some suggestions that these regional projects were functional and they would give Turkey a negotiating card in its relations with the Community; but these discussions died off and regional orientations took a course of their own. Thus, it seems that the Gulf Crisis and its aftermath served to strengthen the tendency which became manifest during the early 1980s, crystallizing the marginalisation of Turkey in Europe. With Turkey's application for full membership in 1987, it seemed, for a short time, that there might be a revitalization of EC–Turkey relations. These hopes now seem shattered as the EC and Turkey appear to be set to follow increasingly divergent paths.

The rejection of Turkey's application for membership has increased anti-Western, particularly anti-European, feelings in Turkey. EC statements on the Cyprus dispute or the Kurdish question have increased public resentment. These sentiments were fashioned and utilized by nationalist and religious political orientations. In particular, the Welfare Party led by Erbakan has stepped up its anti-EC attitude in such a climate and proposed an 'Islamic Common Market' as an alternative to the European Community.

Conclusion

Dramatic changes in the international climate present new options for the Turkish governing elite. During the cold war years, such options were foreclosed given Turkey's geo-political role in the East–West conflict and that links with Europe were perceived as essential. But, in the post-cold war atmosphere, exclusion from Europe is now leading Turkey to search actively for new options. It would seem that the dissolution of the Soviet Union, and the ensuing independence of the Turkic republics, have presented Turkey with such a viable option and there is an unprecented drive to increase economic, cultural and political links with these countries. This orientation further reinforces the negative feelings *vis-à-vis* the EC that were voiced during the Gulf Crisis. Among the Turkish governing elite, there is an increasing feeling that Turkey can do without the European Community.

It seems that the new regional drive is creating a historical turning point in Turkey's relations with the West, particularly with the EC. The possibility increasingly arises that Turkey might have a regional course, isolated from Europe. This new regional trajectory might be based on closer cooperation with the United States rather than with the EC. This situation constitutes a major turning point not only in terms of Turkey's foreign policy but also with regard to Turkey's identity. At the foundation of the Republic, Turkey made the political decision to become part of the West. This decision was also a question of identity: the leaders of the new nation had opted for development and modernization and this was only possible by becoming like the West. And the West had largely meant Western Europe. In the new fluid international climate, Turkish governing circles are increasingly involved in the redefinition of 'the West' and their Westernization project. As the 1990s seem to set the stage for even greater regional involvement for Turkey, questions of identity, religious and ethnic, will occupy greater space in domestic politics while the project of Westernization will be redefined.

Notes

1. This section, and the following three sections, are largely based on my previous work (Eralp, forthcoming).
2. Turkey's commitment to the West was so strong that its policy-makers felt slighted when Turkey was not included in the Marshall Plan immediately after the war.
3. Similar views seem to be prevalent in Greece in the same period (see Verney, 1987).
4. The Foundation (IKV in Turkish) was established in 1965 with the specific aim of coordinating the relations of the private sector with the EC.
5. The fact that the Demirel government needed the outside support of the National Salvation Party, a party that was bitterly opposed to Turkey's accession to the EC, goes a long way towards explaining the reluctance of the Turkish cabinet to heed its foreign minister (see Eralp, forthcoming). In effect, Erkmen was finally removed from office on 5 September 1980 after a parliamentary no-confidence vote in which the National Salvation Party played a key role.
6. It must immediately be mentioned that it was not only in the 1980s that questions of religion occupied an important place in Turkey's political agenda. The difference seems to lie in the mode in which demands for an Islamic way of life are articulated.
7. Sezer mentions other points that indicate the growing tensions between Turkey and the United States. Among these are the American refusal to open up American markets to more Turkish exports and the increased importance accorded by the United States Congress to various Armenian claims.

References

Birand, M.A., 1985, *Türkiye'nin Ortak Pazar Macerasi 1959–85* Istanbul: Milliyet yayinlari.

Ceyhan, H., 1988, 'Türkiye Avrupa Toplulugu 25 Ortaklık Yılının Değerlendirilmesi', *Iktisadi Kalkinma Vakfı Derqisi*, Ankara Antlasmasi 25. Yil Özel Sayisi, no. 59, September, 35–41.

Eczacibasi, N., 1988, 'Ankara Antlasmasinin 25. Yilinda Türkiye AT Iliskileri', *Iktisadi Kalkinma Vakfı Dergisi*, Ankara Antlasmasi 25. Yil Özel Sayisi, no. 59, September, 31–3.

Erlap, A., 1988, 'The Second Enlargement Process of the European Community and its Possible Effects on Turkey's External Relations', *Yapi Kredi Economic Review*, 11, (2–3), 3–24.

Erlap, A., 1990, 'The Politics of Turkish Development Strategies', in A. Finkel and N. Sirman (eds), *Turkish State, Turkish Society*, London: Routledge.

Erlap, A., 1991, 'Turkey in the Changing Post-war World Order: Strategies of Development and Westernization', paper presented to the Workshop on Comparative Study of Turkey and Egypt, Cairo.

Erlap, A., forthcoming, 'Turkey, and the European Community: Prospects for a New Relationship', in A. Eralp, M. Tünay, B. Yesilada (eds), *Socioeconomic Transformation of Turkey in the 1980s*: Praeger Publishers.

Gönlübol, M. and Ölman, H., 1987, 'Ikinci Dünya Savasindan Sonra Türk Dis Politikasi (1945–1965 Yillari): Genel Durum', in M. Gönlübol *et al.*, *Olaylarla Türk Dis Politikasi*, 6th edition, Ankara: Siyasal Bilgiler Fakültesi Yayinlari.

IKV, 1987, *Avrupa Topluluğu ve Türkiye-AT Iliskileri*, IKV pub. no. 49.

IKV, 1989, 'IKV Basin Toplantisi', *Iktisadi Kalkinma Vakfı Dergisi*, Ankara, no. 64, February, 6–7.

Koc, V., 1988, '25. Yilinda Türkiye-AT Ortaklik Iliskileri', *Iktisadi Kalkinma Vakfı Dergisi*, Ankara Antlasmasi 25. Yil Özel Sayisi, no. 59, September, 24–6.

Mardin, S., 1989, 'Culture and Religion: Towards the Year 2000', in *Turkey in the Year 2000*, Ankara: Turkish Political Science Association.

Nicholson, F. and East, R., 1987, *From the Six to the Twelve, The Enlargement of the European Communities*, Essex: Longman.

Van Rij, J., 1989, 'Comments on Turkey and European Community: Towards the Year 2000', in *Turkey in the Year 2000*, Ankara: Turkish Political Science Association.

Sander, O., 1979, *Türk-Amerikan Iliskileri 1947–1964*, Ankara: Siyasal Bilgiler Fakültesi Yayinlari, no. 427.

Sezer, D., 1989, 'Turkish Foreign Policy in the Year 2000', in *Turkey in the Year 2000*, Ankara: Turkish Political Science Association.

Şen, F., 1989, 'AT'nin Türkiye Raporu Sevimsiz', *Ekonomik Panoroma*, 2 (12), 16–7.

TOBB, 1987, *Iktisadi Rapor*, pub. no. Genel 20, APK-4.

Tsoukalis, L., 1981, *The European Community and its Mediterranean Enlargement*, London: George Allen and Unwin.

Turan, I., 1988, 'Turkish Political Parties and the European Community', *Yapi Kredi Economic Review*, 3 (1), 73–88.

Turan, I., 1989, 'Turkey and the European Community: Toward the Year 2000', in *Turkey in the Year 2000*, Ankara: Turkish Political Science Association.

Ülman, H. and Sander O., 1972, 'Türk Dis Politikasina Yön Veren Etkenler (1923–1968), II', *Siyasal Bilgiler Fakültesi, Dergisi*, 27 (1), 1–24.

Verney, S., 1987, 'Greece and the European Community', in K. Featherstone and

D.K. Katsoudas (eds), *Political Change in Greece: Before and After the Colonels*, London: Croom Helm.

Yalcin, N., 1989a, 'AT'da Boykot Hazirligi', *Milliyet*, 5 March.

Yalcin, N., 1989b, 'AT Öyeligi 1992'den önce Hayal', *Milliyet*, 24 March.

Yalmaz, M., 1988, 'Ankara Antlasmasinin Siyasi Yönü ve Dis Iliskilerimiz Bakimindan Değerlendirilmesi', *Iktisadi Kalkinma Vakfi Dergisi*, Ankara Antlasmasi 25. Yil Özel Sayisi, no. 59, September, 9–11.

3
Turkey: the Mediterranean context

Allan M. Williams

Introduction: Turkey through the Mediterranean prism

Turkey's relationships with the European Community are mediated by its location within the ill-defined Mediterranean sphere of influence. Turkey is not simply 'a Mediterranean country', as is evident by its location within the Middle East and its strategic position with respect to the newly independent republics of the former Soviet Union. However, its relationships with the EC, particularly in the past but to a large extent in the present, are coloured by the perception of its Mediterranean features and linkages. In so far as the centres of economic power in Turkey lie in the west, this has some foundation. Moreover, this is how the country is normally analysed and classified in most EC analyses of trade relationships, special associations and preferential agreements. Indeed, one of the critical questions in understanding Turkey–Mediterranean relationships is the balance between those Mediterranean states within and without the EC. It follows, therefore, that one of the keys to understanding Turkey's dialogue with Europe is to see it in context of the Mediterranean region, although this is set within a larger hierarchy of relationships stretching upwards to the global level. These are not necessarily uni-directional relationships. Turkey's relationship with the EC is contingent upon the Mediterranean dimension, but, at the same time, it has sufficient economic weight and strategic importance to give it a key role in shaping this Mediterranean dimension. This is true in terms of population (52 million in the late 1980s), economic dynamism, and military strategic roles.

The original Community of Six was essentially a Northern European construction. France had a Mediterranean south but only Italy could claim to be an essentially Mediterranean state. Even in Italy, the real centres of economic power were in the least Mediterranean region, the north. Given the particular geopolitical and economic considerations that guided the formation of the Community, and the early evolution of its common policies, it was predictable that Mediterranean considerations were not central at this time. The same applied during the critical decade of the 1960s when the two essential economic frameworks of the EC were established: the internal free market, within a common external tariff, in industrial goods; and the Common Agricultural Policy. The latter was heavily orientated towards intervening in the markets for northern European farm products.

Given the early focus of the Community, it was probably inevitable that any eventual Mediterranean reorientation of policies and interests would be characterised by incrementalism. This was especially the case after the First Enlargement brought three further northern European countries into the EC, although one of these — Ireland — shared some economic and social structural characteristics with the future Mediterranean member states. The European Regional Development Fund, established as part of a package of measures to ease the accession of the United Kingdom, was also to prove important in the transfer of structural assistance to, at first, Italy, and later the other Mediterranean member states. Even more important was the 1981 accession of Greece which gave the Community a strong presence in the eastern Mediterranean and a new dimension to relations with Turkey. Furthermore, as part of the internal EC compromise leading to the agreement over the 1986 accession of Spain and Portugal to the Community, the countries with existing Mediterranean interests negotiated the introduction of a new package of structural measures, the Integrated Mediterranean Programme. This effected a further resource distribution from the northern core of the European Community to the Mediterranean regions. Meanwhile, the enlargements of the 1980s led the Community to re-examine its relationships with the other Mediterranean non-member states, including Turkey.

Although Mediterranean issues increased in prominence in the early 1980s, they were soon caught up in much wider issues of European convergence. The Single European Market programme, and later the Maastricht treaty, both served to refocus Community attention on to global issues and the vexed questions of European union. Additional urgency was lent to this by the extraordinarily rapidly changing position in Eastern and Central Europe and in the Soviet Union. The future of the EC's internal Mediterranean policies became caught up with broader issues of convergence in the Community, a linked but different question. External relations with the non-member Mediterranean states were also enmeshed with the attempt to formulate a common foreign and security policy and with specific issues such as recognition of the former Yugoslav republics, legal and illegal immigration into a 'fortress' Europe, and relationships with Islamic countries and groups. It was within this uncertain context that Turkey lodged its formal application for EC membership in 1987. This was clearly a different economic and political Mediterranean and global context to that prevailing at the time of the 1963 Association agreement between Turkey and the EC.

Establishing the European Community: the Mediterranean offstage

There were several major forces behind the drive to establish the European Community. These ranged from political idealism, as in the European federalist movement, to the need to create a third force in global politics, to an attempt to overcome trade distortions and increase market size in Europe (Mowat, 1973). The focus of the new Community was northern Europe. This was evident in the way that the Benelux Customs Union provided a model for the establishment of the Community, and more importantly in that the Community was above all a political construct for the reconciliation of France and Germany. The interests of the Mediterranean region and of the principal Mediterranean member state, Italy, were near the bottom of the prevailing hierarchy of interests. Italy was, in effect, willing to trade off its specific Mediterranean interests against those of its northern manufacturers, a strategy which was seemingly vindicated by the 'economic miracle' of the early 1960s (Rey, 1982). At the same time Italy did win a programme of special assistance for the developments of the Mezzogiorno, recognised as the poorest region within the EC6 rather than as a specific Mediterranean regional problem.

The Treaty of Rome was essentially guided by a number of negative economic principles, the aim being the elimination of barriers to the operation of free markets for capital and labour, and for trade (the customs union and the common external tariff). There was also provision for common policies in the fields of social affairs, transport, and agriculture. However, as Holland (1980, p. 10) writes, the Treaty is 'mainly concerned with preventing abuses to competition and the market mechanism rather than with providing a framework for joint intervention to achieve what the market itself cannot do'. The need for such a minimalist approach was dictated by the speed at which the Community was established, making it necessary to avoid contentious issues or highly detailed policy formation. West Germany was also fundamentally opposed to any large-scale state intervention. This effectively ruled out any attempt to launch a comprehensive development policy for the Mediterranean regions; the Italian 'problem' was always seen as exceptional.

This initial neglect of the Mediterranean region was repeated throughout 1958–73, which were to be the formative years for most Community policies. In some ways the crowning achievement of these years was the shaping of the Common Agricultural Policy (see Hill, 1984). However, it was forged mainly as a compromise between the conflicting interests of French and German farmers. This had two main implications. First, intervention was mainly directed at northern agricultural products so that many Mediterranean products were excluded from the guarantee price system. Second, high guarantee prices and growing levels of intervention purchasing meant that the Common Agricultural Policy soon came to absorb a massive proportion of the total EC budget: 74 per cent by 1972. This severely reduced the scope for other forms of Community structural intervention, both within and without agriculture, thereby constraining contemporary and future Mediterranean policies.

The other major achievement of these years was the establishment of the customs union and the common external tariff. These contributed to a reorientation of European trade (via trade diversion and trade creation) as intra-EC commerce grew at the expense of extra-EC trade (Wijkman, 1989). The long-term significance of this was its effect on the British economy which, together with geopolitical changes, led to the first enlargement of the Community on 1 January 1973, effectively reinforcing the northern European bias of the EC. It also introduced the irritant of the British budgetary rebate which was to add to the difficulties of decision-making in the enlarged Community.

The Mediterranean region was not completely ignored during these years. On the one hand the Community simply could not neglect such a large economic region on its doorstep, especially as individual Mediterranean economies began to expand in the 1960s. In addition, many of the member states had historic ties with the region, based mostly on ex-colonial ties: France with Morocco, Algeria, Tunisia, Lebanon, and Syria: Italy with Tunisia; and latterly, the United Kingdom with Cyprus, Egypt, Israel and Malta. Greece and Turkey, as NATO members, also had defence links with most of the Community member states; and the cold war underlined their strategic importance.

The Community's initial response to the non-member Mediterranean states was a series of individual cooperation or association agreements; 12 of these were signed during the 1960s and the 1970s. The association agreements with Greece, Turkey, Cyprus and Malta were designed eventually to lead to a customs union with the EC. For Turkey there was also the possibility of eventual membership of the Community. The Maghreb countries (Algeria, Morocco and Tunisia) and the Mashreq countries (Egypt, Syria and the Lebanon), Israel and Yugoslavia were linked to the Community by cooperation agreements which covered trade, industrial cooperation and financial assistance (see Table 3.1). The earliest association agreement was with Greece (1961), followed by Turkey (1963) and Morocco and Tunisia (1967). The effectiveness of these agreements was, at best, uneven during the 1960s. These were also bilateral agreements rather than collective arrangements for the Mediterranean basin. Given its colonial history — or more precisely its lack of colonial links with the northern European countries — Turkey was granted its special association agreement at a relatively early date which is probably indicative of the strategic importance attached to this country.

In 1972 there was a major change in the Community's approach when it brought the ad hoc bilateral relationships within the common framework of the so-called Mediterranean global approach, an early example of a macro regional approach. This reflected growing Community awareness of the importance of the region and was also an attempt to harmonise its patchy relationships with individual countries. In effect this offered preferential trading relationships to the region; the Mediterranean countries were given free entry to the Community for their manufactures without immediate reciprocity being demanded by the EC. The two main exceptions were agro-industrial products (and even more so, agricultural products) and, from the

Table 3.1 Mediterranean countries' access to the EC market for industrial goods during the 1960s and 1970s

Country	Free access since	Legal basis
Greece	1968	1961 Association Agreement
Morocco & Tunisia	1969	1967 Association Agreement
Maghreb, Mashreq, Cyprus, Libya, & Yugoslavia	1971	Generalised system of preferences
Turkey	1971	1963 Association Agreement
Portugal	1976	1972 Free Trade Agreement
Maghreb	1976	1976 Co-operation Agreement
Israel	1977	1975 Free Trade Agreement
Mashreq	1977	1977 Co-operation Agreement
Malta	1978	1970 Association Agreement
Cyprus	1978	1972 Association Agreement
Yugosalvia	1980	1980 Co-operation Agreement

Source: based on Ashoff (1983)

late 1970s, textiles which became subject to quantitative restrictions. These were of course the critical industries in which they had some comparative advantage.

Migration was another area of Mediterranean interest to the EC. One of the EC's founding principles was the creation of a single market for labour. Throughout the 1960s there was progressive implementation of freedom of movement and removal of labour-market discrimination against nationals from other member states (Molle and van Mourik, 1988). This contributed to an increase in the number of intra-EC international migrants in the Community from 577,000 in 1950 to 905,000 in 1974 (Straubhaar, 1988). However, during the same period the number of extra-EC migrants increased from 722,000 to 3.5 million. This underlined the fact that the restructuring of labour markets in the EC was part of the larger globalisation of the European economy and also the importance of the Mediterranean region as a source of labour for the Community. This was to prove an exceptional period for emigration.

At this time, Turkey had a relatively high profile within the Community's interests in the Mediterranean region. For example, it was the second country to sign an association agreement with the EC (12 September 1963). There certainly was an economic basis to the agreement based on mutual interests in trade and markets, and indeed these featured heavily in the Treaty of Ankara (see Rosenthal, 1982). However, the largely autarkic economic development strategy followed during the 1960s meant that at that time Turkey was far less exposed to international influences than it would become in later decades after it had opened up its economy. It is not surprising, therefore, that most commentators consider that political as well as economic factors were important in the decision to seek the association agreement. Among these were the need to counterbalance the cooling political alliance with the United States and the pursuit of further

Europeanisation. In addition, there was, as ever, a need to balance out Greece's political relationships (see Gürel, this volume).

Political reasons also lay behind Turkey's decision in 1967 to ask for the transition phase of the agreement to be brought forward, to the additional protocol which was signed in 1970 setting out a new timetable for freedom of movement of labour, and for the dismantling of quantitative restrictions on industrial trade. The specific political motives behind these moves included the opportunity which arose from the freezing of the EC's relationships with Greece and disappointment concerning the lack of support received from the United States during the Cyprus crisis (see Eralp, this volume). There were also growing trade ties between Turkey and the EC (Goodman, 1976). However, in most other respects the Turkish economy was not yet ready for closer trade relationships: for example, in 1969 manufactured products accounted for only 10 per cent of all exports. At this stage, therefore, Turkey had only limited economic and political importance for the EC at a time when the latter's Mediterranean policies were still nascent.

The Mediterraneanisation of the European Community: the 1970s and early 1980s

The 1970s opened brightly for the Community, after a decade of successful integration measures had culminated in the first enlargement. The high point was probably the 1972 summit of heads of governments which agreed to move rapidly to completion of the internal market and to the adoption of a common currency among other measures (Williams, 1991, chapter 4). However, there were already signs that the long post-war economic boom was coming to a close. As a result, the entire context for the EC's development had changed. In the 1960s the expansionary environment had meant that the EC had been 'condemned to succeed' in its integration (Hodges, 1981, p. 6). But by the 1970s there was a cold climate for further economic integration, and this was compounded by general budgetary problems.

The new economic climate affected the EC's Mediterranean relationships in a number of ways. First, the more difficult competitive environment, and especially the challenge offered by Japan and the Newly Industrialising Countries, led to a wave of protectionist sentiment throughout northern Europe. This was particularly evident in the more sensitive sectors: cars, steel and clothing/textiles (Ziebura, 1982). The last of these had serious consequences for the non-member Mediterranean countries. Second, rising average EC unemployment — from 3 per cent in 1973 to 11 per cent in 1984 — led to attempts by individual governments to restrict further immigration from outside the EC. Again, this had implications for the Mediterranean region, which were compounded by the improved access obtained by the new member states. Third, there was continuing growth of agricultural production and surpluses so that the Common Agricultural Policy accounted for 78 per cent of the EC budget by 1978. This squeezed the scope for other policy expenditures and for structural assistance to member and non-member Mediterranean states. For example, the Social and Regional Funds, respectively, accounted for only 7 per cent and 6.5 per cent of total expenditure by 1986. It also became even more difficult for the EC to grant trade concessions for agricultural products to non-member states. Over time these difficulties were exacerbated; during the 1970s, more and more Mediterranean products were brought within the CAP. As a result, higher prices and guaranteed markets stimulated production within the Community. Taken together with the enlargements of the 1980s, these policies would lead to greater Community self-sufficiency and to reduced export opportunities for the non-member states.

Despite these difficulties, there was an effective Mediterraneanisation of the EC during the early 1980s brought about by the second enlargement, following the accession of Greece in 1981 and of Spain and Portugal in 1986. While there was some economic logic for the Community in such a market enlargement, there was equally compelling political motivation to help stabilise the new democracies in these countries. Greece was the first new member. Given its small size it did not seem to pose insurmountable problems for the Community, with the exception of some agricultural products. However, with hindsight it seems that the accession was rushed through prematurely to avoid the difficulties that were expected following the anticipated electoral victory of the anti-EC PASOK. Greece has subsequently found it difficult to adjust to trading and macro-economic conditions in the Community. Its trade balance has deteriorated, its industry has suffered from competition, and it has failed to tackle either its inflationary or public-deficit weaknesses. For example, most economic analysts consider Greece is the member state least likely to meet the convergence criteria set out at Maastricht for transition to the third stage of the Economic and Monetary union. In the 1990s the Community has been taking a harder line with Greece and has withheld further financial assistance until such time as the Greek government actually implements fiscal reforms to which it has previously agreed. The only compensation for Greece, although a burden on the Community, has been the substantial transfers it has received under the structural and other programmes: these were equivalent to 2.5 per cent of GDP in 1984 (Georgakopoulos, 1986).

Outwardly, the accession of Spain and Portugal posed more difficulties for the Community. Spain was a large economy with a potentially very competitive agricultural sector, while both the Iberian applicants were likely to make substantial demands on the Community's structural funds. In terms of their trade links with the Community, these were broadly similar to those of Turkey at the present time. Fifty-seven per cent of Portugal's exports and 39 per cent of its imports were with the EC9; for Spain, the respective figures were 47 per cent and 32 per cent. Irrespective of the economic arguments, some member states — notably Germany — were keen to accept the Iberian members in order to help ensure democracy in those countries.

The Iberian enlargement of the Community has been a relative success. Lengthy transition periods were agreed for the new members, ranging mostly between five and ten years. Thus far, both economies have experienced high growth rates and have displayed some convergence with the

Community in terms of public-sector expenditure, monetary policy and liberalisation, if less so in terms of inflation and current-account deficits. However, this has not been without cost to the new members — in terms of their balance of payments and economic restructuring — or to the Community. Portugal, for example, received transfers from the EC which were equivalent to 2.5 per cent of its GDP in the first three years of membership (Eisfeld, 1989). The Iberian enlargement also brought into being another dimension to the Community's Mediterranean interests. As part of the internal compromise which preceded the 1985 agreement on enlargement, the Integrated Mediterranean Programme was introduced partly to compensate the existing Mediterranean regions for the increased competition that was expected to result; 50 per cent of this programme was earmarked for Greece. In summary, therefore, the cost implications of the Mediterraneanisation of the EC during the 1980s were likely to have made it more circumspect about further accessions.

The non-member Mediterranean state had to adjust in the 1980s to two conditions: the first was the enlargement. The scale of the challenge was underlined by the fact that Spain alone exported more non-fuel products to the Community than did all the non-member Mediterranean states taken together. There were specific concerns about agriculture and that the new members would pre-empt the traditional markets of non-members. The most vulnerable products are citrus fruits, early potatoes, tomatoes, olive oil, olives, grapes and wine. Spain, in particular, had massive agricultural surpluses in most of these products. As a result, the Community of Twelve was likely to move into surplus in most of these products, whereas wine lakes were the only serious 'Mediterranean' surplus in the Community of Nine. Furthermore, the CAP's high prices were expected to have a dynamic effect, stimulating additional production in the new member states. The problems were underlined by an EC analysis which suggested that 45 per cent of Mediterranean non-member states' agricultural exports to the Community were at a 'high risk' from the Second Enlargement (Commission of the European Community, 1985). Yugoslavia, Turkey and Egypt were least vulnerable, while Cyprus, Morocco, Israel and Tunisia were most at risk. Whereas Turkey had EC exports of ECU 375 million in 1982, only EC 26 million ECU were considered at risk. In contrast, 251 million of Morocco's ECU 295 million were considered at high risk, and by the 1980s Morocco was accumulating mini-mountains of unsold oranges. Turkey's exports were considered to be least at risk because of their uniqueness: hazelnuts, sultanas, dried figs and apricots, tobacco and lentils met less competition from within the Community, either before or after the Second Enlargement.

The second difficulty for the non-member states was that the economic boom had come to an end, particularly in northern Europe. This had implications for their manufacturing sectors: 'The Community's economic performance, far from sustaining growth as in the heady 1960s and until the mid 1970s, had become a source of constriction and anxiety for development planners throughout the region' (Commission of the European Communities, 1985, p. 20). The countries most directly at risk were

Morocco, Tunisia and Turkey as almost 70 per cent of their industrial trade was directed to the Community in the early 1980s (Ashoff, 1983, p. 112).

In trade with the Community most of the non-member Mediterranean countries have specialised in light industrial products, especially textiles and clothing, leather items and footwear. These were all covered by the preferential access provided under the Global Mediterranean Policy. However, by the late 1970s the EC's own textiles/clothing industries were in deep crisis. The Community responded by 'persuading' the principal textile producers in the Mediterranean region to sign voluntary export restraint agreements. It suggested that otherwise it would invoke the safeguard clause in the Global Mediterranean Policy. Turkey refused to accept self-limitation and had unilateral import restrictions imposed upon it. Ashoff (1983) estimates that Morocco, Malta and Tunisia were little affected by these agreements. In contrast, Turkey had the highest proportion of production considered by Ashoff to be 'probably affected'; 44 per cent of Turkey's exports were considered to be vulnerable. The problem centred on the high proportion of Turkish exports destined to the Community and the predominance of cotton yarn within its export profile. Despite these limitations, the Mediterranean region still maintained a favoured relationship with the EC. The state-trading economies and the Asian producers had much tougher and less flexible quotas imposed on their textile industries.

These difficulties were exaggerated by the Second Enlargement as all three new member states were important producers in these industrial sectors. In 1982 the three new members had exports to the EC which were approximately equal to those of all the other Mediterranean countries. Turkey was most at risk in simple quantitative terms, as it had exports to the EC of ECU 655.7 million in 1982. Yugoslavia ranked second with exports of ECU 525.2 million. The Second Enlargement did not lead to any significant change in the access of either the new member states or the non-members states to EC industrial markets as these had already been duty-free for some years. However, there were fears that the accession would lead to increased use of safeguard measures by the Community; the demands were expected to come either from the northern states as a response to the guaranteed access obtained by Greece, Spain and Portugal or from the new members themselves in order to protect them against other low-labour-cost producers.

Even before any such political and dynamic changes took place, there is strong evidence that the economic ties between Mediterranean non-member and member states had weakened in the first half of the 1980s (Aliboni, 1990). The Mediterranean member states' trade grew fastest with northern Europe, and then with each other, while trade ties with non-EC Mediterranean states stagnated. This means that 'the EC–South Mediterranean solidarity is weakening and its future appears linked less to an inherent economic logic than to political options. This is the meaning of the applications made by Cyprus, Malta and Morocco, and of Turkey's insistence on speeding up its accession to the EC' (Aliboni, 1990, p. 159).

The preceding discussion has given the impression of uni-directional flows with the Community sustaining the economies of the Mediterranean region — with the exception of textiles/clothing. This, however, was not the case, for the Community has consistently exported more to the region than it imported from it. It has been much more a 'dynamic market than . . . a productive threat'. All the member states had positive trade balances with the Community, especially West Germany which already had a surplus of over ECU 3,000 million in 1982. The non-member Mediterranean states, including Turkey, provide an important market for the EC's agricultural and industrial exporters. In agriculture they bought 18 per cent of the EC's dairy exports and 22 per cent of their cereal exports in 1982.

Quite apart from the immediate trade effects, the Second Enlargement also changed relationships within the Mediterranean region. There were now four Mediterranean member states and if they were able to co-operate effectively, then such solidarity could provide the basis to exert considerable influence on Community policy. In practice, however, the Mediterranean member states have not worked effectively as a common interest group. They have mostly been content with special pleading at the margin of policy-making rather than seeking to dictate the overall direction of policy.

The shift in EC–Mediterranean relationships is also to be seen in other contexts. For example, during the 1970s and 1980s there has been a growing divergence between the member and non-member states in terms of emigration. Until the 1970s there was little to distinguish the pattern of emigration from all the Mediterranean countries to northern Europe. However, by the 1980s the Mediterranean member states were becoming less important as sources of emigrants to the north, but were becoming more pronounced as countries of immigration from the south; this was especially the case with Italy with an estimated one million of the two million immigrants in the four southern member states (King, forthcoming). Because of this, there has been growing concern in other EC governments about the security risks and labour-market threats emanating from what is perceived to be the relatively weak and porous frontier of the Community in the Mediterranean region. The issue is not as simple as this because there are important differences in the attitudes towards immigration in the southern members states themselves. Italy had been relatively relaxed because of the need for imported labour, also wishing to avoid making this an issue which could generate racial conflicts. Recent developments in the former Yugoslavia and Albania have, however, led to a hardening of Italian attitudes in this respect. Spain wishes to stem immigration, which has come to be seen as a threat to security and to domestic labour. The unanswered question is whether the Mediterranean member states will be able, or will wish, to act together to influence EC immigration policy. If so, they are likely to wish to protect their relatively privileged position within the EC's international division of labour, at least until such time as they experience significant labour-market constraints. The same consideration is likely to influence the attitude of the EC as a whole.

Turkey's relationships with the EC, relative to the rest of the Mediterranean region, slipped during this period. In the early 1960s, it was the only non-member Mediterranean country, other than Greece, to have a special relationship with the Community. This was weakened by the

Community's adoption of the global Mediterranean policy and, sub-sequently, by the Second Enlargement. Meanwhile, a number of other events also strained relationships with the Community: the 1974 Cyprus crisis drew criticism from some Community member states, notably France; Greece's application and acceptance for full membership was viewed with grave distrust; and the imposition of import quotas on textile imports after 1978 hindered Turkish exporters. However, relationships warmed after 1985 as Turkey opened up its economy and adopted economic stabilisation measures. Industrial interests also began to talk about seeking full member-ship of the Community as soon as possible (Rosenthal, 1982, p. 15), so as to improve Turkey's relative position among the Mediterranean states. Political reforms and the return to parliamentary democracy after the 1983 election also helped in this respect.

The Globalisation of the Community: the Mediterranean in retreat

During the 1970s and the early 1980s the Community had become more inward looking, but at the same time there had been a greater awareness of Mediterranean issues as a result of the Second Enlargement. In the mid- and late 1980s, however, Mediterranean issues were to be overshadowed by major developments both within and outside of the Community. It was in this context that Turkey applied for full membership of the Community in 1987; it was arguably one of the least propitious moments in the history of the Community for such an application.

By the early 1980s there was growing realisation in the Community of a loss of global competitiveness. Western European growth rates were seen to have fallen behind the global average, most notably those of the other two economic superpowers, Japan and the United States. Europe was much slower in recovering from the 1973–4 oil crisis than its major rivals, and there was a view that it had 'a population of sleeping giants who were ill-equipped to meet the challenge of the 1970s and the 1980s' (Geroski and Jacquemin, 1985, p. 175). The Community was perceived to be particularly weak in the areas of high-technology goods for which it had a mounting trade deficit. This gave rise to the fear that the EC was suffering from 'Eurosclerosis' — a technological paralysis compared to its major economic rivals. It was inevitable that the interests of the Mediterranean countries — with the exception of Italy (home to transnationals such as Olivetti) — would appear to be less than central in the debate that surrounded this economic malaise. For example, the technology programmes which were introduced by the Community — such as RACE, CUBE and ESA — to en-courage intra-EC cooperation, tended to favour the northern European member states (Sharp, 1989) in terms of their construction and the allo-cation of funds.

The Community's principal response to these economic weaknesses was to launch the Single Market Programme. This was, in effect, an attempt to complete the process of establishing the single EC market. It was, therefore, very much an extension of the Community's earlier emphasis on negative measures, that is, the elimination of internal barriers. There were three types of measures: to remove physical, fiscal and technical barriers. These had important consequences for all the member states but some measures were particularly important for the Mediterranean countries. The removal of physical barriers such as customs and passport controls focused attention on the Community's 'porous' southern border in the Mediterranean member states; both security and illegal migration issues were raised. Eliminating fiscal barriers required adjustments — such as realigning VAT rates — by all the member states and did not pose specifically Mediterranean issues. However, some of the measures to remove the so-called technical barriers were expected to impinge strongly on the southern member states: among these were the harmonisation and liberalisation of financial services, the opening up of public procurement, the reduction of state subsidies, and greater freedom of movement for labour. Whether these measures will bring about the great economic leap forward envisaged in the Cecchini report (1988) is questionable, but they will certainly change the context for relationships with the Mediterranean region.

The indirect consequences of the Single Market Programme are expected to be even greater. An issue of particular importance here is the pressure for greater economic and political union, in large part as a logical consequence of the creation of the Single Market. This culminated in the Maastricht intergovernmental conference in December 1991, at which the 12 members committed themselves to a vast array of new policy and institutional arrangements. In part, the Maastricht agreements represented extensions of existing areas of EC competence in such areas as the environment and transport. There were also major new initiatives in the fields of foreign policy and coordination of policy on refugees and illegal immigrants. Mediterranean issues, especially events in the former Yugoslavia, influenced these policy initiatives. However, the most important initiative agreed at Maastricht was the staged conditional transition to Economic and Monetary Union by 1997/9. Member states would automatically pass to the third and final stage of monetary union if their economies met certain criteria. These are dependent on economic convergence in terms of public sector deficit, inflation, exchange-rate stability and public debt. There are stringent conditions and there were serious doubts as to the ability of several member states — including all the Mediterranean ones — to achieve the targets. The painful process of economic adjustment is to be eased by a cohesion fund affecting North–South transfers within the Community. The Maastricht agreement also made an unspecific committment to greater political union. If the agreement is ratified by the member states, then this will, effectively, increase the 'price' of future membership.

The Maastricht agreement may also have other implications for the EC. The Community is moving slowly, but decidedly, towards a cohesive foreign policy. This has been heightened by the need to develop a coordinated policy response to such major international events as the Gulf Crisis, the disintegration of the Soviet Union and the civil wars in the former Yugoslavia. As a consequence there should in future be a more coordinated EC approach to the Mediterranean region in respect of political as well as economic issues. There is also, potentially, the birth of Social Europe following the adoption (excepting the United Kingdom) of a Social Agreement at the Maastricht conference. This moves the EC towards harmonising working and living conditions as an essentially parallel move to economic union. It is inspired by the need to harmonise competitive conditions within the EC and also by fears in northern Europe of 'social dumping'. There is a real possibility that, if and when the Social Agreement develops, the EC may begin to insist on similar conditions being accepted by those non-member states to which it offers privileged trading relationships. It is an open question as to how this will effect the more labour-intensive economies of Mediterranean Europe.

The Single Market Programme was launched against a background of unease relating to economic and social inequalities in the EC, at both the national and the regional levels. The Treaty of Rome had considered these to be temporary phenomena which would be eliminated or at least reduced during the process of integration. However, these inequalities have proven remarkably resilient, and the enlargement of the Community has intensified them. They now have an essentially North–Mediterranean complexion — with the exception of Ireland. Income differentials between the ten richest and the ten poorest regions in the EC are of the order of a three-to-one ratio. The Community has approached these inequalities via its structural funds which, in effect, bring about transfers of resources to the poorer regions and member states; the most important of these are the CAP, the Regional and Social Funds, the European Investment Bank, and the special programmes of assistance for Greece, Portugal and Spain.

With the adoption of the 1992 programme, there were widespread fears that this could lead to increasing inequalities in the community. In 1988, therefore, the so-called Delors programme was introduced which committed 63 billion ECU to help bring about convergence among the member states. Two-thirds of funds are to be spent in the laggard regions with per capita income below three-quarters of the EC average; most of the rest is for regions in industrial decline. Portugal, Greece and Ireland are wholly covered under the first criterion, as are large parts of Spain and southern Italy. The planned distribution of funds to 1993 is shown in Table 3.2: Portugal is the largest net recipient followed by Greece and Ireland, with Spain being the only other significant beneficiary. This is considerably greater than the aid offered to any of the Mediterranean non-member states. For example, Turkey was offered ECU 600 million under the Fourth Financial Protocol of the EC with the Mediterranean countries. This was later frozen but, even if the aid had been transferred, it would only have amounted to about 1 per cent of GNP in one year. This is significantly less than Portugal and Greece now receive annually as part of the Delors' package.

However, there is depressing evidence that even after considerable structural transfers, and a sustained period of growth, convergence between the Mediterranean states and the remainder of the Community has been painfully slow. Between 1986 and 1990 the four less-developed member states of the Community grew, on average, at 1.4 percentage points faster than the

Table 3.2 EC structural fund transfers as percentages of GDP

Country	1988	1993 (projected)
Belgium	0.1	0.1
Denmark	0.1	0.1
Germany	0.0	0.1
Greece	1.6	2.9
Spain	0.5	0.8
France	0.1	0.1
Ireland	1.5	2.7
Italy	0.2	0.3
Luxembourg	0.2	0.2
Netherlands	0.1	0.1
Portugal	2.4	3.7
United Kingdon	0.2	0.2

Source: European Commission

other (northern) EC states. However, their GDP per-capita levels only increased from 66 per cent to 69 per cent of the EC average. Greece actually fell back during this period from 56 per cent to 53 per cent. Even if these rates of growth were to be sustained over twenty years, the figure would still only rise to 90 per cent of the Community average. The probability is that while Spain may surge ahead, and Portugal and Ireland will perform adequately, Greece is in danger of falling further behind. It had already had the experience of falling behind Portugal in terms of GDP per capita in 1991 and, thereby, becoming the poorest member state.

The response of the poorer members has been to intensify their demands for greater structural assistance to help bring about convergence. Spain led the way during 1991, calling for a new compensation fund for this purpose. It argued that, in particular, a future single European currency, with its attendant monetary and financial discipline, could permanently condemn the poorer member states to the bottom of the EC development league. In the background there is also the spectre of the possible double negative effects of closer ties with Eastern Europe: competition from low-wage countries and increased geographical marginalisation within Europe. Spain articulated three particular demands: an inter-state compensation fund to invest in physical and human capital in the poorer member states; a progressive taxation system for an enlarged EC budget; and more generous terms for matching finance for Community projects. While the 1992 programme was the immediate catalyst behind these demands, they also expressed an underlying concern at the overall construction of the Community. Most sectoral expenditure tends to favour the more prosperous regions (Molle and Capellin, 1988). For example, 80 per cent of the Common Agricultural Policy goes to just 20 per cent of farmers in the north and centre of the Community.

The compensation issue surfaced again at the Maastricht intergovernmental conference, and a cohesion fund was one of the preconditions for eventual agreement on moves to further economic and political union.

Subsequently, there has been a reaction to this in Germany which is faced with mounting costs for the integration of the former east Germany. Given also the increasing difficulties over financing the CAP and the Community's needs to increase the ceiling on its own budget, this is likely to become one of the more controversial issues facing the Community in the 1990s. The budget issue is particularly difficult because the package of convergence assistance measures is having to compete with the needs of Central and Eastern Europe, as well as with the ambition of expanding the Community's industrial development programme. It took a year and two very difficult summits, in 1987 and 1988, to agree the first Delors' package of financial assistance for the Mediterranean members (and Ireland). The second Delors' package promised at Maastricht could pose even greater challenges to the political will-power of the Community.

For the Mediterranean non-member states these developments have a particular relevance. First, the high costs of convergence are likely to make the Community even less willing to consider applications from large, relatively poor applicants. To take a hypothetical example: if Turkey were to have been given structural assistance by the EC of the same order as the 3.7 per cent of GDP received by Portugal, then in 1990 alone this would have amounted to $5,536 million. Second, the Community convergence programme, taken together with the possible benefits of the 1992 programme, may lead to more rapid sustained growth in the southern member states. This could result in further differentiation between the member and non-member Mediterranean states. The application from Turkey has already been deferred, and those from Cyprus and Malta are on the EC negotiating table. However, they are hemmed in, politically, by the concurrent or expected applications from the EFTA and the Eastern European countries. This above all underlines the structural change — perhaps even bifurcation — which has occurred in Mediterranean–EC relationships between the early 1980s and the early 1990s.

Turkey and the Mediterranean member states

Turkey's 1987 application for full membership of the EC, and the Community's reaction to it, has to be seen in context of the Mediterranean region. There were numerous internal and external political and economic reasons for both the application and the decision to defer consideration at least until after 1993. In the context of this chapter, however, there were a number of salient points with regard to the larger Mediterranean region. First, by the late 1980s the relative importance of the Mediterranean to the EC was decreasing as new global and world regional issues, such as the disintegration of the Soviet empire, impinged on the international scene. Second, Spanish, Portuguese and Greek membership brought home to Turkey the disadvantages of being outside the Community. This was evident in the shifts in trade as well as the continued opposition by Greece to the unfreezing of the 1981 ECU 600 million Community financial-aid package for Turkey. Turkey was also the only significant southern

European NATO country which was outside of the EC. Third, there was the
vexed question of Turkish emigration to Northern Europe. Under the 1963
Association agreement there was a general commitment to offer free movement of labour between Turkey and the EC as of 1 December 1986. While
there was some ambiguity as to whether this was dependent on other
aspects of integration, over time it had become clear that Turkish emigration was not being assessed in isolation but was viewed in context of
other streams of Mediterranean emigration to the EC and the growing
political tensions surrounding these. Fourth, there was the question of the
Cyprus conflict, although this was really a part of the larger tapestry of
Greek–Turkish relationships which coloured all aspects of the Community's
dealings with Turkey. Finally, the Second Enlargement showed that the
advantages of being a Mediterranean member state outweighed those of
being a non-member state.

The problem for the Turkish application was that, by the late 1980s,
what might have been seen as a Mediterranean issue had become linked to
larger global issues and to the internal politics of integration. The Common
Agricultural Policy remained an enormous obstacle to the development of
the Community and at that time seemed virtually unreformable. The Single
Market Programme was also being implemented at the time that the decision was taken on the Turkish application. Apart from diverting attention
from the application, it also made the terms of any likely accession far more
difficult; for example, the competition, liberalisation and harmonisation
rules, and the reductions required in state procurement and state subsidies
significantly increased the problems of adaptation for any new member. The
Maastricht agreement on European Monetary Union later served to increase
further the difficulties for prospective members. Turkey's high inflation rate
(over 70 per cent in early 1992), interest rates and public-sector deficit
would have been particular obstacles.

While global issues were dominant, it is possible, in retrospect, to see how
important the Mediterranean dimension was to the Turkish application.
There is no doubt that Turkey's accession could have been economically
advantageous to the Community. During the 1980s there had been a
relative shift in Turkey's trade from the EC to the Middle East and other
world regions. As a result, enlargement held out the prospect of significant
trade-diversion benefits. There was also the prospect of trade-creation
effects within the EC market, particularly given Turkey's high economic
growth rates and large market. Turkey's level of development did lag behind
the EC average, but in comparison to the Mediterranean member states the
gap was large but probably not unbridgeable. Turkey's GDP per capita (at
purchasing power parity) was at a level equivalent to 59 per cent and 58 per
cent of those pertaining in Greece and Portugal, although it was considerably adrift of Spain and Italy (see Table 3.3). While Turkey's aggregate
economic growth tended to outstrip that of the Community (an exceptional
4.7 per cent 1980–90), high population growth rates meant that per capita
growth rates remained broadly similar during the 1980s. The sectoral
distribution of gross value added was also not substantially out of line with
the Mediterranean member states; the proportion in agriculture was high

Table 3.3 Turkey and the EC–Mediterranean states: GDP per capita and gross value added by sector

GDP per capita at purchasing power standard, 1989 (dollars)		Gross value added by sector, at market prices, 1988 (%)			
		Agri.	Ind.	Srvc.	Total
EC12	17,229	3.0	35.4	61.6	100.0
Greece	9,353	15.8	28.3	55.9	100.0
Spain	13,324	5.1	37.4	57.5	100.0
Italy	17,841	3.7	34.3	62.0	100.0
Portugal	9,452	6.3	38.0	55.7	100.0
Turkey	5,503*	16.4	37.5	46.1	100.0
*1988					

Source: *Eurostat*

compared to the EC average but similar to that in Greece, while the proportion in industry was close to the EC and the Mediterranean member-state averages. While there were problems of high inflation and high public-debt levels, the latter was not completely out of line with the experiences of individual member states such as Belgium.

There are, however, some important differences between Turkey and the EC–Mediterranean states. There are very great regional income differences within the country, and the eastern and south eastern regions continue to lag behind the national average. In addition, in 1990 Turkey's population was equivalent to 16 per cent of the EC total and was significantly larger than that of any other Mediterranean member state except for Italy (see Table 3.4). Furthermore, it was projected that by the year 2000 Turkey's

Table 3.4 Population in 1990 and 2000 (millions)

	1990	2000 (projected)
EC12	327.1	333.8
Greece	10.0	10.2
Spain	38.9	39.4
Italy	57.6	57.6
Portugal	10.3	10.9
Turkey	52.4	66.6

Source: *Eurostat*

population would have outstripped even that of Italy by 9 million. There were also (officially unvoiced) concerns about the cultural and religious differences between Turkey's Islamic population and the (largely Catholic and Protestant) Christian denomination of the Community. It should be noted however that Turkey is not unique in this respect for Albania and some of the constituent republics of the former Yugoslavia also have Islamic characters. Moreover, Turkey is very different from most other Islamic countries in that it is officially a secular state.

Table 3.5 Employment by sector, 1989 (%)

	Agric.	Ind.	Svcs.	Total
EC12	7.0	32.5	60.6	100.0
Greece	26.6	27.2	46.2	100.0
Spain	13.0	32.9	54.0	100.0
Italy	9.3	32.4	58.2	100.0
Portugal	18.9	35.3	45.7	100.0
Turkey	50.6	20.4	29.0	100.0

Source: *Eurostat*

Another important difference centred on the distribution of the labour force. Unlike the sectoral distribution of income, there were considerable differences in the composition of employment. Even in 1989 50.6 per cent of Turkey's population was employed in agriculture, compared to an EC average of 7 per cent and a maximum of 26.6 per cent in Greece (see Table 3.5). Turkish statistical definitions do tend to overstate the proportion employed in agriculture, but there are real differences in labour-force composition.

Another difficulty with a Mediterranean dimension was trade in sensitive agricultural and industrial products (see Table 3.6). The most important

Table 3.6 (a) Production of cotton yarns and fabrics, 1989 ('000 tonnes)

	Yarn	Fabric
EC12	1,072	788
Greece	120	53
Spain	132	105
Italy	213	165
Portugal	163	87
Turkey	334	249*

*1986

Table 3.6 (b) Agricultural production

	Wheat 1987–9 ('000 tonnes)	Fresh Veg 1987–9 ('000 tonnes)	Sheep & goats 1989 ('000s)
EC12	74,990	42,585	113,515
Greece	2,247	3,886	16,257
Spain	5,924	10,348	29,092
Italy	8,249	11,781	12,815
Portugal	516	1,800	4,202
Turkey	16,221	16,720	47,950

Sources: *Eurostat*

industrial products were cotton yarn and fabrics, for Turkey's output was equivalent to 31 per cent of EC output for both of these. Moreover, it had considerably higher production than any of the southern member states, which were themselves important producers and would therefore experience strong competition from Turkish accession. In passing, it can be noted that the industrial benefits of membership do not always turn out to be those that were anticipated. For example, textiles and clothing had been considered to be one of Portugal's few competitive sectors within the Community, but by the early 1990s it had been driven to seek special EC assistance for its crisis-riven woollen-textiles sector. In agriculture, wheat (21.6 per cent of the EC total), vegetables, and beef were the principal competing products, and these are items in which there are Community surpluses. However, Turkey's largest meat production is sheep and goats (42 per cent of total EC output), while its most competitive exports are nuts, apricots, sultanas, lentils and dried fruits; these provide relatively little threat to existing EC producers.

Future perspectives on Turkey and the Mediterranean

In recent years there has been a realignment of the EC's world position, at the same time as the Single Market Programme and the Maastricht agreement have been changing internal organisation. First, the disintegration of the Eastern bloc and of the Soviet Union has led to the emergence of large numbers of new democratic or partly democratic states on its doorstep. Given their strategic positions, historic ties and resource endowments, some of these — especially, Hungary, Poland and Czeckoslovakia (granted special association agreements in 1991) — appear to be relatively attractive future partners for the Community. There is already talk of an enlarged community with perhaps as many as 35 members but operating at more than one level of integration. This will offer opportunities as well as constraints to the Mediterranean non-member states.

The Community is also being recognised as a major international political force. The United States is encouraging the EC to play a more active role in coordinating assistance for Eastern Europe; hence its insistence that the European Bank for Reconstruction and Development should come under the EC's aegis. The EC is also increasingly being recognised as a voice in international forums, and it has taken steps to strengthen its mechanisms for foreign-policy intervention. However, the growing world presence of the EC has also led to increasing conflict with the United States, both in terms of political intervention and in terms of trade. The United States has been concerned about the possibility of the EC evolving into 'Fortress Europe' after 1992 and this fear has spilled over into the Uruguay round of GATT negotiations. One direct result has been the attempt by the United States to force a reduction in the level of agricultural protection in the EC. This was the largest single external influence leading to the May 1992 agreement to reform the Common Agricultural Policy by replacing production incentives with direct income supports, cutting price levels (especially wheat) and eliminating export subsidies. This agreement may increase opportunities for Mediterranean non-member states, including Turkey, to intensify their competition with the EC's own producers, although it will depend on the precise details of the final GATT negotiations.

By 1992 Turkey's relationship with the EC had become bound up with these wider issues. Some form of enlargement of the Community was being discussed to incorporate the EFTA, East European and some Mediterranean countries. It is possible that any such ambitious enlargement will probably have to involve the creation of different tiers of Community membership or association, that is, the concept of 'variable geometry'. Mediterranean countries such as Turkey may only be offered places in the second tier with limited participation in Community policy-making and institutions. However, the question is not simply going to be seen in terms of economic issues and internal EC politics. Turkey also occupies a strategic position. It is in many ways the hinge between the Community and the Eastern Mediterranean/Middle East and is also capable of playing an influential regional role with regard to the southern republics of the former Soviet Union. However, Turkey's relationships with the EC will continue to be mediated fundamentally by the fact that this is above all a key country in the Mediterranean region.

References

Aliboni, R. (1990), 'The Mediterranean dimension', in W. Wallace (ed.), *The Dynamics of European Integration*, London: Pinter Publishers.

Ashoff, G. (1983), 'The Mediterranean policy of the EC — the case of industry', *Intereconomics*, 3, pp. 111–9.

Barchard, D. (1990), 'Turkey's troubled prospect', *The World Today*, **46**, pp. 107–10.

Brown, J. (1988), 'The politics of transition in Turkey', *Current History*, 87, (526) pp. 69–72.

Cecchini, P. (1988), *The European Challenge: 1992, the benefits of a Single Market*, Aldershot: Wildwood House.

Commission of the European Communities (1985), *The European Community and the Mediterranean*, Luxembourg: European Documentation, Office of the Official Publications of the European Communities.

Eisfeld, R. (1989), 'Portugal in the European Community 1986–1988. The impact of the first half of the transition period', *Iberian Studies*, **18**, (2), pp. 156–65.

Georgakopoulos, T.A. (1986), 'Greece in the European Communities: a view of the economic impact of accession', *Royal Bank of Scotland Review*, 150, pp. 29–40.

Geroski, P.A. and Jacquemin, A. (1985), 'Industrial change, barriers to mobility, and European industrial policy', *Economic Policy*, no. 1, pp. 170–218.

Goodman, S.S. (1976), 'Turkey', in E.N. Baklanoff (ed.), *Mediterranean Europe and the Common Market*, Birmingham: University of Alabama Press.

Hill, B.E. (1984), *The Common Agricultural Policy: Past, Present and Future*, London: Methuen.

Hodges, M. (1981), 'Liberty, equality, divergency: the legacy of the Treaty of Rome?', in M. Hodges and W. Wallace (eds), *Economic Divergency in the European Community*, London: George, Allen and Unwin.

Holland, S. (1980), *Uncommon Market*, London: Macmillan.

King, R. (forthcoming), 'Migration and the single market for labour; an issue in regional development', in M. Blacksell and A. M. Williams (eds), *The European Challenge*, Oxford: Oxford University Press.

Molle, W. and Cappellin, R. (eds), (1988), *Regional Impact of Community Policies in Europe*, Aldershot: Avebury.

Molle, W. and van Mourik, A. (1988), 'International movements of labour under conditions of economic integration: the case of Western Europe', *Journal of Common Market Studies*, **26**, pp. 317–42.

Mowat, R.C. (1973), *Creating the European Community*, London: Blandford Press.

Neundorfer, K. (1983), 'The problems of the Southern enlargement of the EC', *Intereconomics*, **6**, pp. 255–64.

Rey, G.M. (1982), 'Italy', in A. Boltho (ed.), *The European Community: Growth and Crisis*, Oxford: Oxford University Press.

Rosenthal, G.G. (1982), *The Mediterranean Basin: its Political Economy and Changing International Relations*, London: Butterworth Scientific.

Sharp, M. (1989), 'The Community and new technologies', in J. Lodge (ed.), *The European Community and the Challenge of the Future*, London: Pinter Publishers.

Straubhaar, T. (1988), 'International labour migration within a Common Market: some aspects of EC experience', *Journal of Common Market Studies*, **27**, pp. 45–61.

Wijkman, P.M. (1989), 'Exploring the European Economic Space', *EFTA Bulletin*, **30**, (1) pp. 10–15.

Williams, A. M. (1991), *The European Community: the Contradictions of Integration*, Oxford: Blackwells.

Ziebura, G. (1982), 'Internationalisation of capital, international division of labour and the role of the European Community', *Journal of Common Market Studies*, **21**, pp. 129–42.

Part Two
Economic relationships

4
External pressures and the new policy outlook

Gülten Kazgan

Introduction: is the EC an external pressure?

Turkey joined the Common Market as an associate member in 1963 on the signing of the Ankara Agreement. Beginning with this date Turkey also embarked upon quinquennial indicative planning, and its mixed economy was sustained so as to support policies geared to attaining plan targets. Apart from opening up the economy to international competition or joining the process of globalization, even those policies orientated to promoting its integration in the ongoing customs union formation in a part of Western Europe remained laggard. Surprisingly, this laggardness notwithstanding, in official discourse the ultimate aim was almost invariably expressed as full membership in the Community.

Given the underdeveloped industrial structure, the lack of sound market institutions and the fairly closed nature of the economy to international competition, policy-makers as well as academics or the business community were clearly conscious of the difficulties involved in the transformation called for to integrate such an economy with those of the highly industrialized Western European countries. The hardships that society at large might have to experience in the course of this transformation seemingly galvanized policy-makers into inaction. In effect, barring some reductions in customs tariffs on imports from the EC in the mid-1970s, the Ankara Agreement remained almost ineffective with regard to policy implementation.

A total change in policy stance commenced in early 1980 under external pressures — from international financiers — quite independently of integration with the EC or the stipulations of the Ankara Agreement and its Additional Protocol. Outward-orientated economic growth under a free-market economy via structural adjustment policies came to be the target to be attained within a short time frame. Policy-makers were aware that successes achieved on this front would also enhance Turkey's possibilities on the other front, that is accession to the EC. It was the recognition of this interrelationship that led the government then in office to apply for full membership in early 1987.

The Ankara Agreement and its Additional Protocol did not appear as an external pressure in the 1970s. Both the EC and Turkey felt free to delay the policies stipulated in the Agreement if these policies were deemed to be untimely from the standpoint of their domestic interests. But, in the 1990s, the situation has been completely altered in Turkey's case, whereas the EC's indifference seems to be enhanced. The substantiation of the customs union in industrial products with the EC — as well as the free-trade area with EFTA — by the second half of the decade is considered to be a must if ultimately Turkey is to accede to the EC and/or to integrate into Europe at large. Here it is the threat of remaining outside of arrangements that shape today's and tomorrow's Europe which creates the external pressure. This pressure is additional to that exerted by external financiers to substantiate an outward-orientated free-market economy. Completion of the customs union in industrial products as an associate member involves the total elimination of protection on imports from and exports to the EC — a requirement that goes beyond those called for under structural adjustment, though covering, by and large, the policies involved in this latter programme.

This chapter purports to study Turkey's transition to an outward-orientated free-market economy under external pressures for structural adjustment. The first part discusses the chain of events that led to the emergence of external pressures and their impacts on changes in policy stances as well as the features, tools and phases of the liberalization process. The second part deals with the pros and cons of the outcomes of the implemented policies; it is a candid appraisal of the favourable consequences as observed over the last twelve years, as well as the adverse effects which are directly or indirectly related to policy implementation under the new policy outlook. The observed outcomes will in the concluding paragraph be briefly related to the process of integration in the EC. The time-series data related to the statistical estimates cited in the text are given in the statistical appendix at the end of the chapter.

The new policy outlook and structural adjustment

EMERGENCE OF EXTERNAL PRESSURES

The Turkish economy ran into a serious foreign-exchange crisis between 1978 and 1980 concomitant with its failure to meet the debt-servicing obligations on its outstanding foreign debt. Although its outstanding foreign debt indicators were moderate, its short-term liabilities aggravated its debt profile. By 1977, its short-term liabilities had come to constitute 57.9 per cent of its total outstanding debt.

The negative real interest rates charged by international banks on loans offered to developing countries in the years following the first oil crisis

(1973) had served as a pitfall in which a large number of developing countries were entrapped between the end of the 1970s and the beginning of the 1980s. The lure of these loans lay not only in their low interest rates but also their extension without any conditionality constraints.

Thanks to easy borrowing, Turkey's outstanding foreign debt almost tripled over a period of three years — from $4.7 billion to $13.8 billion between 1975 and 1978. The IMF entered the scene in 1978, drawing up a standby agreement in accordance with its conditionality stipulations but with no success; hence there were no fresh funds forthcoming. Turkey was strangled by a foreign-exchange shortage and was thus gripped with stagflation and shortages of basic necessities.

The following year was marked by a worsening of the conditions in the international market from the standpoint of oil-importing indebted countries, following a new rise in oil prices. The IMF entered the stage a second time and the new standby agreement signed came into effect by mid-1979. Turkey succeeded in converting a part of its private short-term liabilities into long-term public liabilities and in stretching out somewhat the maturity term for the latter. But out of the $989.3 million pledged by the OECD Aid Consortium countries, only $253.7 million were disbursed and Saudi Arabia's pledge went unfulfilled.

The economic policies marking the period beginning with 1980 came into effect in the wake of the government's realization that unless Turkey resorted a second time to debt rescheduling, it was doomed to failure in meeting its debt obligations. And unless ample fresh funds were forthcoming, the domestic economy was likely to become unmanageable (Kazgan, 1988: 336–43). As Turkey's creditworthiness had shifted to an all-time low, it could no longer borrow from international banks, which, by now, had revised their lending policies to cooperate with the IMF.

Adoption of a new policy stance in the economy

The democratically elected Demirel government drafted the 24 January 1980 programme in perfect recognition of Turkey's constraints and of the revision expected in its policy stance by international creditors. The aim was to pledge to the OECD Consortium and the World Bank, along with the IMF, the implementation of policies which they would heartfully endorse and thereby secure their approval for a new debt rescheduling and the extension of fresh funds. The government thus committed itself to the realization of an outward-orientated free-market economy at a time when its bargaining power, vis-à-vis its international creditors, was at its lowest and when it had no other choice than to accept those policies perennially proposed to indebted countries in difficulty. The task of the full implementation of these policies, however, fell on governments other than the one which initially drew up and announced the programme.[1]

Turkey was characterized by an inward-looking and highly administered economy (save for a brief period in the early 1950s) between 1930 and 1980 where exporting received little attention. Its exports constituted of some traditional agricultural crops with low-demand elasticities but well-established markets in Western Europe. Attempts to open up the economy to world-wide competition in the late 1940s and early 1950s — again under external pressures — had been a complete failure. This is quite understandable in view of the country's weak industrial base at the time when a private manufacturing sector, along with an urban industrial labour force, was almost non-existent. By the late 1950s and early 1960s — the period of Turkey's first IMF surveillance experience — external pressures had arisen in the opposite direction for drawing up quinquennial economic development plans. Thanks to the implementation of investment planning, a private manufacturing base as well as some public industrial enterprises were set up in the two decades preceding 1980. It was on the basis of this burgeoning industrial base that some manufactured products appeared among the list of exportable products from the early 1970s onwards. It is thanks to the sizable industrial capacity created by dint of substantial capital inflows at favourable terms in the 1970s that the export boom in the 1980s was rendered possible. That is, the change in the government's stance, as announced in the 24 January 1980 programme, had some underpinnings in the domestic economic structural transformation that had taken place earlier, in addition to pledges from creditors for support.

Phases of structural adjustment

Stabilization phase (1980–3)

POLITICO-ECONOMIC SETTING
The stabilization phase of the structural adjustment programme was marked by extremely unfavourable conditions in the international economy. New rises in oil prices in 1979 and 1980, the climb in real interest rates and the appreciation of the US dollar in international markets added to the stagnation in industrialized countries to aggravate conditions for indebted countries in debt-servicing difficulty. Moreover, the deterioration in the international terms of trade for agricultural products continued its downward trend, except for a brief break in 1980 and 1981, and further aggravated the conditions that agricultural exporters like Turkey faced.

None the less, Turkey was fortunate to enjoy the benefits of some favourable conditions associated partly with its geographic location and partly with its domestic economy. The rise in oil prices had created an import and investment boom in the neighbouring oil countries; the outbreak of the war between Iraq and Iran in the late 1970s constantly gave rise to new opportunities in the export of a wide variety of manufactured products, as well as of food products and several services. Since Turkey was considered a bulwark against potential Soviet aggression, the OECD countries together with the World Bank and the IMF, stood ready to provide fresh funds in addition to debt rescheduling.

The favourable conditions were furthered by the existence of high rates of idle capacity in manufacturing, and business circles that were eager to exploit the regional opportunities. In the crisis years of the late 1970s manufacturing production had plummeted and, by the early 1980s, about one-half of productive capacity lay idle. Additionally, businessmen had accumulated some expertise in exporting to the Middle-East market, as well as in undertaking contracting services in the first post-oil-crisis years. Finally, the iron hand of the military regime and its civilian bureaucrats had come to the support of the invisible hand of the market, suspending union activity and taking measures to reduce real wages/salaries as well as real agricultural prices. Hence, profit prospects had been raised substantially for the private sector in all activities

In brief, the implementation of the stabilization package and the first steps taken to transform the Turkish economy to an outward-orientated free-market economy benefited from the existence of some unique opportunities specific to time and place.

POLICY TOOLS

From 1980 till the end of 1985, substantial official credits were extended to Turkey by the IMF, the World Bank and the OECD Aid Consortium countries.[2] In addition, thanks to the IMF endorsement of the programme, Saudi Arabia, the Islamic Bank, the Opec Fund and the European Settlement Fund also contributed to support the stabilization package. The yearly average for the current-account deficit reached 3.3 per cent of GNP while the non-interest current account ran a deficit of the order of 1 per cent of GNP. This massive official support had a large say in the redressal of the economy.

The substantiation of a free-market economy called for a substantial reduction in the government's role in direct productive activity and in its intervention in the price mechanism. Subsidies to state economic enterprises were to be reduced and they were to be transformed into profit-making organizations. The government was to confine its economic activity to undertaking infrastructure investments, in particular in energy production. There was to be an overall deregulation in all markets while agricultural price supports, including subsidies to inputs, were by and large to be eliminated.

The inflation rate was to be reduced by strict control of the money supply. The money market was to be deregulated so as to permit the formation of positive real interest rates. Direct controls over foreign trade and the foreign-exchange market were to be relaxed. As a first step, the crawling peg system was to be adopted following a substantial devaluation of the Turkish lira (TL). Additionally, the multiple exchange rates were to cede their first place to a uniform rate, and the clearing agreement with the Soviet Union was to be replaced by payments in convertible currencies. The Central Bank was to be conferred as the jurisdiction to run the system. Measures were to be taken for promoting the inflow of foreign direct investments to offset the reduction in domestic investments, and controls over capital inflows were to be lifted. In addition, in order to transform the inward-looking economic structure to an outward-orientated one, other measures — institutional or monetary — were to be taken so that exports could expand. Debt management institutions were to be strengthened (Ekzen, 1984: 165–87).

The foregoing measures were brought into effect through a heavy reliance on relative price changes to engender the expected structural transformation in the economy. First, domestic demand was substantially curtailed to bring down the inflation rate and to promote exports. Domestic terms of trade were shifted against agriculture by way of manipulating agricultural price-support policy and imports. Thus, in real terms per capita income in agriculture could be lowered. Labour union rights to strike and employer union rights to lay off workers were suspended, and a militant trade-union federation was banned from activity. In state economic enterprises, wages were brought under control by substituting a so-called 'coordination committee'[3] in lieu of collective bargaining; the salaries of government employees could be directly adjusted in accordance with requirements via budgetary allocations; the prices of public goods and services were raised so that the supplying state enterprises could reap substantial profits. High positive real interest rates, plus real devaluations, also contributed to the curtailment of domestic demand.

Therefore, in restructuring the economy towards outward-orientation, the major policy tools implemented relied on reductions in income and consumption by social classes making their livelihood out of labour income or, as in the case of agricultural producers, of a meagre mixed income. The investment rate, however, was sustained at its previous level of around 20 per cent of GNP.

Second, the foreign-exchange and trade regimes were substantially liberalized. In lieu of the previous officially fixed exchange-rate system, the crawling-peg system was introduced in May 1981, based on daily adjustments of the foreign-exchange rate by the Central Bank. The commercial banks were to follow this central rate, with rates to be fixed within a narrow band around the former. This system helped eliminate the overvaluation in the TL and reduce the gap between the official rate and the black-market rate through constant adjustments — according to differences in inflation rates at home and abroad, changes in the foreign terms of trade, movements in the current account deficit etc. It also permitted the undertaking of ample real devaluations without making it a public issue. In effect, the index of the real effective exchange rate of the TL[4] declined from 145.3 in 1979 (May 1981 = 100) to 80.3 in 1983; that is, its value declined by 45 per cent in real terms.

Tax rebates provided a further incentive to export orientation. In addition, the previous prohibitive approach to imports was altered, even if import liberalization was postponed to the second phase.

Third, interest rates were deregulated by mid-1980. However, by mid-1983 this implementation had to be discontinued. This is because of the outbreak of a serious financial crisis in the money market in 1982 which ended in the collapse of a large number of (deposit collecting–money lending) private loan institutions along with some small private banks. The savings of many low-income or middle-income urban savers — most of them retired persons — were lost in consequence, causing great hardship. They had been entrapped by the high positive real interest rates offered on their savings by bankers, whereas the latter had relied on the high positive real interest rates offered to them by small and medium-sized business owners strangled by stringent finance. As the businesses of the latter collapsed, so did the savings of the former. In consequence, centralized control of the money market and the banking system was reintroduced. None the less, the commitment to sustaining positive real interest rates was also observed by official authorities, the ministry of finance. Underlying the high positive real interest rates was the strict control exercised by the IMF on the money supply, primarily by limiting credits extended by the Central Bank to the public sector (Kazgan, 1988: 353–6).

These radical policy alterations lacked a radical tax reform to increase government fiscal revenue. Whatever change did take place in the tax system was orientated to alleviating the tax burden on income from capital and to shifting the burden of taxation from direct to indirect taxes. The policymakers of the military regime had adopted the — then highly in vogue — supply-side economics approach to taxation as a means to boost business activity.

Thanks to these policies significant changes occurred in the functional distribution of domestic net-factor income in favour of capital at the expense agricultural income, as well as income from labour (Özmucur, 1990: 6).

PERFORMANCE INDICATORS

The unique advantages that Turkey enjoyed in the neighbouring countries and within its domestic economy, accompanied by the policy tools discussed in the preceding paragraph, led to a notable improvement in basic performance indicators. In particular, if the year 1980 (when shock measures were put into effect) is left out of the calculations, performance indicators for 1981–3 show even more impressive achievements.

First, exports doubled between 1979 and 1983 — from $2.26 billion to $5.73 billion — notwithstanding the considerable appreciation in the value of the US dollar.[5] The current account deficit — including 1980 — hovered around a yearly average of 3.3 per cent of GNP, permitting a considerable expansion in imports. This was crucial in view of the import bottlenecks faced in raising manufacturing output prior to 1980. Thus, idle capacity in the industrial sector could easily be mobilized thanks, on the one hand, to export expansion creating the required demand for its output and, on the other to import, expansion supplying its inputs. After the drop in manufacturing output in 1979 and 1980, output picked up again and the annual growth rate averaged 7.4 per cent, from 1981 through 1983. The performance of agriculture, however, turned out to be quite poor due to a deterioration in its domestic and international terms of trade; its growth rate for the same years averaged out to a mere 0.7 per cent per annum. GNP growth, although below the rate in normal years, increased to 4.5 per cent per annum between 1981 and 1983. That is, export expansion dragged back an upward growth performance.

None the less, when looked at in terms of US dollar estimates, the picture was different; Turkey turned out to be one of the two middle-income countries, together with Argentina, whose per capita income declined by about 7–8 per cent in the first half of the 1980s — from $1,330 in 1979 to $1,270 by 1983. Substantial real devaluations, added to the deterioration in Turkey's international terms of trade, worsened the relative income position of the population. Given the large shifts in the functional distribution of income against agricultural producers, as well as wage and salary earners, economic hardship mounted for the majority of the lower-income social classes. It was, by and large, receivers of income from capital — whose share jumped from 38 per cent of domestic income in 1978 to 54.7 per cent in 1983 (Özmucur, 1992: 6) who benefited from these policies. Within this group the large industrial conglomerates with a foreign trading company and commercial bank participation were especially favoured.

Second, Turkey's outstanding debt profile improved considerably thanks to debt rescheduling. Whereas in 1977 and 1978, 57.9 per cent and 52 per cent respectively of total outstanding debt consisted of (private) short-term debt, this ratio remained as low as 12 per cent until the end of 1983. But the other debt indicators worsened: the debt/GNP ratio jumped from 28 per cent in 1980 to 35.6 per cent in 1983 because of laggard GNP growth in US dollars and, notwithstanding the substantial expansion in exports, the debt service/exports of goods and services ratio jumped from 22.7 per cent to 29.5 per cent during the same years. Turkey's total outstanding debt went up from $14.23 billion in 1979 to $18.3 billion in 1983. Throughout this period, Turkey benefited from net resource transfers from abroad; the non-interest current-account deficit amounted to 1 per cent of GNP which facilitated the attainment of the targets set. The international reserves/ imports ratio also improved, increasing from a mere 15.9 per cent in 1979 to 22.7 per cent by 1983. In consequence, Turkey was able to regain creditworthiness in international markets towards the middle of the decade at a time when, following the outbreak of the debt crisis in Latin America, many developing countries had lost theirs.

Third, there were also substantial achievements in the monetary domain. In the pre-1980 crisis years inflation had accelerated, accompanied first by a decline in the GNP growth rate but finally ending up in a negative growth rate in 1979; in this latter year the wholesale price increase index rose to 60.3 per cent while GNP growth dropped to –1.1 per cent. This stagflation-ary trend continued in 1980 with a further rise in prices to 107.2 per cent per annum and a further decline in GNP by 2.9 per cent. But the shock therapy policies implemented worked efficiently and pulled the inflation rate down to an average of 30 per cent per annum, while the GNP growth rate turned positive, at an average of 4.5 per cent per annum, between 1981 and 1983. Real positive interest rates helped channel financial savings which, at that time, were mainly deposits in commercial banks. This shift also helped dampen the inflation rate, even though the overall domestic saving rate dropped by a few percentage points.

Finally, some crucial steps were taken towards reducing state intervention in the economy. Price subsidies to state economic enterprises and agriculture were substantially reduced, whereas they were increased for exports of manufactures; price controls, previously exercised on a large number of goods, were either reduced or completely lifted.

It needs to be emphasised that the foregoing policies did not work smoothly as soon as they were implemented. As the decision-making process had become totally centralized, policies went into effect with a trial-and-error methodology and the outcome was a dizzying atmosphere of constant change.

Liberalization phase (1984–91)

POLITICO-ECONOMIC SETTING

General parliamentary elections were held in November 1983, and beginning with 1984 steps were taken by the new government for the gradual restoration of democracy. This implied that the repressive and rigid policy implementation of the previous phase, disregarding popular discontent, would gradually have to cede its place to policies that took into account — at least to some extent — their impact on different social classes. Although the impact from the military regime lasted until the late 1980s, democratization set the stage for the approach of policy-makers.

A further change was the termination of IMF surveillance, together with the ample official credit programme of the previous phase. The former rendered the implementation of more relaxed monetary policies possible, whereas the latter implied that the government would have to resort to international financial markets for further borrowing — which was now possible thanks to Turkey's restored creditworthiness. Consequent upon the termination of the official support programme, from 1985 onwards Turkey had to produce a surplus on its non-interest current account to stem an exponential explosion of its outstanding foreign debt. That is, the net resource transfer from abroad of the previous phase came to an end. Over time, an increasing proportion of interest payments had to be met out of domestic savings (World Bank, 1990: 1–4).

The private short-term foreign debt incurred in the 1970s had been transformed into long-term public debt in the process of debt rescheduling in the previous phase. Due to this, the government budget henceforth was likely to come under increasing strain on account of increases in interest payments. As the government had gradually to reduce its reliance on foreign borrowing for fiscal balance, this new policy stance called for new adjustments with respect to the domestic saving rate, tax revenue and government expenditures.

The opportunities that had emerged in the neighbouring countries in the early 1980s gradually faded away as oil prices dropped in the international market and as the Iran–Iraq war finally ended in 1988. By the end of the decade, these opportunities had ceded their place to adverse effects as the Gulf Crisis, the Gulf War, and the oil embargo on Iraq came in a chain, accompanied by an upsurge of ethnic problems. These called for an increase in military expenditures, thus exerting a further strain on the fiscal balance. Furthermore, Turkey incurred considerable income losses in tourism, transportation, transit trade and contracting trade, as well as merchandise exports to the region.

None the less, world trade growth picked up somewhat and Turkey's terms of trade improved as oil prices dropped, compared to the beginning of the period. These improvements could hardly offset, however, the losses incurred on account of the turbulence in the region. By the early 1990s, new opportunities sprang up in the Turkic republics of Central Asia, as well as in Ukraine and the Russian Federation. Thus, Turkey's outward-orientation had to undergo a shift in regional targets in order to be sustainable. Additionally, Turkey's associate membership of EFTA opened up some new opportunities. As Turkey's application to accede to the EC as a full member had been shelved and the opening of negotiations postponed to an uncertain date, and as the Community was likely to become a closed entity by the mid-1990s, governments had to create new opportunities for the viability of the outward-orientated policy outlook.

POLICY TOOLS

The phase beginning with 1984 is characterised by efforts to liberalize further the goods, foreign exchange, money and capital markets and to ensure the integration of the economy into regional trading blocks as well as the international economy.[6]

Beginning with 1984, the transition to a more liberalized import regime was initiated with the abolishment of the prohibitive approach to imports. Nominal tariff protection was substantially reduced: the arithmetic average of rates dropped from 76.3 per cent to 48.9 per cent. The outstanding feature of the import liberalization process was the substitution of price levies in lieu of bureaucratic controls and quantitative restrictions. Initially, in order to protect some of the domestic industries, import surcharges played a crucial role together with tariffs and real devaluations (Baysan and Blitzer, 1990: 9–36). In 1989 and 1990 both tariff rates and import surcharges were reduced further; however, in early 1992, on the advent to power of the coalition government, both were raised on some specific products to protect domestic productive sectors. By the end of the 1980s and the early 1990s, imports had been liberalized up to a rate of 94 per cent. This rendered meaningful the application to the IMF for the endorsement of the convertibility of the TL.

The liberalization of imports was followed by reductions of tax rebates on exports because they conflicted with the stipulations of the GATT subsidy code — of which Turkey is a signatory — and since they gave rise to fictitious exports. Reductions commenced in 1986 and the system was discontinued from 1988 onwards. The Eximbank was instituted in 1987 with the purpose of financing foreign operations, and an export insurance system was instituted in 1989 to help reduce exporters' risk exposure.

Liberalization of the foreign-exchange market accompanied the foregoing changes. Residents and non-residents were allowed to open foreign-currency deposit accounts with commercial banks by the end of 1985. In 1988 and 1989 the foreign-exchange and gold markets were instituted and capital-account transactions were liberalized. In August 1990 market-determined prices for foreign exchange replaced the Central Bank-determined prices, the system which had been in effect since May 1981.

The foregoing policy changes and institutionalization processes were paralleled by similar moves in the money and capital markets. In the autumn of 1988 the Central Bank freed commercial bank-deposit rates; the free setting of non-preferential lending rates had remained in effect since the early 1980s anyway. From April 1986 onwards, an interbank money market started operations. In early 1987 the Central Bank initiated open market operations and from 1986 onwards started to prepare monetary programmes, targeting M2 until 1990 and from then on a monetary aggregate called the 'Central Bank money'.

The capital-market board had been established as early as 1981 but had remained inoperational. It was only with the institution of the Istanbul Stock Exchange in 1986 that capital-market operations became meaningful. The reliance of the government in office on domestic borrowing — beginning with 1985 — rather than tax-revenue increases to meet budget expenditures fed enough material to keep the market going. In addition, the start of the privatization of public enterprises in 1986, by floating their shares on the market, contributed to the same end. Private corporations, squeezed by high real interest rates on bank credits, followed suit so as to obtain access to cheaper finance. On the liberalization of the capital-account transactions, beginning with 1989, foreign portfolio capital inflows were also added to the list. By the early 1990s, capital-market operations had become a part of daily life.

Turkey had passed a liberal law in the early 1950s to lure foreign direct investments, but the total amount invested until the end of the 1970s remained meagre. From the early 1980s onwards measures were taken to ease the red tape associated with the issuing of permits. Furthermore, the revision in the laws related to oil exploration, and to the encouragement of the tourism industry, as well as the government decree encouraging foreign direct investments introduced a much more liberal approach to the operation of foreign capital in the domestic economy. This was furthered by the 1985 law on the establishment of Free Zones in several parts of the country. Free border trade with the neighbouring country residents, encouragement of foreign banks to open branches etc. all point to the degree of government commitment to outward-orientation. It should be underlined that this policy stance has also been valid for domestic capital so that Turkish business-persons have been undertaking a wide variety of economic activities abroad in a large number of countries.

The liberalization of trade-union activity commenced in the last months of the military regime and went into effect on the advent to power of the civilian government in the autumn of 1983. New revised laws for trade-unions and collective bargaining were passed, and the previously suspended rights of collective bargaining and to strike were restored by 1984. The abolition of the coordination committee, however, came later in 1987. From 1988 onwards more freedom was granted to trade unions and real wage increases became the rule.[7]

However, taxation policy continued to remain a lame duck of the policy package implemented in this phase. None the less, an important step — in the way of adapting indirect taxes to EC policies — was taken by putting into effect the value-added tax in 1985 and abolishing outmoded indirect taxes. The tax revisions undertaken in 1987 aggravated the tax burden on wage workers and government employees. This was followed by steps to increase the tax burden on income from capital by restoring the withholding tax (abolished in the early 1980s) on interest income from TL- and foreign-currency deposits and government internal borrowing papers.

The fact that an increasing surplus on the non-interest current account was targeted by the government implied that the domestic saving rate would have to be raised, in comparison with the previous phase, given the invest-ment rate. Additionally, since the burden of foreign-debt servicing fell, by and large, on the public sector, the government would have to be able to lay hands on an increasing proportion of domestic savings. Furthermore, in order to boost economic growth, the government had to sustain public investment but abstain from being involved in directly productive domains. Thus, it had to confine its investment activity to infrastructure in order to abide by its pledge to privatise economic activity.

The domestic saving rate was raised, in part, via real positive interest rates on financial assets and, in part, by the redistribution in income in favour of high-income capital owners through inflation and other policies. Since government tax revenue increases — as a means of forced savings — displayed an elasticity coefficient around unity with respect to GNP growth, from 1985 onwards domestic borrowing was resorted to in order to transfer a part of increasing private savings to the public sector. Sale of government securities and treasury bonds, by and large to commercial banks, has been the basic means by which this transfer takes place. Together, these changes have engendered three undesirable outcomes which are closely related to each other: high real interest rates (on commercial bank credits), the stepping up of the inflation rate from 1985 onwards, and increasing inequa-lity in income distribution. It can be argued that the same policies are unlikely to be sustainable in the coming years.

PERFORMANCE INDICATORS

The second phase of the implementation of the restructuring programme basically may be divided into two subperiods. In the first subperiod, which lasted from 1984 through 1987, most of the economic performance indi-cators improved compared to the previous phase. However, in the second subperiod covering the years 1988 through 1991, not only did they worsen, but there was also extreme financial instability in the foreign-exchange, capital and money markets. The buoyant economy of the first subperiod ceded its place to a stagflationary process.

From 1984 through 1987 GNP growth (7.3 per cent per annum), saving and investment rates in GNP (20.3 per cent and 22.4 per cent per annum respectively) and growth rates in agriculture and manufacturing (2.0 per cent and 8.9 per cent per annum respectively) improved noticeably com-pared to the previous phase. Additionally, not only did the current-account deficit — as a percentage of GNP — substantially decline (from −3.3 per cent to −2.2 per cent per annum), but the economy also started to yield a surplus on the non-interest current account. That is, the net resource inflow of the previous phase gradually ceded its place to net resource transfers abroad. International reserve holdings almost tripled to meet more than 25 per cent of yearly imports. There were also substantial improvements on a sectoral basis: the public-sector deficit between public savings and investments declined, as a proportion of GNP, while the surplus in the private sector increased.

Export growth rate could be sustained at almost the same rate as in the previous phase; exports jumped from $5.7 billion in 1983 to $10.2 in 1987. However, a part of the increase was fictitious. Export values were inflated to benefit from the tax-rebate system. This fraudulent activity was one of the underlying reasons for the termination of the system by 1988. The composition of exports went on changing in favour of manufactures in the course of rapid export expansion; its share reached 79.2 per cent in 1987, compared to 63.9 per cent in 1983.

On the other hand, some important indicators considerably worsened. First, some foreign-debt indicators reached all-time peaks: the foreign debt/resource ratio[8] almost doubled — from 24.8 per cent in 1980 to 35.6 per cent in 1987; second, the real effective exchange rate of the TL went on deteriorating and the index dropped to 64.5 (May 1981 = 100) by 1987 from 80.3 in 1983; third, the average annual rate of inflation jumped from 31.1 per cent in the previous phase to 41.5 per cent. The persistent worsening of income distribution, despite a considerable improvement in the performance of the economy and in some basic indicators as well as the ongoing democratization process, was perhaps the most striking feature of this subperiod. The change in the shares of agriculture, wages and salaries as well as capital income in the functional distribution of net domestic product followed the same trend as in the previous phase; that is, about 85 per cent of the active population hardly benefited from the improvement in economic performance. The share of capital income went on climbing relentlessly and claimed 62.2 per cent of net domestic-factor income by 1987. Inadequate domestic demand turned out to be a crucial factor curtailing private investments and manufacturing output in the following years. The economy had been choked by high real devaluations, high real positive interest rates and sharp drops in the real incomes of the majority of the working population.

Beginning with 1988, the economy entered a stagflationary stage and most of the performance indicators started to deteriorate. Some exogenous factors were added on to the endegenous factors and worsened economic conditions in the domestic market. For two successive years, substantial surpluses in the current account of approximately $1.6 billion in 1988 and $1.0 billion in 1989 involved considerable net resource transfers abroad; the ratio of non-interest current-account surplus to GNP attaining 6.2 per cent and 4.9 per cent respectively. Seemingly, stagflation plus the heavy deterioration in income distribution and these surpluses were two facets of the same process. The index of the real effective exchange rate of the TL, which hit a rock bottom value of 62.5 (May 1981 = 100) in 1988, was permitted to appreciate in the foreign-exchange market in the following year to ease the pressure on available resources. The index went up to 68.2 thanks to a substantial inflow of foreign direct investments and portfolio capital: $1.5 billion in 1988 and $2.25 billion in 1989. The current-account surpluses, plus capital inflows, permitted the repayment of a part of short-term debts, while the appreciation in the TL permitted a drop in the debt/resource ratio: the former came down to 14 per cent of total outstanding foreign debt and the latter to 42.5 per cent.

Performance indicators, other than those pertaining to the current-account and foreign debts, considerably worsened in these two years: exports stagnated at around $11.6 billion, GNP growth dropped to 1.5 per cent and 0.9 per cent, while the inflation rate almost doubled to 75.4 per cent and 68.8 per cent in 1988 and 1989 respectively. Both agriculture and manufacturing stagnated.

In 1990, policies were revised to reduce the rate of inflation and to ease pressure on available resources. The TL was allowed to appreciate in value further through promoting capital inflow by sustaining a high real interest rate through monetary restraint. The real effective exchange-rate index of the TL went up to 76.5; the inflation rate dropped to 60.4 per cent; GNP growth rose to 9.2 per cent; so did growth rates for agriculture and manufacturing while employment expanded. Notwithstanding the appreciation in the TL, exports also expanded by 10 per cent, reaching $12.96 billion. Income distribution, beginning with 1989, started to turn in favour of wages/salaries as organized labour pressed for higher wages: the share of this factor income, after the dip in 1988 (18.2 per cent) reached 21.7 per cent and that of agriculture 18.9 per cent, while the share of capital income dropped to 59.4 per cent of net domestic capital income.

The foregoing improvements were obtained by an unsustainable deficit in the current account: this reached 3 per cent of GNP while the non-interest current-account surplus dropped to 0.7 per cent. But thanks to the appreciation of the TL, the debt/resource ratio came down to 36.7 per cent.

In 1991, performance indicators reverted to their 1988 and 1989 values; that is, GNP growth rate dropped to around 0.3 per cent, the inflation rate went up to 71.4 per cent and the public-sector deficit reached an all-time high of 10.5 per cent of GNP. The functional income distribution continued its amelioration in favour of wages and salaries — 23.6 per cent of net-factor income — but this time it was agriculture which lost in its share (16.9 per cent). The appreciation in TL in the foreign-exchange market ceded its place to a small real depreciation, and the deficit in the current account gave way to a surplus; exports expanded by 7.6 per cent while imports contracted by 5.9 per cent. The non-interest current-account surplus is expected to be around 3.5 per cent of GNP and that of the current account around 1 per cent.

The picture drawn above of the subperiod 1988–91 leads to the conclusion that economic policies ran into difficulties in striking internal and external equilibrium at one and the same time. It seemed that the one could be ensured only at the expense of the other.

Consequences of structural adjustment policies

Structural adjustment policies (SAP) have been in effect for twelve full years (1980 through 1991), thus making possible a realistic evaluation of their outcomes. This is all the more important since Turkey has been lauded abroad for its achievements and has been depicted as a highly successful example of the transition to a free-market economy via the SAP. The myriad of countries that look forward to undertaking the same transition have, before them, the Turkish case as the quintessence of laudable performance.

Favourable outcomes

The first point to emphasize is that the most notable achievement of SAP is that lately it seems to have solved Turkey's perennial foreign-exchange shortage problem. Whether this solution is due to a deep-rooted structural transformation in the economy, however, is a moot question. None the less, new export sectors have evolved, and some of the existing industries have become export-orientated; import bottlenecks no longer hamper economic growth; and debt servicing proceeds without disruption. The latter point is of prime importance from the standpoint of foreign-loan institutions in their assessment of SAP.

Second, the economy has been further integrated into international markets through an enlarged foreign-trade sector. Whereas merchandise exports plus imports made up about 10 per cent of GNP in the late 1970s, by the early 1990s this figure had reached 40 per cent. The economy has broken the fetters imposed by meagre export revenues in return for exporting a few agricultural and semi-processed products to largely stagnant foreign markets. By the early 1990s, about 80 per cent of total merchandise exports were made up of manufactured plus processed agricultural products — of which the share stood only at 30 per cent in the late 1970s. Additionally, many service industries have expanded such as tourism, transportation, and contracting. These now yield more than half as much revenue as merchandise exports. The spirit of globalization is well-entrenched in large companies: they form joint-ventures with foreign companies both at home and abroad. Undertaking direct investments abroad has, by now, become a part of the profit plans of the large conglomerates.[9] That is, the Turkish economy has been able to orientate itself in the direction of the world economy at large and has been able to keep pace with the other semi-industrialized countries in attempts to globalize their activities. In this sense, it has become a contemporary economy.

Third, greater international integration, plus market-determined prices at home, have invoked greater cost consciousness in business executives; an enhanced entrepreneurial spirit characterizes the younger generation who, unlike their risk-averse predecessors, stand ready to take risks at home and abroad. Women have been driven to take up income-earning employment at home or outside under the pressure of enhanced desires to raise the material well-being of the family. Asset holders have become highly yield-conscious in their portfolio selection, thus helping the free play of market forces. Unquantifiable changes, such as the foregoing, have helped shatter the image of the benevolent and omnipotent state which is responsible for the well-being of its citizens. People have come to assume greater responsibility for their own welfare, an attitude which is the *sine qua non* of the modern individual. A similar change is observed in the attitudes of policy-makers who have become driven more by concerns of economic rationality than heretofore.

Fourth, policy-makers have exploited effort to develop the basic market institutions thanks to the pressures created by the implementation of the SAP. Such key prices as the interest rate and the foreign-exchange rate are now determined by market forces, rather than government rule, as the requisite institutions have been created. There is, therefore, far less state intervention in the goods and assets markets and hence less bureaucracy and the disequilibria associated with administrative price-setting. On the agenda is the setting up of a new institution, TOYOK, which is expected to enable the state economic enterprises to participate fully in the market as economic agents free from government intervention in price-setting and other activities as well as to rehabilitate those to be privatized.

Finally, these favourable changes have been accompanied by non-negligible increases in per capita income, thanks to the discontinuation in real devaluations and the 20 per cent appreciation in the external real effective value of the TL after 1987. Whereas per capita annual income stood at approximately $1,350 at the end of the 1970s and at $1,318 in 1988, by the early 1990s it exceeded $1,900 in current US dollars. Although a part of the observed appreciation in TL is accounted for by the stagnation in the economy, the other part is associated with the emergence of new domestic sources of foreign-exchange revenue, as well as increased autonomous foreign-capital inflows — foreign direct investments and portfolio capital[10] — which are expected to continue. Given the stagnation in some debt-ridden Latin American countries, the income increase seems non-negligible even if it looks modest when compared to the growth rates in the Far East.

These favourable changes in the economic domain, as well as in individual attitudes, have been engendered by the direct and indirect effects of the SAP. There are, however, several adverse consequences of the programme which constitute costs that society has had to, or is having to, pay for its implementation; they have not only been very costly but they also threaten the sustainability of the programme and/or the viability of the economy.

Aggravation of external debt

THE OPEN ECONOMY

Turkey's SAP were accompanied by massive capital inflows in the form of concessional credits in the first half of the 1980s and later, by and large, in the form of loans received from the international financial market thanks to its enhanced creditworthiness. These helped the country over the hardships of the stabilization phase as well as sustain its growth rate and, more or less, its macroeconomic stability, at least until 1988. But the exogenous factors associated with changing conditions in the world economy, added to the domestic policies deemed necessary for structural adjustment with export orientation, resulted in a 3.5-fold increase in outstanding foreign debt, as well as an aggravation in its real burden.

Turkey's outstanding total external debt stood at $14.24 billion in 1979 and at $16.23 billion in 1980; by the end of 1990 the figure had reached $49.03 billion. The $33.2 billion increase over the decade between 1980 and 1990, however, was only partly associated with current-account deficits which accounted for as little as 27.4 per cent of the total. Almost an equivalent amount of the increase is attributable to cross-currency changes in the world market (26.1 per cent) and to foreign-exchange reserve accumulation (26.0 per cent) (Ercel, 1991: 6). To this one should also add lending abroad (6.4 per cent) which is often a must if exports are to be expanded. That is, about 60 per cent of the increase in outstanding foreign debt is accounted for by the effects or requirements of the open economy.

The aggravation of the outstanding foreign debt — about one-half of GNP in the late 1980s and early 1990s — is of the utmost importance from different standpoints: on the one hand, it exerts strong pressures on available resources and on economic growth for its servicing; on the other hand, it is the major source of external pressures on the country.

REAL DEVALUATIONS

Turkey's SAP have relied heavily on real devaluations to shift domestic relative prices in favour of the foreign-trade sector as well as to reduce domestic demand to gain a competitive edge in foreign markets.

In relation to external debt repayment, real devaluations give rise to two opposite effects. In so far as they help reduce the current-account deficit, or result in a current-account surplus, debt servicing proceeds smoothly. Creditworthiness can, thus, be sustained and spreads over LIBOR; hence interest rates on loans may be reduced. This is their favourable impact effect. In effect, Turkey's current-account deficit, on average, has been reduced from 3.3 per cent of GNP in the 1980–3 period to 2.2 per cent in the second phase, to almost zero in the last phase, when the surplus on the non-interest current account attained 3.6 per cent of GNP. Its creditworthiness has been sustained uninterruptedly. Thanks mostly to the fall in interest rates in international markets, the average interest rate in debt servicing also dropped from 11 per cent in the early 1980s to around 7 per cent in the late 1980s.

Real devaluations can, however, also have effects in the opposite direction. The economy incurs capital losses on the outstanding foreign debt as the prices of its exportables are reduced in terms of foreign currencies. The real debt burden is, therefore, aggravated in this sense. The real effective value of the TL experienced a continuous drop between 1980 and 1988; the index (May 1981 = 100) dropped from 103.9 to 62.2. The approximately 40 per cent drop over these years, therefore, involved considerable capital losses. None the less, there was a non-negligible improvement later, and the index went up to 76 in 1990 and 1991. That is, capital losses have been stemmed somewhat in recent years.

In addition to giving rise to capital losses on external debt, real devaluations also exert significant adverse pressures on fiscal balance and internal stability.

Macroeconomic instability

The implementation of the SAP went hand in hand with domestic macroeconomic instability as non-interest current-account surpluses increased and liberalization was enhanced during the three phases discussed previously. Recently, the economy has reached a stage where it seems incapable of striking internal and external equilibrium simultaneously. Monetary policies have become ineffective, whereas fiscal policies continue their laggard trend.

FROM 1980 THROUGH 1987

The relatively high rate of inflation over the first two phases originated in some major structural shifts engendered via relative price changes: the jump of the exports/GNP ratio from approximately 4 per cent in 1978–9 to 15.2 per cent by 1987; the increase from 40 per cent to 65.4 per cent in the share of capital income, plus income from self-employment, in the distribution of domestic net-factor income; or the movement of the current-account balance from around −3 per cent of GNP in the pre-foreign-exchange crisis years to 2.3 per cent by 1988 show the scale of transformation in the economy engendered by relative price changes over a decade. In the same way, one may also cite the increase in the surplus of saving over investment in the private sector which was made available to the public sector as well as the upward trend in the domestic-saving rate from about 18 per cent in 1973–7 to 24 per cent by 1987.

The major policy tools in this radical transformation were relative price changes. Technological change and productivity increases, and autonomous jumps in the private-saving rate, played a relatively minor role. Constant real devaluations of the external value of the TL, positive real interest rates, adverse terms of trade for agricultural products and falling real wages helped shift income to the foreign-trade sector and capital-income receivers, that is away from social classes that are assumed to spend their disposable income on consumption. Avoiding inflationary price increases — about 40 per cent per annum between 1984 and 1987 — in the course of this structural transformation would have called for absolute declines in the nominal incomes of the latter social classes, a change deemed to be impossible in contemporary societies. Therefore, the transformation was achieved by relative price changes in the course of inflationary price increases, making the best of the money illusion of the low-income social strata.

Obviously, if significant technological changes and productivity increases had occurred, in particular in the export sector, and if the domestic propensity to save had jumped upward autonomously, such high inflation rates could have been avoided. But short of such changes, inflation turns out to be a major policy tool for governments. On the one hand, the government enjoys the yield of the inflation tax, but on the other hand the conditions call for ensuring that smooth debt servicing can be achieved.

It should be emphasized that the inflationary pressures in this period can hardly be ascribed to public-sector deficits, which hovered around 3–4 per cent of GNP; instead, real devaluations underly the inflationary spiral. The vicious circle hypothesis — which posits that under a floating exchange-rate regime; exchange-rate devaluation will be transmitted to domestic prices and costs and thereby back to the exchange rate — was borne out in Turkey's case, as some empirical studies show (Önis and Özmucur, 1990: 133–53).

Furthermore, the effect of devaluations on expanding the issuance of banknotes was strong throughout this period. As the Central Bank's international liabilities exceeded its international assets, banknote issues became an endogenous variable consequent upon devaluations. This is because the bank capitalized foreign-exchange losses in an item called 'the revaluation account'. Thus, an asset item which is potentially conducive to issuing banknotes, increases automatically. This item made up only about 14 per cent of the external and internal assets of the Central Bank in 1978–9, whereas it stood at 42.4 per cent by the end of 1987. Retrospectively, one can say that, in terms of macroeconomic instability, a relatively high inflation rate, originating in real devaluations, seems to be the major socioeconomic cost of the SAP in the latter part (1984–7) of the period.

FROM 1988 THROUGH 1991

Import liberalization, plus the sustaining of a liberal foreign-exchange market, calls for the availability of adequate foreign-exchange reserves. In effect, the banking system carefully accumulated reserves by borrowing abroad. Turkey's gross total foreign-exchange reserves increased from $1.3 billion in 1980 to $3.96 billion in 1987, followed by a long jump in the following phase, to $13.15 billion at the end of 1991, thanks partly to hot-money inflows. Thus, reserve accumulation became a crucial source of monetary expansion.

Central bank net foreign assets, which continued to be negative, though declining until 1988, turned positive in that year. Together with the slowing rate of devaluation over the period, this reduced the expansionary impact effects of the revaluation account on banknote issues, although it did eventually constitute about 45 per cent of the value of the Central Bank balance sheet.

The expansionary effects of foreign-reserve accumulation on the banknotes had to be sterilized. Therefore, the Central Bank tried to restrict credits to the public sector. This policy overlapped with the government increasing domestic borrowing requirements as a result of the effects of financial and capital account liberalization, as well as the exogenous factors discussed previously. Free capital flows ensure the equalization of domestic real interest rates with real rates abroad plus a risk margin. High rates of expected devaluation, and the uncertainty and risks they involve, are thus reflected in domestic nominal interest rates, which soar as devaluations continue and the risks of domestic asset holders are enhanced. High interest rates are anyway required to shift the preferences of domestic asset holders to holding financial assets rather than real assets, so that inflationary pressures may be brought under control, and to shift to holding financial assets denominated in TL rather than in foreign currency so that speculative attacks on foreign exchange can be avoided. But this requirement aggravates the interest burden of the public sector due to domestic debt.

The public sector carries about 75 per cent of the outstanding foreign debt. Since 1985 it has been borrowing, by and large, from domestic commercial banks in order to pay the interest on foreign debt and on the accumulating domestic debt as well as to carry out infrastructure investments. That is, surplus savings in the private sector are transferred to the public sector via borrowing rather than taxation. Government borrowing — in lieu of monetary expansion — helps sustain high interest rates. Both high interest rates and devaluations are thus reflected in the 'interest' item in fiscal expenditures. This item — covering interest on foreign and domestic debt — hovered around 7–8 per cent of budgetary expenditures in the early 1980s, but exceeded 20 per cent by the early 1990s. Surpluses on the non-interest budgetary balance switched to a deficit in 1991.

The government is under pressure to sustain infrastructure investments since high domestic interest rates, devaluations and macroeconomic instability crowd out private fixed investment. To this one should also add the significant expansion in military expenditures as a result of the political events in the country and in the region. That is, inflationary pressures originating in fiscal deficit overlapped with the period of increasing reserve accumulation.

Speculative flows of domestic funds between the domestic money market and the foreign-exchange market add to the speculative inflow and outflow of foreign funds to complete this picture (Haque and Montiel, 1991: 38–40). When the government relaxes domestic borrowing and resorts to the Central Bank for financing deficits, there is a short-term drop in domestic interest rates but attacks on foreign exchange with increases in their prices and vice versa when borrowing is heavily increased.[11]

When nominal devaluations remain below the domestic inflation rate and the TL appreciates in value in the foreign-exchange market under high interest rates, speculative capital inflows from abroad to capitalize on high fund yields follow and vice versa in cases of real depreciation. Such flows have been dizzying policy-makers as well as the business community but have no steady solutions.

In brief, foreign-reserve accumulation, expansion in public-sector borrowing requirements, plus speculative activity emerged as the major sources of macroeconomic instability in this period. Given the high foreign-debt servicing and domestic borrowing requirements, it is warranted to conclude that the financial- and capital-account liberalization policies have been untimely. It has conferred a very high social cost to the economy in the form of stagflation — GNP growth per annum on the average around 2 per cent and inflation rate of 71 per cent — and extreme macroeconomic instability, with fluctuating key prices between 1988 and 1991.

Shift of resources from tradables to non-tradables

The basic assumption of the SAP/export orientation model is that, given booming exports markets, export sectors will grow at rates exceeding the overall GNP growth rate. The income increase accruing to these sectors will be channelled to investments, since high rates of profitability will be ensured thanks to the right exchange rate. Moreover, competition will engender rapid productivity increases in the tradables sectors via technological improvements embodied in the new investment goods. Thus, export industries will grow fast enough to become the 'growth-leading' sectors in the economy.

The foregoing model, derived mainly from the experiences of the Four Tigers of the Far East, is, however, far from being the unique outcome possible under SAP.[12] The set of internal and external conditions that characterize the economy and the time period can yield quite different outcomes if they differ from those assumed in the model (Kazgan, 1989: 59–81). In effect, Turkey's experience has been at a variance on this account.

Shifts in private fixed investments

Throughout the period of its implementation, SAP has given rise to two major shifts in private total (financial plus fixed) investments: (i) Private investments have partly shifted away from fixed investments to financial assets due to high yields on and high expected (speculative) capital gains from holding the latter; (ii) private fixed investments have been increasingly diverted to such non-tradables as housing and some service industries at the expense of the major tradables — producing sectors, namely agriculture and manufacturing.

A high and riskless real return on the increased supply of assets due to public domestic borrowing, plus bank deposits in foreign currency and — from time to time — in TL, have been conducive to increased financial deepening in the economy (Akyüz, 1990: 98–131).

The capital market functions more as a casino under speculative expectations than as an institution channelling investible funds to long-term industrial investments. Expectations of high capital gains via speculation in the foreign-exchange market add to this. Turkey imports about $1–1.5 billion of gold yearly to satisfy local demand.[13] Foreign-currency deposits held by residents in commercial banks jumped from $4.1 billion in 1987 to $9.1 billion by the end of 1991 (TCMB, 1991: 158). The process of financial deepening was further promoted by increased government borrowing. It should be stressed that the process gained momentum in 1985, when domestic government borrowing accelerated and when the holding of foreign-currency deposits was liberalized and was reinforced in 1988 with capital-account liberalization.

Housing increasingly became the preferred sector for private fixed investments (Conway, 1990: 78–97). Between 1974 and 1984 investments in housing took up 28–33 per cent of the total, whereas their share had reached 51 per cent by the end of the decade. In absolute real amounts, the increase was of the order of threefold. This was accompanied by sharp drops in fixed investments in manufacturing: whereas between 1975 and 1977, their annual average stood at TL 4.3 thousand billion (in constant 1988 prices), by the end of the 1980s, they had dropped to TL 2.9 thousand billion. The drop in the case of agriculture was even more dramatic; in the same period they fell from TL 1.1 thousand billion to TL 0.650 thousand billion. These falls occurred notwithstanding the approximately one-fourth increase in private fixed investments. Tourism, and some other services, in addition to housing, proved to be the major attractions for private interests (TOBB, 1990: 20–7). The reasons underlying this sharp alteration in re-source allocation are directly or indirectly associated with SAP. High real interest rates seem to have crowded investors in manufacturing out of the market for loanable funds, to be replaced by internal and external trade sectors. The share of these last two sectors stood at 19 per cent in 1980, at 35.6 per cent in 1987 and at 40 per cent in 1990, of the credits extended by the commercial banking system,[14] whereas the share of manufacturing dropped from 33.8 per cent to 22.8 per cent and to 13.2 per cent respectively. The profitability of investments in manufacturing has also been adversely affected by continuous devaluations, domestic demand curtailment, the deterioration in income distribution, import liberalization and macroeconomic instability. It is true that manufacturing output did grow at non-negligible rates until 1988; but by and large, this was due to the mobilization of idle capacity, which actually deters new investment.

As a result of the decline in government support and the adverse terms of trade, agricultural stagnation has been more persistent; and Turkey has gradually switched from an economy with a considerable net agricultural surplus to one with a meagre surplus. Unless the trend is reversed, the economy could become a net importer, leaving huge amounts of labour and land resources idle.

Shifts in public investments

In the 1970s about 45 per cent of total investments in manufacturing were undertaken by the public sector. In the early 1980s, when private investments in the sector receded, this rate went up to about one-half. But beginning with 1983, the pendulum swung in the other direction: the increase gave way to a continuous reduction, from about TL 3.8 thousand billion in the second half of the 1970s to TL 2.2 thousand billion in 1983, to only TL 0.5 thousand billion in 1989–90 (in constant 1988 prices) (TOBB, 1990: 20–7). The requirement that the public sector should not be involved in directly productive activity was the major cause of this sharp decline. To sustain the previous level of fixed investments, the public sector diverted its resources to infrastructure investments, mainly in energy, telecommunications and transport; their share went up from 28 per cent of total fixed investments in the 1970s to one-third by 1990. Total fixed investments by the public sector, between 1980 and 1990, varied between TL 1 thousand billion and TL 1.38 thousand billion (in constant 1988 prices) without showing any downward or upward trend. But an ever-increasing proportion was allocated to non-tradable infrastructure investments.[15] Adding private housing investments to infrastructure investments shows the sharp switch in total fixed-investment allocation to non-tradables: these two items constituted 58.5 per cent of the total in 1990 compared to 45 per cent in the 1970s.

Retrospectively, SAP seem to have yielded self-defeating results. The policies were designed to engender export-orientated growth via relative price changes under free-market conditions in an economy run by private enterprise. However, they have given rise to a new resource allocation that is inimical to the realization of these targets.

Shifts in foreign investments

The climate that discouraged domestic capital from undertaking fixed investments in manufacturing had similar effects on foreign direct investment. Whereas 80 per cent of foreign direct investment was in manufacturing prior to 1980, this share had fallen to 52 per cent by the early 1990s. None the less, foreign direct capital inflows increased several fold: in cumulative terms from $228 million between 1950 and 1979 to $8.3 billion [16] between 1980 and 1991. Therefore, in absolute terms, there has been a notable investment increase in manufacturing as well. Among service industries, tourism ranks as the preferred sector; by and large this is an export-orientated sector. Free zones set up to lure foreign capital have, thus far, had little success.

Privatization and foregone targets

The topic of privatization initially came up, in the early 1980s, as an expedient way of converting a part of the outstanding foreign debt to foreign-capital inflows. The so-called debt/equity swap operation was expected to alleviate the burden of debt servicing since interest payments would cede their place to profit transfers, assuming the latter would be smaller than the former. Turkey did undertake such an operation in the course of debt rescheduling. Holdings of rescheduled convertible TL deposits could be repaid in TL through being swapped for equity in new foreign investments (TCMB, 1984: 34). Suppliers' arrears on non-guaranteed trade credits, extended by foreign exporters, were partly settled in a similar way: the creditors could opt to be paid immediately in TL for undertaking new investments or other activities in Turkey. About one-half of suppliers' arrears ($1.2 billion) were eventually repaid through this debt/equity swap procedure (Celasun and Rodrik, 1989: 756).

Privatization has remained on the agenda after Turkey attained the capacity to service its foreign debts regularly. One of the arguments is that this will help expand government revenue and thus reduce the fiscal deficit and, hence, inflationary pressures. This argument assumes that the sales revenue from public enterprises will be additional to funds raised from the private sector through taxation plus domestic borrowing; that is, their sale will result in a rise in the private saving rate or they will be sold to foreign enterprises. Otherwise, this transaction is likely to end up reducing the lending capacity of the domestic private sector and, therefore, lead to increased interest rates. The other argument is that public enterprises are poorly managed and lead to a waste of resources.[17] Obviously, such an argument should be conducive to the sale of enterprises sustaining losses through poor management. But pressure is brought to bear on governments to privatize the most profitable companies that enjoy monopoly power in the domestic market as well as strong international competitiveness and to close down the non-profitable ones, irrespective of their role in the domestic economy.

Many governments embarked upon privatization in the second half of the 1980s, using various policy tools. As a first step in Turkey, about ten plants set up in the least-developed regions — northeast, east and southeast — for the purpose of regional development were sold to local small businesses. These were engaged in such light industries as milk-processing and the production of animal feed, textiles, apparel and shoes. This type of privatization turned out to be a failure. Not only did the government only collect about 10 per cent of the expected sales revenue, but the purchasers were also given large loans as working capital for running the plants. The outcome was that the plants were closed down and regional development concerns were set aside.

The other method has been the en bloc sale of public shares — in private or public companies — or the floating of the shares on the stock market for sales to the public at large. Of the 106 companies included under the privatization programme, 51 had been privatized between 1986 and the first half of 1992. Public shares were sold en bloc in twenty, while eight were sold to foreign and domestic private enterprises or asset holders en bloc but with pledges to float a part of the shares later; and twenty-three were sold by en bloc sales in combination with a share flotation (Cumhuriyet, 1992: 6). En bloc sale of plants to foreign companies — five cement factories and the catering company of the Turkish Airlines — gave rise to some legal and economic problems. None the less, external pressures invariably favour this type of privatization.

In the past, governments had set up state economic enterprises in manufacturing mainly to achieve three objectives: (i) to ensure regional development as, notwithstanding ample investment incentives, the private sector has failed to invest in underdeveloped regions; (ii) to transfer new technology from abroad and to diffuse it through the private sector as well as to create external economies via manpower training etc; (iii) to reap economies of scale in activities which call for large capital investment when the private sector abstains from doing so on account of its inability to assemble such large funds and/or the high risks involved in the undertaking.

These enterprises contributed in the past, and go on doing so today, to Turkey's economic development, even though many officials pay lip service to the ideologically shaped values behind them. Policy-makers will have to create new ways and means for substantiating the same goals, once it is no longer possible to use the same instrument. Otherwise huge social costs are likely to arise by increasing income cleavages between regions, in the stagnation of private fixed investments in manufacturing, and in the absence of some crucial industries from the domestic scene.

Conclusion: have SAP brought the Turkish economy closer to the EC?

The implementation of SAP have, by and large, put Turkey's economy on the right track for integration with the EC or Europe at large, notwithstanding the huge problems that have emerged. Previously non-existent market institutions and market mechanisms have been introduced and, in consequence, price structures as well as the attitudes of individuals have undergone a notable change.

A perusal through the Ankara Agreement and its Additional Protocol shows that a considerable part of these is related to the gradual relaxation of foreign-exchange and trade controls by Turkey in its trade with the Community. By now, most of the articles addressing such changes have become redundant. Obviously, the completion of the transition stage to the formation of the customs union calls for the total elimination of protection for manufactured exports to and imports from the EC, as well as the adoption of the common external tariff. This goes somewhat beyond the degree of liberalization achieved under SAP. Furthermore, Turkey's agricultural policy has moved farther away from the CAP, as it now stands, whereas the Agreement expects a convergence. As regards capital flows, however, the degree of liberalization that Turkey has achieved goes far beyond that foreseen in the Agreement. Free circulation of labour, one of the main pillars of the Agreement, has been suspended by the EC, thus distorting its consistency.

A second notable move towards the EC is related to the shift in Turkey's exports in favour of manufactured products, a change which renders participation in a customs union in industrial products meaningful. Given Turkey's export structure in the late 1970s, such a customs union arrangement had then seemed rather irrelevant. It is, by and large, the pressure to expand exports via implementing SAP that have elicited this notable shift.

In conclusion, it should also be noted that for a semi-industrialized country to come closer to the highly industrialized countries of Western

Europe under free-trade conditions implies some deep-rooted alterations in its relative technological standing. Its state-of-the-arts technology should be improved, total productivity should be increased, industrial structure should be diversified and, to substantiate such technological progress, its investment climate should be favourable. SAP have had nothing to contribute on this front, and if anything, some of its policy tools have adversely affected the investment climate. However, Turkey should be able to overcome this barrier by cooperating with the EC, thus paving the way to full membership of the Community.

Notes

1. In September 12, 1980 the Demirel government was toppled by a military coup, but the military were committed to the faithful implementation of the same programme.
2. The IMF loaned $1.2 billion with an additional $225 million in 1984, the World Bank $1.6 billion in five structural adjustment loans, and the OECD Aid Consortium countries $4.6 billion between 1980 and 1985.
3. This committee, which conflicted with the ILO charter of which Turkey is a signatory, was dissolved as late as April 1987.
4. In calculating the real effective exchange rate of the TL, the Central Bank assigns a weight of 75 per cent to the US dollar and of 25 per cent to the DM.
5. In the crisis years, to reap the benefits of selling foreign exchange receipts at the black-market rate, exporters concealed a significant proportion of export revenues from the authorities. Hence, official export revenue figures for those years underestimate the true revenue.
6. Along with associate membership of the EC and EFTA, Turkey holds full membership in a number of regional organizations such as the Economic Cooperation Organization, the Black-Sea Regional Economic Cooperation Organization, and the Islamic Conference Organization.
7. The coalition government that came to office in the autumn of 1991 also pledged to legalize union activity for government employees.
8. The foreign debt/resource ratio is a weighted average of the debt GNP and debt service/exports ratios. The former is given a weight of 40 per cent and the latter of 60 per cent on the basis of estimates made for Turkey.
9. Recently small businessmen have also joined the globalization process by setting up shop in Eastern Europe, in particular in Romania.
10. Between 1989 and 1991, there was also substantial hot-money inflows to capitalize on the high domestic interest rate while the TL appreciated in value.
11. Foreign currency deposits have become a major source of credit expansion in the economy between 1987 and the end of 1991: whereas M1 increased by 4.4, M2 by 5.9-fold, M2Y (which covers these deposits) increased by 6.8-fold. An IMF study addressing the degree of capital mobility in developing countries over the 1969–87 period classifies Turkey among countries with partial capital mobility (Haque and Montiel, 1991: 39). But following capital-account liberalization, from 1988 onwards, this degree has definitely increased.
12. The Four Tigers, namely South Korea, Taiwan, Singapore and Hong Kong, differ in most aspects from other developing countries (Kazgan, 1989: 78–81).
13. A part of this is used in gold jewellery and other industries as well as in medicine.

14. That is, private investments in manufacturing have been crowded out by other private activities and not only by public investments as the theory argues.
15. An overwhelming proportion of subsidized foreign official credits are given to the public sector for undertaking infrastructure investments. The loan policy of these institutions also underlies the extreme distortion in resource allocation.
16. The figure for 1980–91 refers not to actual entries but to the permits issued.
17. It is worth noting that some large private companies on the verge of or already in bankruptcy were nationalized and turned into state economic enterprises to improve their economic performance. That is, the process at work in the 1980s involved the nationalization of the losses of private companies and the privatization of the profits of public companies.

References

Akyüz, Y., 1990. 'Financial System and Policies in Turkey in the 1980s', in T. Aricanli and D. Rodrik (eds), *The Political Economy of Turkey*, pp. 98–131, London: The Macmillan Press Ltd.

Baysan, T. and Blizter, C., 1990. 'Turkey's Trade Liberalization in the 1980s and Prospects for its Sustainability', in T. Aricanli and D. Rodrik (eds), *The Political Economy of Turkey*, pp. 9–36, London: The Macmillan Press Ltd.

Celasun, M. and Rodrik, D., 1989. 'Debt, Adjustment and Growth: Turkey', in J.D. Sachs and M.S. Collins (eds), *Developing Country Debt and Economic Performance*, pp. 617–820, Chicago and London: The University of Chicago Press.

Conway, P., 1990. 'The Record on Private Investment in Turkey', in T. Aricanli and D. Rodrik (eds), *The Political Economy of Turkey*, pp. 78–97, London: The Macmillan Press Ltd.

Cumhuriyet, 1992. 'Özellestirme Hedef Sapiyor', 6 Mayis, Istanbul Cumhuriyet Matbaacilik ve Yayincilik TAS.

Ekzen, N., 1984. '1980 Stabilizasyon Paketinin 1958, 1970 ve 1978–1979 Paketleri ile Karşilastirmali Analizi', *Türkiye'de ve Dünya'da Yaşanan Ekonomik Bunalim*, pp. 165–87. Istanbul: Yurt yayinlari.

Erçel, G., 1991. 'Diş Borç Kaynaklari ve Stratejisi'. Istanbul: Mimeo.

Haque, N.U. and Montiel, P.J., 1991. 'How Mobile is Capital in Developing Countries?', *Finance and Development*, 28 (3): 38–40.

Kazgan, G., 1988. *Ekonomide Dişa Açik Büyüme*. Istanbul: Altin Kitaplar Bilimsel Sorunlar Dizisi.

Kazgan, G., 1989. 'Internal and External Constraints of Export-Oriented Growth Strategy', *New Perspectives on Turkey*, 3, (1): 59–81, Great Barrington, M.A., Simon's Rock of Bard College.

Önis, Z. and Özmucur, S., 1990. 'Exchange Rates, Inflation and Money Supply in Turkey: Testing the Vicious Circle Hypothesis', *Journal of Development Economics*, 32: 133–54.

Özmucur, S., 1992. *Gerlirin Fonksiyonel Dağilimi: 1948–1991*. Bebek, Istanbul: Bogazici Universitesi.

TCMB, 1984. *The Republic of Turkey*. Ankara: TC Merkez Bankasi.

TCMB, 1991. *Türkiye'nin Ödemeler Dengesi Istatistikleri*. Ankara: TC Merkez Bankasi.

TCMB, 1992. *Yillik Rapor: 1991*, Ankara: TC Merkez Bankasi.

TOBB, 1990. *Planli Dönemde Rakamlarla Türkiye Ekonomisi*. Ankara: Odalar Birligi.

World Bank, 1990. *Turkey: A Strategy for Managing Debt, Borrowings and Transfers under Macroeconomic Adjustment*, Washington DC.

Statistical appendix

Table I PC Income in Turkey (1970–90)

Years	PC Income US$
1970	365
1983	1077
1985	1066
1988	1318
1990	1964

Source: State Institute of Statistics

Table II Average annual growth rate in GNP, consumer price index agriculture and manufacturing (%) (1978–91)

Years	GNP (%)	CPI (%)	Agriculture (%)	Manufacturing (%)
1978–80	–0.5	70.2	1.9	–2.3
1981–3	4.5	31.1	0.7	7.4
1984–7	7.3	41.5	2.0	8.9
1988	1.5	75.4	7.9	1.6
1989	0.9	68.8	–7.4	2.9
1990	9.7	60.4	8.2	9.7
1991	0.3	71.4	–1.5	2.3

Source: State Institute of Statistics, national accounts data in constant 1987 prices and consumer price index series

Table III Outstanding foreign debt ($ million), debt/GNP, debt service/exports and, gross foreign exchange reserves ($ million) (1977–91)

Years	Foreign debt ($ million)	Debt/GNP (%)	Debt service/exports (%)	Forex gross reserves (%)
1977	10886	—	—	727
1978	14681	—	—	902
1979	14620	—	—	795
1980	16227	28.0	22.7	1308
1981	16861	28.6	21.4	1571
1982	17619	32.8	26.4	1873
1983	18385	35.6	29.5	2098
1984	21258	41.5	27.0	3099
1985	25349	48.1	32.9	2615
1986	31228	55.6	33.8	3187
1987	38304	59.3	36.4	3959
1988	37694	58.0	40.4	5228
1989	40282	51.5	36.7	7762
1990	49035	45.0	31.2	10349
1991	49210			13148

Source: The Central Bank of Turkey and State Institute of Statistics
N.B. Exports cover exports of goods and services. Reserves include reserves with the Central Bank and commercial banks

Table IV Sources of the increase in external debt (1980–90)

Items	Share (%)
Current account deficit	27.4
Forex reserve increase*	26.0
Change in cross-currency rates**	26.1
Debt restructuring***	10.5
Lending abroad	6.4
Errors and omissions in the balance of payments	3.5
	100.0
Increase in external debt ($ billion)	33.2

Source: The Central Bank of Turkey.
  * Excluding gold
 ** Including the World Bank pool differences
*** Conversion of FMS high-interest rate credits into commercial loans with lower interest rates and postponement of interest payments on OECD loans

Table V Nominal and real effective exchange rate of TL, exports and exports/ imports, exports/GNP (1978–91

	Exchange rate of TL			Exports	
Years	Nominal TL/$	Real effective (Weighted)	($ million)	(%) ratio to GNP	(%) ratio to Imports
1978	25.0	128.7	2288.2	4.3	50.0
1979	35.0	145.3	2261.2	3.4	44.6
1980	88.9	103.9	2910.2	5.0	36.8
1981	129.6	97.8	4702.9	8.1	52.7
1982	185.1	85.2	5746.0	10.7	65.0
1983	274.0	80.3	5727.9	11.2	62.0
1984	432.5	75.8	7133.7	14.8	66.3
1985	567.9	64.3	7958.0	16.1	70.2
1986	755.2	64.9	7456.6	12.8	67.2
1987	999.2	64.5	10190.0	15.2	72.0
1988	1794.8	62.2	11661.8	16.4	81.4
1989	2304.4	68.2	11624.7	14.8	73.8
1990	2951.1	76.5	12959.5	12.0	58.1
1991	3795.8	75.6	13672.0	13.0	63.6

Source: The Central Bank of Turkey and the State Institute of Statistics.
N.B.   The real effective exchange rate of TL is the weighted average with US dollars assigned a weight of 75% and DM a weight of 25%; the base date of the index is May 1981.
         Exports and imports refer to merchandise trade only.

Table VI Current account and non-interest current account balance and basic balance (average annual) (1977–91)

	CA balance		Non-Interest CA balance		DI plus portfolio I	Basic balance
Years	($ million)	in GNP (%)	($ million)	in GNP (%)	($ million)	($ million)
1977–9	−1939	—	−1333.0	—	45	−1894
1980–3	−2054	−3.3	−641.0	−1.0	54	−2000
1984–7	−1180	−2.2	784.3	1.3	218	−962
1988	1596	2.3	4368.0	6.2	1532	3128
1989	961	1.2	3868.0	4.9	2249	3210
1990	−2625	−3.0	653.0	0.7	1247	−1378
1991	272	0.5	3702.0	4.5	1431	1703

Source: State Institute of Statistics, State Planning Organization, The Central Bank.
CA: Current account
DI: direct foreign investment
Portfolio I: portfolio investment

Table VII Total domestic saving and investment rates, foreign saving rate, private and public investment — saving balance rates (as % of GNP) (1978–90)

Years	I_t (%)	S_d (%)	S_f (%)	$I_{pr}-S_{pr}$ (%)	$I_{pu}-S_{pu}$ (%)
1978–9	18.4	16.0	−2.4	3.1	−5.5
1980–3	20.8	17.1	−3.6	0.2	−3.8
1984–7	22.4	20.3	−2.1	0.9	−3.0
1988	24.0	26.3	2.3	4.4	−2.1
1989	22.4	23.6	1.2	4.7	−3.5
1990	25.2	22.8	−2.4	4.5	−6.9

Source: State Planning Organization.
I_t: total domestic investment rate yearly.
S_d: total domestic saving rate yearly.
S_f: foreign saving flow rate (minus sign shows inflow, plus sign outflow) yearly.
I_{pr} and S_{pr}: private investment and saving rate yearly.
I_{pu} and S_{pu}: investment and saving rate yearly.

Table VIII Share of agriculture, wages-salaries and others in net domestic factor income (%) (1976–91)

Years	Agriculture (%)	Wages-Salaries (%)	Others (%)	Total (%)
1976–7	30.2	34.8	35.0	100.0
1978–9	25.5	34.0	40.5	100.0
1980–3	22.3	24.8	52.9	100.0
1984–7	19.8	18.3	61.9	100.0
1988(*)	18.5	17.4	64.1	100.0
1989(*)	17.6	20.5	61.9	100.0
1990(*)	18.9	21.7	59.4	100.0
1991(*)	16.9	23.6	59.5	100.0

Source: S. Özmucur, Gelirin Fonksiyonel Dağilimi: 1948–1991, Boğaziçi Üniver-
stesi, Istanbul, 1992, p. 6, Table 2.
(*): Provisional estimates.
N.B.: Others column covers interest, profit, rent and the income of the urban self-employed.

5
Turkey and the European Community: foreign trade and direct foreign investment in the 1980s

Canan Balkır

Introduction

While much of the debate about Turkey's EC membership has focused on the political relationship, the reasoning that led Turkey in 1959 to take the first step on the long road to full membership was mainly economic. The situation became more complex along the road, but in 1987, when Turkey applied for full membership, economic considerations were again at the forefront of the discussion. This should not surprise anyone, since in the previous enlargements of the Community, economic factors had been central to all the applications.

Turkish policy-makers have turned to Europe when domestic economic difficulties have made them search for new policy alternatives abroad. Trade and investment have always been the key factors in the consideration of this alternative. This became more pronounced after the accession of the three Mediterranean countries to the Community.

To understand Turkey's trade relations with the EC in the 1980s, one has to look to a wider context, Turkey's global trading position, which was changing in the 1980s. The 1980 Stabilization and Structural Adjustment programme has aimed to integrate the domestic economy with the world economy by liberalizing trade. This integration in world markets outflanked Europe at the beginning, but after the mid-1980s gained momentum once again, as the markets of the oil-producing countries in the Middle East proved to be unreliable. Thus trade relationships between Turkey and the European Community did not follow a linear trend. From time to time Turkey diverted its trade from the EC to other regions, with similar effects on capital inflow and trade, later returning its attention to Europe with renewed enthusiasm.

This chapter aims to provide a detailed analysis of trade and investment relations between Turkey and the EC and also a detailed analysis of the Association Agreement. This agreement not only provides the frame of reference in trade relations but also underlies much of the discussion in some of the other chapters. An analysis of trade and direct foreign-investment policy in the post-1980 period also sheds some light on the structural changes taking place in Turkey's economy and its position *vis-à-vis* the European Community.

The chapter is divided into two main parts. The first part focuses on the 1980 Programme which was launched independently of the stipulations in the Association Agreement but which brought Turkey's economic policies much closer to those of the Community than any previous policy shift. Since the Programme targeted a high export-growth rate to serve as an impetus to overall economic growth, export promotion and import liberalization became the main policy tools of this new economic model. The inflow of foreign direct investment from abroad was also promoted in order to raise competitivity in the economy. These three policy tools will be briefly reviewed in three separate sections in part one.

The second part of the chapter discusses specifically the trade and investment relations between Turkey and the Community. It starts with the Association Agreement, outlining the framework of these relations and later giving an overview of these relations. Trade in agricultural products and industrial products will be examined in more detail. This will be followed by an analysis of certain aspects of the direct foreign investment flowing from the Community to Turkey in the post-1980 period. Finally, the conclusion will look at future prospects. The data related to the statistics cited in the chapter, as well as the timetables concerning the customs union, are given in the statistical appendix at the end of the chapter, although data reinforcing the arguments is also to be found in the text.

Turkey's foreign trade and direct foreign investment policy in the 80s

From import substitution to export promotion

Turkey followed an inward-orientated development strategy beginning in the 1950s, when domestic production was first directed towards replacing the imports of non-durable consumer goods. The trade regime exhibited the characteristics of import-substituting industrialization with high rates of trade protection, use of quantitative restrictions, administrative allocation of foreign exchange, and other measures which biased incentives away from the export sector to the domestic market. Government intervention in the price mechanism and strict control in the foreign-exchange market were the main features of economic policy. The import-substitution strategy enabled Turkey to embark upon a process of industrialization, generating substantial industrial capacity especially during 1973–77, after which foreign-exchange bottlenecks resulted in sharp declines in capacity utilization rates.

The first stage of import substitution proceeded smoothly until the mid-1960s with annual growth rates, in real terms, between 6–7 per cent. After this, Turkey was faced with the choice of either moving on to the second stage of import substitution or exporting manufactured goods already produced. Turkey chose to move on to the second stage of import substitution, producing consumer durables and intermediate goods. This stage required more imported inputs and advanced technology, which increased foreign-exchange requirements considerably. However, this could not be fulfilled as Turkish exports had consisted of traditional agricultural crops with no significant foreign exchange earnings. The quadrupling of oil prices between 1973 and 1974 and the resulting world recession aggrevated the balance of payments, while the economic recession in Europe led to a slowdown of labour emigration and therefore a decline in workers' remittances, an important source of foreign exchange. Compared to most of the European economies, Turkey recovered very slowly from the first crisis. The same cannot be said for the second oil shock when recovery in Turkey came much earlier than in the northern European economies.

Successive coalition governments in the second half of the 1970s were reluctant to restructure economic policy according to changes in the international economy. They continued to pursue expansionary policies financed by short-term foreign debt which, combined with the mounting foreign deficit, led to balance-of-payment crises in mid-1977. The unsuccessful implementation of the IMF standby agreement strained relations with the international financial community. In addition there was adverse movement in international terms of trade against agricultural commodities, a rise in real interest rates, domestic inflationary slowdown of growth in real terms, public discontent with economic policy, and political instability at home. As a result, the government resigned and a minority government was formed by Demirel. The new government on 24 January 1980 introduced a stabilization programme along the lines approved by the IMF and the World Bank with the aim of securing their consent for new debt rescheduling and obtaining fresh funds to overcome severe external and internal imbalances. The military government in power after the 1980 coup was fully committed to the implementation of the programme.

In the early stages, the 1980 programme emphasized macroeconomic stabilization supported by debt relief and new borrowing, as well as an income policy which restricted wage/salary rises and increases in agricultural support prices. The programme was designed to bring about radical changes in the economic structure by achieving a more liberal and outward-orientated policy. By implication the international price mechanism and international capital flows would have a substantial impact on economic restructuring.

After inflation was reduced from over 100 per cent in 1980 to almost 30 per cent in 1981 and the growth resumed, the policy-makers began to focus on liberalization reforms in the economy and pursued export-led output expansion. Export growth was essential to restore international creditworthiness and also to establish the credibility of liberalization reforms at home. This period after 1983 represents the Structural Adjustment phase of the programme.

During the first three years of the programme almost all price controls were abolished and a plausible price stabilization was achieved through orthodox measures. Agricultural price supports and input subsidies were gradually reduced. Financial-sector reforms and the encouragement of foreign direct investment were the main supplementary measures. Extrabudgetary funds, financed by indirect taxes and the sale of revenue-sharing certificates of public utilities, were established. A value-added tax system was adopted. The decentralization of public finance and the strengthening of the fiscal autonomy of local government were the other important steps. In State Economic Enterprises (SEEs), the emphasis was on price flexibility to lessen the burden on the economy. Privatization studies for the SEEs were initiated in 1985. The government was expected to confine its economic activity to constructing infrastructure and providing basic services, leaving the rest to the private sector.

One can see that the policy measures embodied were not only crucial to the economic stabilization programme but also for the orientation of economic policy away from government control towards greater reliance on market forces. Foreign investment and foreign competition were considered means to promote efficiency and better resource allocation.

Exchange-rate management became one of the main policy tools after 1980, aiming at adjustment of the external value of the Turkish Lira (TL) to take account of the differential between domestic and foreign price developments and the need to provide a competitive edge for exports. A devaluation in January 1980 was followed by frequent mini-devaluations and, beginning in May 1981, depending on the requirements of the economy, the exchange rate of the TL was adjusted daily against a currency basket. This resulted in a real depreciation of the TL at around 5 per cent annually until 1988, the index dropping from 103.9 (May 1981=100) to 62.2, after which the TL appreciated. Real devaluations gave rise to capital losses on foreign debt and had an adverse impact on fiscal balance and internal stability.

The financial liberalization which started in July 1980 with the deregulation of interest rates on time deposits resulted in severe competition among banks and brokers, leading to a financial crash in 1982. The outcome of this was the reconsideration of the interest-rate policy and the authorization of the Central Bank in determining ceilings on deposit rates. The deposit rates were later reliberalized in October 1988.

A special factor affecting economic performance after 1980 has been debt relief and new lending made available. The Western powers' strategic concern after the Iranian Islamic Revolution triggered the support provided to Turkey at the beginning of the 1980s. A three-year standby arrangement was concluded with the IMF which was followed by a one-year standby in June 1983, later replaced by a one-year arrangement in April 1984. The debt relief granted through the OECD Aid Consortium was $4.6 billion during 1980–5.

The World Bank provided five structural adjustment loans in support of liberalization reforms and nationalization programmes in agriculture, energy and the financial sector. This firm support by the IMF and the World

Bank encouraged concessional bilateral lending by major creditors. These new loans boosted Turkey's foreign-exchange with the result that the imports needed in overcoming structural bottlenecks in industry were resumed.

The successful macroeconomic performance under the programme staggered at the end of 1985, after which inflation started to reaccelerate, the budget deficit rose and the distributional impact of the programme began to be questioned. Positive real interest rates, declining real wages, adverse terms of trade for agricultural products and real devaluations shifted income to the foreign-trade sector and capital-income receivers.[1] As these subjects will be discussed in detail elsewhere (Kazgan, this volume), here we will dwell more on the two positive features, namely export promotion and import liberalization policies which were expected to raise the competitiveness of domestic productive sectors via integration with the international price system. This part will also provide an evaluation of trade regimes in the post-1980 period, which form the basis of Turkey's contemporary trade relations with the EC.

EXPORT PROMOTION POLICY

The significance of export growth to the success of post-1980 policies should not be underestimated. In the ten-year period (1980–90) exports grew at an average annual rate of 17.2 per cent, while industrial exports increased in current dollars at an average annual rate of 26.2 per cent. Turkey's export growth rate was above the world export growth rate leading to an increase in Turkey's share in world exports (Table 5.1).

Table 5.1 The share of Turkish exports in world exports, 1979–90 (US$ million, %)

Year	Total world exports (FOB)	% Change	Total Turkish exports (FOB)	% Change	Share of Turkish Exp. in world Exp.	% Change
1979	1,640,325	—	2,261	—	0.14	—
1980	1,998,600	21.8	2,910	28.7	0.15	5.6
1981	1,971,801	−1.3	4,703	61.6	0.24	63.8
1982	1,829,288	−7.2	5,746	22.2	0.31	31.7
1983	1,809,600	−1.1	5,728	−0.3	0.32	0.8
1984	1,909,400	5.5	7,134	24.5	0.37	18.0
1985	1,930,000	1.1	7,958	11.6	0.41	10.4
1986	2,122,800	10.0	7,457	−6.3	0.35	−14.8
1987	2,492,000	17.4	10,190	36.7	0.41	16.4
1988	2,828,700	13.5	11,662	14.4	0.41	0.8
1989	3,039,200	7.4	11,627	−0.3	0.38	−7.2
1990	—	—	12,959	11.5	—	—
AVG	—	6.71	—	18.57	0.34	12.55

Source: SSI, *Foreign Trade Statistics*, various Years; UNCTAD (1990), *Handbook of International Trade and Development Statistics*.

Although this increased share may not seem noteworthy, certain commodities such as textiles, ready-made garments, tobacco and shelled fruits had increased export share up to 4–10 per cent of world exports.[2]

Turkey's satisfactory export performance in comparison with developing countries also led to an increase in its share in the overall exports of developing countries from 0.69 per cent in 1980 to 2.27 per cent in 1987.

The internal factors which contributed to this performance were export-promotion policy, depressed domestic demand, exchange-rate policy and the government's strong commitment to export growth. The decline in real wages in manufacturing and deterioration of the domestic terms of trade against agriculture were seen as prerequisites for the competitiveness of the labour-intensive export sector which was heavily based on agricultural inputs. The external factors important in this export miracle were the Iranian Islamic Revolution which isolated this country from its major suppliers, and the Iran–Iraq War which increased the demand for Turkish exports by both countries due to geographical proximity. The share of these two countries in total exports rose to around 23 per cent during the first half of the 1980s. Thus the increase in exports had come mainly from increases in sales to Islamic countries in the Middle-East and North-African. (See Appendix Table A).

Exports grew rapidly, increasing from 2.9 billion dollars in 1980 to 12.7 billion dollars in 1990, and the export/GNP ratio rose rapidly, surprising in a period when the international terms of trade were deteriorating (Table 5.2). The export/import ratio improved and the export composition was

Table 5.2 Foreign trade indicators, 1980–90 (%)

	1980	1981	1982	1983	1984	1985	1986	1987	1988	1989	1990
Export/import ratio	36.8	52.7	65.0	62.0	66.3	68.5	66.6	71.4	81.1	73.6	58.1
Export[a]/GNP	5.0	7.9	10.6	11.1	14.2	14.8	12.7	14.9	16.5	14.4	11.9
Import[b]/GNP	13.6	15.0	16.3	17.9	21.4	21.7	19.1	20.9	20.2	19.6	20.5
Foreign trade/ GNP	18.6	22.9	26.9	29.0	35.5	36.5	31.8	35.9	36.7	34.0	32.4
Share of industry in total export	36.0	47.9	59.7	63.9	72.1	75.3	71.4	79.1	76.7	78.2	79.0

[a] Exports of goods (fob)
[b] Imports of goods (cif)

Source: State Planning Organization

altered in favour of manufactured products. The share of agroindustry in total manufacturing exports declined from 25.8 per cent in 1984 to 19 per cent in 1990. The export boom was predominantly in manufactured products. Although textiles and clothing, iron and steel were the leading subsectors, several other subsectors also enjoyed significantly increased expansion (See appendix Table B). Along with manufactured exports, many service export industries such as transportation, contracting and tourism also expanded. Large holding groups undertook initiatives abroad, especially in construction.

⭑ Compared to the other Mediterranean countries, Turkey's export performance became noticeable during the decade, as can be shown from the share of exports in GNP in 1988, higher than the figures for Greece (10.03 per cent) and Spain (11.63 per cent) respectively. The export growth was supported by export subsidies in the form of tax rebates, exemption from certain taxes, subsidized export credits and preferential allotment of foreign exchange, and duty-free imports.[3] Most of these incentives were present to a limited degree before 1980, but their impact was curtailed by the overvaluation of the TL.

The policy of promoting exports with financial incentives encouraged rent-seeking activities: in particular, fictitious exports where export values were inflated and created distortions in the allocation system. On average, the actual level of exports to OECD markets appears to have been overstated by 13 per cent during the 1981–5 period. This over-invoicing contrasts with the under-invoicing which took place prior 1980 due to the existence of a black-market premium for foreign currency.[4]

Another problem for the export promotion policy was its adverse impact on the small exporters as a consequence of giving incentives to the large exporters, especially with the introduction of the concept of Foreign Trade Corporate Companies (FTCCs) whose share in exports surpassed 50 per cent in 1989. The FTCCs enjoyed additional tax rebates for exports exceeding a set volume and were also the sole beneficiaries of Eximbank's special rediscount credit as a result of its minimum eligibility requirement.[5] They also had the opportunity to be the sole importers from Comecon countries.

The Turkish FTCCs were established after the Japanese model, but, unlike their Japanese counterpart (Sogo Shosha), they were not successful in financing small- and medium-sized producers and exporters. Since they were not vertically integrated with the productive sectors, the profits accrued could not trickle down to the producers. The special incentive system available to these firms caused serious concern when the privilege of obtaining additional tax rebates gave rise to the FTCCs preying on small export firms. The system worked in such a way that the small exporters would sell goods to the FTCCs, which would export them and would then split the additional tax rebate.

The major criticism of the financial incentive system, especially tax rebates, came during the mid-1980s and those who welcomed the incentives at the beginning became critical of the application. Public discontent eventually led to modification of the system in 1984.[6]

The domestic industrialists who wanted the promotion of exports to be linked to the selective encouragement of industry also favoured the modification. The decision concerning the adaptation to the prevailing GATT rules of Articles 6, 16 and 23 required a revision of export incentives and, more specifically, the gradual elimination of tax rebates until January 1989. The reduction of direct incentives spawned another subsidy mechanism, namely the real exchange-rate depreciation in promoting exports. However, exports slowed down in response to the reduction of direct incentives which, unfortunately, were implemented at a time when the decrease in oil prices reduced the Middle-Eastern countries' ability to import. Thereafter, a preferential export-credit scheme was reinstated in November 1986, and a new export scheme financed by the Support and Price Stabilization Fund was established. By granting different rates of subsidies to a limited number of products, the latter was more selectively targeted.

Export growth during the 1980s primarily occured by exploiting idle capacity based on the investments realized before 1980; this was then mobilized, thanks to import liberalization supplying inputs and export growth creating demand for its output. The diversion of loanable funds from productive sectors to public infrastructure — and the absorption of the remaining available funds by the foreign-trade sector, accompanied by domestic demand curtailment and the high interest rates on loans — discouraged private investors. A decline in total fixed investments in the main sectors of exportables was the result. The share of manufacturing in total investments presented a continuing decline after 1978 which adversely affected productivity by retarding the growth of capital stock and the incorporation of new technologies, As a result, the sustainability of export growth was questioned. Private investors preferred investments in real property and in the less risky service sector. The financial difficulties involving working capital and the stagnation of domestic demand beginning in 1989 also contributed to a decline in capacity utilization in manufacturing, causing the diversion of available funds into high-profit sectors such as tourism and construction. The manufacturing sector was crowded out by domestic and foreign trade and services. Of course, this should not be considered as being totally unfavourable since many service industries expanded: such as tourism, transportation and contracting with varying international outlets, especially in the Middle East and North Africa.

In 1988, the economy entered a stagflationary stage, with exports hovering around $11–12 billion. It became evident that export-promotion policy was able to give the initial impetus to exports, but further growth required restructuring of the economy and investment in tradables.

IMPORT LIBERALIZATION

The main characteristics of the import policy prior to 1980 were the high rate of protection made available through widespread use of quotas, selectivity and discretion in licensing, and administrative allocation of foreign exchange. These measures not only encouraged rent-seeking activities but also biased production toward the domestic market.

From 1980 onwards, Turkey launched a programme of revising its import regime in favour of further liberalization. The aims of liberalization were to provide a continuous supply of raw materials and intermediary goods at competitive prices, to encourage investment and to keep prices under control, while securing reasonable protection for domestic industry. For this purpose, nominal tariff rates were reduced substantially, quantitative restrictions were abolished, and the bureaucratic controls over imports were reduced. There were other supplementary measures such as

Table 5.3 Quantitative restrictions (QRS)

	1980	1981	1982	1983	1984	1985	1986	1987	1988	1989	1990
Liberation list #1	71	935	959	972	—	—	—	—	—	—	—
Liberation list #2	870	813	798	821	—	—	—	—	—	—	—
Quota list	330	—	—	—	—	—	—	—	—	—	—
Imports under permission	—	—	—	—	450	520	111	111	33	16	16
Items whose import not permitted	—	—	—	—	224	127	(4)	(4)	(4)	(4)	(4)

Source: State Planning Organization

delegating greater authority to Chambers of Commerce and Industry with regard to import procedures, thereby localizing the bureaucratic formalities. The prohibition of private sector imports from the centrally planned economies was abolished.

Despite fears regarding the competitiveness of the Turkish manufacturing industry, import liberalization proceeded smoothly. The main reason for this was that the protection provided to domestic industry by direct controls was partly replaced by the imposition of variable import surcharges to protect those manufacturing industries which lacked competitivity. Import surcharges, together with tariffs and real devaluations, not only provided protection to domestic industries from competition abroad but also modified the composition of imports, in line with the objective of the structural adjustment programme.

The radical change to the reduction of direct controls came with the announcement of the 1984 import regime when a large-scale elimination of quotas took place. The list of importables was replaced by import lists specifying only the banned products or those subject to licence (Table 5.3). The transition from a positive list to a negative one made it possible to import all products not specifically listed. The number of banned import commodities was reduced from 1,800 to 224 in 1984 and later to only a few specific commodities such as narcotic drugs, weapons and their intermediate products. Goods subject to special permission were limited to those controlled for reasons of human health and environmental protection. Thus at the end of 1985, around 80 per cent of the total imports were liberalized not counting those requiring an official permit.[7]

Prior to the 1984 tariff revision, the nominal protection rates on most sectors were substantial, the arithmetic average being 76.3 per cent. This came down to 48.9 per cent in 1984.[8] In 1989 and 1990, both tariffs and import surcharges were reduced further and the widely spread rates on different goods were brought closer to each other. The result of the indicated amendments in import regime had been the marked reduction in effective rates of protection on imports, ensuring the further integration of the economy into the international economy.

Before the fundamental tariff revision of 1984, imports from the EC enjoyed lower tariff rates on average. The arithmetic average of the nominal tariffs on imports from the EC was 64.8 per cent as against 76.3 per cent from the rest of the world. After the 1984 revision, the tariff on imports from the EC exceeded the new average for the rest of the world, which was 48.9 per cent.[9]

The natural consequence of import liberalization has been the enactment of the 'Legislation on the Prevention of Unfair Competition in Importation' put into force in October 1989. The formulation of the legislation and the rules relating to procedures and measures to be taken were formulated in accordance with similar legislation in the EC.

Turkey also accepted the International Convention on the Harmonized Commodity Description and Coding System in 1988. Finally, concerning the free circulation of capital, liberalization was realized in a number of areas: real-estate investments, personal capital movements, guarantees, securities, security rights and related transfers, transfers relating to the execution of the insurance of contracts, the transfer of loan repayments, the transfer of the free usage of blocked money belonging to non-residents and transfers which are required within the framework of the invisible transactions.

DIRECT FOREIGN-INVESTMENT POLICY

Beginning in the early 1950s, Turkish policy-makers, aware of the contribution of foreign capital to economic development, have taken steps to encourage the inflow of foreign capital. However the policy was not successful in attracting significant direct foreign investment. The capital inflow which resulted under the Foreign Investment Law No. 6224 was a meagre $228 million as of 1979. In the following decade, it reached around $7 billion, under the Structural Adjustment Programme which emphasized the catalysing role of foreign capital to export orientation while restoring the country's international creditworthiness. The classical examples cited in Turkey were South Korea, Singapore, Taiwan and Hong Kong, called 'the Gang-of-Four', where foreign direct investment had played a significant role in spurring exports.[10]

The policy-makers of the post-1980 period introduced a more encouraging framework within which foreign capital could operate,[11] as well as simplifying bureaucratic formalities in connection with the issuance of permits allowing the operation of foreign firms. As a result, Turkey's direct foreign investment environment has improved significantly.

The foreign investment policy began to be governed under three major regulations:

— The law concerning the encouragement of foreign capital (Law No. 6224, dated 18 January 1954);
— Foreign Capital Framework Decree (Supplement to Decree No. 86/10353, dated 12 February 1986);
— Comminiqué No. 1 concerning the Foreign Capital Framework Decree (Official Gazette Date: 25 May 1986, No. 19117).

The main framework, Law No. 6224, was designed to encourage foreign investments in Turkey on the condition that they would contribute to the development of the country, were made in a field of activity open to Turkish private enterprise and did not entail any monopoly. The purpose of the Foreign Capital Framework Decree was to state the principles of foreign capital permission within the framework of the afore-mentioned law. Communiqué No. 1 was to determine the principles of application and implementation of permits to be granted according to the decree. This liberal approach towards foreign capital was also extended to the foreign operations of local firms. A programme for the setting of free-trade zones was also launched, offering foreign investors tax exemptions and more liberal foreign-currency regulations. Four free zones were already in operation in 1990. Free border trade with residents of neighbouring countries was also encouraged.

All fields of activity which are open to the Turkish private sector became equally open to foreign investment and participation, with no limitation in the equity participation ratio. Foreign portfolio equity investment in Turkish firms has been made easier. The international protections made available for the security of foreign capital were the OECD codes of Capital Movements and Invisible Transactions, memberships in the Multinational Investment Guarantee Agency and Settlements of Investment Disputes, and bilateral double-taxation agreements and bilateral accords on investment protection.

In consequence of these measures, the number of foreign companies during the ten-year period increased from 100 to 1,813, and the authorized entries began to rise although the actual inflow of foreign capital increased at a more modest rate. The total amount of foreign direct investment between 1980 and 1990 was $6.2 billion.

Before 1980, foreign companies investing in Turkey were mostly import substituting in manufacturing branches due to high protection from abroad. Import liberalization after 1980 diverted foreign investment away from manufacturing into the service sector, characterized by high profits and requiring less fixed investment. Thus, the share of manufacturing during the decade declined from 73.0 per cent to 52.2 per cent, while the share of services rose to 44.7 per cent (Table 5.4).

The success of the foreign-investment policy of the 1980s in contributing to the export-orientated model has been limited not only in the composition of investment but also in the volume of inflow. The Portuguese example is illustrative enough to indicate that Turkey did not come near to the levels attained by new members of the Community in the 1980s. In 1980 the direct foreign investment figure for Portugal was only Esc 6.2 billion, which soared to Esc 509 billion in 1990. After the Treaty of Accession was signed with the EC in 1985, there was a significant increase in investment from the Community; by 1986, 76 per cent of FDI was coming from the EC, while the importance of the United States and non-EC Europe fell sharply.

The subsectoral breakdown of foreign investment in the manufacturing sector in Turkey clearly showed that, even after 1980, the foreign capital entering manufacturing still preferred import-substituting industries that

Table 5.4 Foreign direct investments by years 1980–90 (US$ million)

	Agriculture		Manufacturing		Mining		Services		Total foreign firms	Share of For. inv. in total investment	No. of invest- ments
	million $	%	million $	%	million $	%	million $	%		(%)	
1980	–	–	88.76	88.8	–	–	8.24	8.2	97.00	34.0	100
1981	0.86	0.3	246.54	73.0	0.98	0.3	89.13	26.4	337.51	40.1	127
1982	1.06	0.6	98.54	59.0	1.97	1.2	65.43	39.2	167.00	43.6	170
1983	0.03	0.0	88.93	86.6	0.02	0.0	13.76	13.4	102.74	41.7	185
1984	5.93	2.2	185.92	68.5	0.25	0.1	79.26	29.2	271.36	46.3	267
1985	6.37	2.7	142.89	60.9	4.26	1.8	80.97	34.5	234.49	44.7	421
1986	16.86	4.6	193.47	53.2	0.86	0.2	152.81	42.0	364.00	42.8	610
1987	6.69	1.2	273.75	51.0	6.86	1.3	249.18	46.4	536.48	45.4	839
1988	27.32	3.3	484.14	58.2	5.18	0.6	307.83	37.3	824.47	49.1	1,109
1989	9.80	0.7	900.99	61.3	10.63	0.7	549.04	27.3	1,470.46	49.6	1,542
1990	37.42	2.0	930.94	52.2	18.24	1.0	797.30	44.7	1,783.90	48.7	1,813

Source: SPO, *Developments in Turkish Economy*, Ankara, May 1991, p. 39.; SPO, *Main Economic Indicators*, Ankara, August 1990, p. 61

were highly protected in the domestic market.[12] The heavily invested sectors were the cement industry (1.32 per cent), automative industry (9.6 per cent) and automative spare parts (2.1 per cent), iron and steel (3.5 per cent), industrial chemicals (2.2 per cent), other chemicals (6.8 per cent), food industry (3.2 per cent), electronics (6.3 per cent), tire industry (2.6 per cent), beverages (2.0 per cent) and electrical machinery (1.6 per cent). The service sectors preferred by foreign capital were tourism, banking and insurance.

During the post-1980 period, much has been achieved in direct foreign investment, but much more remains to be achieved if Turkey is to take full advantage of foreign technology and capital.

The Community: the main trading partner

The Ankara Agreement: drawing the framework of trade relations under Associated Membership

Turkey's application to the Community on July 1959, after the Greek application made two months earlier, was mainly the result of economic and political difficulties experienced by the Turkish government after the mid-fifties. The Democrat Party government which came to power in 1950 followed a liberal trade policy and an expansionary domestic economic policy based on large sums of credit coming from the United States and the international financial institutions. The encouragement of the agricultural sector through cheap credits and support purchasing, public investment in infrastructural construction projects and expanded bank credits to the private sector resulted in the rapid growth of the economy, at around 16.6 per cent per annum between 1950–3 while price rises were only 3.3 per cent. For the same subperiod agricultural growth averaged an impressive 12.2 per cent, industry 10.5 per cent and construction 15.7 per cent per annum. However, after 1954, as international terms of trade turned against agricultural commodities, the foreign-trade deficit increased and the government resorted to protectionist measures so that the economy reverted to its traditional inward orientation. Inflation accelerated to an annual rate of 16.9 per cent, the worsening balance of payments slowed investment which relied heavily on imported inputs, and the growth rate declined. These factors finally forced the DP government to agree to an IMF stabilization programme in 1958 which was to start with a large-scale devaluation and an anti-inflationary programme, provoking public discontent. The erosion of political support forced the government to look for other policy alternatives and an application to the Community was seen as the best available option.

The Community had already signed a treaty of association with Greece and, always careful to balance its relations with these two competing countries, and with an eye to its security concerns, was ready to welcome Turkey's application. As a result, Turkey gained the status of associate membership on signing the Ankara Agreement with the Community of Six on 12 September 1963; this came into effect on 1 December 1964. Turkey's membership was to be completed in three stages over an extended time period. Article 28 of the Agreement envisaged the possibility of ultimate full membership for Turkey at a future unspecified date, provided Turkey proved to be capable of fulfilling her commitments as stipulated in the Agreement.

The objective of the Agreement, set out in Article 2, Section 1, is to promote a constant and well-balanced intensification of trade and economic relations between the contracting parties. This is to take full account of the need to ensure rapid growth in the Turkish economy, an increase in employment, and better living conditions for the Turkish people.

The Ankara Agreement foresees the economic association between Turkey and the EC in three stages, namely: the preparatory, the transitional and the final stages.

The first stage was the 'preparatory stage', covering the five years following the coming into effect of the Ankara Agreement and which could be extended to a maximum of eleven years. During this stage, Turkey's commitment was to take the required measures to liberalize its foreign trade gradually.

The Community, on the other hand, was to lower, within certain quota limits, the customs tariffs on the imports of Turkey's major traditional agricultural export products. In addition, concessionary credits of 175 million units of account were to be extended by the European Investment Bank to Turkey over the five-year period.

The preparatory stage was completed in five years without any problems and Turkey took the necessary steps to initiate the second stage of the Association Agreement. During the preparatory stage, Turkey had followed an import-substitution strategy coupled with high protection rates. Its exports orientated towards the Community market were confined to a few traditional agricultural crops.

The second stage in the process of accession was the 'transitional stage' aimed at setting the timetable towards the establishment of a customs union between the parties. The Additional Protocol, establishing the second stage, was signed on 23 November 1970 in Brussels but came into effect in January 1973.

Under the terms of the Additional Protocol, the EC was to remove customs duties and equivalent taxes on industrial imports from Turkey with the exception of certain sensitive products such as machine-woven carpets, cotton yarn and cotton textiles. Oil products were to be subject to tariff reductions within quota limits.

Turkey was given a longer period of adjustment to make successive reductions to the customs tariff applied to imports from the EC within the framework of two separate lists with different timespans. The twelve-year list, which constituted 55 per cent of the value of Turkey's imports from the EC in the reference year 1967, included the imported inputs for existing industries and the products of those industrial branches which were thought to be in a position to compete in foreign markets in twelve years. For items on this list, each customs-tariff reduction, upon commencement of the Additional Protocol, would be 10 per cent of the base duty. Second and third reductions would be at the end of the third and fifth years respectively. The fourth and following reductions would take place each succeeding year so that the final reduction to zero duty would be effective at the end of the twelve-year period. (See Appendix Table E).

Customs duties on goods corresponding to 45 per cent of the value of Turkey's imports from the EC in 1967 were to be removed over a twenty-two-year period. At the first stage, a 5 per cent reduction of each base duty would be made; additional 5 per cent reductions at the end of three, six and ten years and a 10 per cent reduction at the end of twelve, thirteen, fifteen, seventeen, eighteen, twenty, twenty-one and twenty-two years were to be put into effect. Financial assistance would be provided to Turkey to ease the transition to a customs union.

For its part, at the commencement of the Additional Protocol, the EC was to remove all quantitative restrictions on industrial imports from Turkey, with the exception of restrictions on imports of cocoons and raw silk. Quotas and other restrictive measures applied by Turkey were to be gradually lifted over twenty-two years. Turkey would immediately remove quantitative restrictions on her imports corresponding to 35 per cent of the value of 1967 imports from the EC. This would gradually be raised to 80 per cent over eighteen years.

The integration policy to be applied to agricultural products was to be determined at the end of twenty-two years. The agricultural products which were granted tariff concessions were specified in the Additional Protocol. The rest of the agricultural exports from Turkey were treated as coming from a third country, being subject to the Common Customs Tariff.

Turkey was pledged to adjust its agricultural policy to the Common Agricultural Policy (CAP) of the Community so that, by the end of the transition period, free circulation of agricultural crops would be realized if circumstances warranted.

When the Additional Protocol came into force, both parties were to refrain from introducing new foreign-exchange restrictions affecting capital movements between them. Turkey was also expected to harmonize its legislation relating to taxation and competition with that of the EC.

The final stage was to start after the parties had fulfilled the requirements of the preceding stage, at the end of the twenty-two years following the coming into effect of the Additional Protocol. The details concerning this stage were not elaborated in either of the two main documents.

The financial relations between Turkey and the EC date back to 1964 when the First Financial Protocol, annexed to the Ankara Agreement, aimed at promoting the accelerated development of the Turkish economy as stated in Paragraph 1 of Article 2 of the Agreement. With this protocol, Turkey was allocated a loan of u.a. 175 million on special terms.

The Second Financial Protocol (23 November 1970), together with the Additional Protocol, introduced for 1971–7 a loan of u.a. 220 million, 25 million of which were from the EIB, on market terms. The object of the loan was to assist Turkey's development efforts, as stated in Article 1 of the Protocol.

The Third Financial Protocol was signed on 12 May 1977, in order to realize the same objectives, and entered into force on 1 May 1979 for a two-year period, 1979–81. ECU 310 million, 90 million of which were in the form of EIB credits, were granted to Turkey. The Community also decided, on 30 June 1980, to constitute a special fund in the form of grants amounting to ECU 75 million, to support economic and technical cooperation efforts between Turkey and EC. These grants were to be used only for projects approved by the European Commission in the fields of education, training, health service, and the environment. Of this grant only ECU 46 million was committed up to the end of 1981, and the remainder was frozen until 1987 when its use was resumed.

The Fourth Financial Protocol was initialled on 19 June 1981. It committed ECU 600 million: ECU 225 million in the form of loans from the EIB, ECU 325 million in the form of loans on special terms, and ECU 50 million as grants. However, at the end of 1981, the Fourth Financial Protocol was suspended due to the coup in Turkey and remains so. Nevertheless, the recent Cooperation Package prepared by Commission is in favour of re-establishing financial cooperation.

An overview of the development of trade relations between Turkey and the EC

EC countries have always played an important role in the foreign trade of Turkey, having a share of over 45 per cent in the overall trade. The same cannot be said of the reverse of the picture which shows Turkey having a share of around 1 per cent in the total imports of the Community originating from third countries. Germany ranks number one both in Turkey's imports and exports, followed by Italy, the United Kingdom, and France (Table 5.5). Trade relations with countries like Greece and Portugal, that

Table 5.5 Turkey–EC trade by countries (percentage distribution)

Country	1985		1990	
	Exports	Imports	Exports	Imports
Germany	43.4	34.8	44.5	37.5
Belg.-Lux.	5.0	6.1	4.5	5.6
Denmark	0.7	0.8	1.3	1.1
France	6.7	13.2	10.7	14.4
Netherlands	6.7	5.6	6.3	6.1
United Kingdom	16.9	12.1	10.8	10.9
Ireland	0.3	0.1	0.4	0.7
Italy	15.6	17.0	16.0	18.5
Greece	2.5	1.2	2.0	1.4
Spain	1.7	8.4	2.9	3.7
Portugal	0.5	0.7	0.6	0.2
Total	100.0	100.0	100.0	100.0

Source: Undersecretary of Treasury and Foreign Trade

have similar export products, did not develop over time. (See Appendix Tables F and G).

The period 1963–73, covering the signing of the Ankara Agreement and the Additional Protocol, was one of collaboration and harmony in economic relations. The flow of remittances from Turkish workers in Europe, whose numbers increased greatly due to the boom in the European economy, the implementation of the financial protocol, and the tariff and quota concessions given to traditional Turkish exports all contributed to this harmony.

The only important factor which strained relations had been the Cyprus dispute, which was really part of a larger conflict between Turkey and Greece.

Foreign-trade relations between Turkey and the EC during the period 1963 to 1976 indicate that, although the Community was the main trading partner, it was not a success story, with the exception of textiles and agricultural products (Table 5.6). The foreign-trade deficit against Turkey increased, due to the erosion of tariff concessions granted to Turkey *vis-à-vis* third countries, as well as the low income elasticity of Turkish export commodities and their limited number.

An assessment of Turkey's economy during the 1970s indicates that it was in a situation where the availability of cheap loans, the enhancement of the market of oil-producing Muslim countries, and the development of the domestic industry could all have added to the liberalization of foreign trade to a certain extent. In fact, exactly the opposite occurred: the overvalued exchange rate provided a high degree of protection to domestic industry and impeded the integration of the Turkish economy into the international system and hence into the EC.

The period 1976 to 1987 was one of strained relations. The first disappointment emerged after the first oil crisis, as stagflation and rising unemployment in Europe affected labour recruitment from Turkey, demonstrating the Community's inability to comply with the provisions

Table 5.6 Turkey–EC* foreign trade by major commodity categories ($ millions)

	Import			Export			Foreign-trade balance		
	1963	1970	1976	1963	1970	1976	1963	1970	1976
Agricultural Products (0, 1, 22, 4)[a]	3	10	42	77	116	304	75	106	262
Industrial Products (5, 6, 7, 8)[b]	188	286	1,712	3	22	293	–185	–264	–1,419
Total Trade	197	305	1,815	140	239	806	–57	–66	–1,009

Source: F. Senses, *Foreign Trade Impact of Turkey's EC Membership*, Turktrade
 Publications, Ankara, 1988, p. 35

* 6 member countries

[a]- SITC   0 — Food and live animals
             1 — Beverages and tobacco
            22 — Oil seeds and oleaginous fruits
             4 — Animal and vegetable oils, fats and waxes

[b]- SITC   5 — Chemicals and related products
             6 — Manufactured goods classified chiefly by material
             7 — Machinery and transport equipment
             8 — Miscellaneous manufactured products

concerning the free circulation of labour at a time when Turkish policy-makers had begun to see the association as a means of promoting economic development in Turkey.

Another major problem sprang from the extension of concessions by the EC to many LDCs under the General System of Preferences and the Lomé Convention, more importantly, under the Global Mediterranean Policy which considerably eroded the preferences granted to Turkey in agriculture and industry. The EC's direct or indirect import restrictions against raisins, fresh fruit and vegetables, and textile exports, together with the postponement of the Fourth Financial Protocol, almost ended Turkey's hopes for the anticipated benefits of integration.

In Turkey the main problem was delays in the adjustment of economic policies and its inability to fulfil its obligations for the customs union. Tariffs on goods on the twelve-year and twenty-two-year lists were reduced only twice, in 1973 and 1976. Faced with grave economic and balance-of-payments problems, Turkey presented a plan to revise the stipulations of the Association Agreement and asked for another five years in the hope of fulfilling its tariff-reduction obligations. The argument behind this delay was that the period specified by the Protocol was too short for the necessary restructuring of industry. The unfavourable effects of an early customs union were voiced by both industrialists and bureaucrats, particularly those of the State Planning Organization. Turkey also requested an aid package to revitalize its economy, troubled following an American-imposed arms embargo. However, this did not meet a favourable response from the Community due to economic difficulties in Europe after the second oil crisis.

Thus, in 1978 Turkey resorted to Article 60 of the Additional Protocol, which allowed both parties to take requisite measures in case of fundamental sectoral or regional disruption or disruption of general economic stability. It froze the terms of the Association Agreement, and it was not until 1988 that Turkey resumed tariff cuts.

In late 1979, the private sector submitted a memorandum to the government declaring that Turkey should apply for full membership without delay. Following the disclosure of such an intention by the government, the Revolutionary Labour Union Confederation (DISK) applied for membership of the European Labour Confederation in May 1980. However, it did not happen because of the military take-over on 12 September 1980 which was the last straw in the freezing of relations between the two partners.

While Turkey pursued an outward-looking strategy in the 1980s, its relations with the Community experienced a severe set-back. The volume of Turkey's trade with Europe began to decline and, moreover, there was a reduction in financial assistance to Turkey because of disapproval of domestic politics in Turkey. The Fourth Protocol, which was ratified on 19 June 1981, was suspended at the end of 1981. The resumption of this financial aid, non-tariff barriers on Turkish textile items, and the suspension of the free circulation of Turkish workers in the Community as of December 1986 remained the central unresolved issues in Turkey's relations with the Community in the 1980s.

The Community's insistence on democracy and human rights (see Eralp, this volume), and its publication of reports attacking inhumane practices in Turkish courts and jails created pressure regarding the question of democracy in Turkey. Turkey's increasing *rapprochement* with the United States in foreign policy was coupled with its intensification of trade relations with the Middle-East countries. The Iranian revolution, which had cut off Iran from its major suppliers, and the Iran–Iraq War which increased demand for Turkish exports by both countries due to their geographical proximity contributed to the increase in the share of trade with Middle-Eastern countries to 31.2 per cent in 1986, while the share of the EC countries declined to about 30 per cent. Of course, the recession experienced by the Community at the beginning of the 1980s also contributed to this decline. However, the unpredictability of Middle-Eastern markets, which relied predominantly on oil revenue, was shortly acknowledged, leading Turkish exporters once more to revive relations with the Community.

Although the government elected to power in 1983 tried to normalize relations with the EC, it was not until 1986, when the Community reversed its stance, that reactivation of the Association Agreement started. Still, the application for full membership on 14 April 1987 came as a surprise to Turkish citizens as well as Community members. Since the foreign policy factors have been widely discussed by Eralp (this volume), we will consider the probable economic reasons.

Turkey's success story under the export-orientated programme of 1980 had raised hopes about her potential performance under Community rules, although the import liberalization and export-orientated policy reflected IMF and the World Bank conditionality, rather than steps towards alliance with the EC customs union. Another factor in the hasty application was the likely adverse impact of the second and third enlargements of the Community on Turkish exports, since the new members were exporters of competing agricultural products and textiles. The entrepreneurs and exporters, seeing full membership as a way of securing exporting capability to Europe, also put pressure on the government to revitalize economic relations with the more reliable European market when trade relations with the Middle East suffered a set back. The availability of funds through regional and social policies all contributed to Turkey's decision to apply for full membership on 14 April 1987, under Article 237 of the Rome Treaty. This states that any democratic European state may apply to become a member of the EC. With the application, Turkey demonstrated its determination to carry its association with the Community to the ultimate goal of becoming a full member.

The European Council of Foreign Ministers, by its decision of 27 April, referred the application to the Commission for its opinion, in accordance with the procedure followed in previous cases. For the preparation of the opinion, the Commission sent a number of high-level missions to Turkey in 1988, to gather the information needed to assess the implications of Turkish accession. A report was prepared and presented to the Turkish government in December 1989 on which the Commission's opinion on Turkey's request for accession to the EC was based. The report reaffirmed the Community's esteem for Turkey, but pointed out that there were extensive difficulties in immediate full entry and suggested the reactivation of the Association Agreement and a set of measures for obtaining closer cooperation.

Since the full membership application in 1987, Turkey has made it clear that it will fulfil its obligations regarding the customs union. The degree of liberalization of the products consolidated in favour of the EC was raised from 45 per cent (3 July 1989) to 60 per cent (22 August 1990) and, eventually, to 80 per cent (27 May 1991).

On 7 November and 20–1 December 1988 the Ad-Hoc Committee meetings concerning the economic and trade problems between Turkey and the Community took place. A new timetable for customs tariff reductions and adoption of the Common Customs Tariff by Turkey was also set (see Appendix Table H). Within this timetable, the cumulative reduction of tariffs was deemed to reach 70 per cent by 1992 for commodities under the twelve-year list and 60 per cent for commodities under the twenty-two-year list; as regards adoption of the Common Customs Tariff, the cumulative reduction rate would be 40 per cent for both groups.

Although the relative share of the Community trade had shown a decline in the early 1980s, by 1986 it had almost returned to its previous level. Exports and imports from the EC had followed closely the change in the overall foreign-trade pattern. Imports grew at a relatively slower rate than exports, in consequence of which the export/import ratio improved considerably. This ratio, however, has been above the respective ratio for Turkey's total trade. (See Appendix Table F).

What factors underlie this achievement? The success of Turkish export products in Community markets in the 1980s did not stem from the

Community policy favouring Turkey. Agricultural exports were still barred by non-tariff barriers, tariff concessions were not altered and the main export item, textiles, faced quotas. The increase in competitivity was related to export-promotion measures, improvements in industrial structure, and the decline in real wages and in real agricultural prices.

Akder[13] tries to reveal through constant market share analysis, the factors which underlie this achievement. According to his calculations, 66 per cent of export growth is due to increased competitiveness and 32.2 per cent is due to increased world exports to the Community. The commodity composition of exports, or the marketwise distribution, exerted a negligible effect, accounting for only 1.7 per cent of the total increase. This indicated that exports orientated to EC markets were composed of commodities in which international trade expands slowly. The substantial increase in competitivity stems from export-promotion measures and factors associated with improvements in industrial structure.[14]

In line with the structural change in total exports in the post-1980 period, the share of agriculture in exports orientated towards the EC declined from 51.1 per cent to 15.2 per cent, while the share of industrial products increased from 41.4 per cent to 82.7 per cent. The decline in agricultural exports was mainly associated with the lack of export incentives for agricultural crops under the 1980 programme. In addition, agricultural support prices have been depressed while subsidies have been reduced, thus adversely affecting agricultural production.

The subsectoral breakdown of manufacturing in the 1980s implied that Turkey was still continuing to specialize in manufacturing subsectors with lower-skill and technology intensity which was directly reflected in the factor content of manufactured exports. This was also reflected in the export shares of the subsectoral breakdown of manufacturing gross output at the end of the decade.

Export shares in manufacturing gross output were highest in consumer goods (27.5 per cent) followed by intermediate (15.2 per cent) and investment goods (8.4 per cent). The subsectors with the highest ratios were textiles (53.6 per cent), clothing (65.7 per cent), iron and steel (41.9 per cent), and tobacco (31.3 per cent). The same subsectors had the highest export ratio at the beginning of the decade.

A recent study by Senses and Yamada[15] reveals that the manufactured exports of Turkey in the post-1980 period consisted predominantly of labour-intensive categories. This group, including textiles, represented over 90 per cent of exports directed to Community markets, while it declined to 50 per cent for exports to Middle-Eastern markets. With respect to skill-intensive export commodities, their share in total exports to the EC had risen from 9.1 per cent (1984) to 19.1 per cent (1987).

The factors that contributed to the expansion of imports from the Community during the post-1980 period differed completely from those for exports.[16] Of this expansion, 67.8 per cent was due to commodity composition, implying that imports were concentrated on commodities in which international trade expanded rapidly; 66.7 per cent was due to the increase in total imports, while the competitiveness effect carried a negative sign

(−34.5 per cent) which implied that Community exports in Turkey's market have lower competitivity *vis-à-vis* products from third countries.

The structural change in imports was negligible. The share of agricultural products increased from 0.8 per cent to 3.5 per cent, while that of industrial products decreased from 98.7 per cent to 96.2 per cent. Motor vehicles, metal goods and air transport vehicles were the main imported items (see table 5.7).

Table 5.7 Structural change in Turkey's trade with EC, 1980–90 (%)

Share in exports to the EC	1980	1990
Industrial products	41.4	82.7
Agricultural products	51.1	15.2
Mining	7.5	2.1
Total	100.0	100.0
Share in imports from the EC		
Industrial products	98.7	96.2
Agricultural products	0.8	3.5
Mining	0.5	0.3
Total	100.0	100.0

Source: Undersecretary of Treasury and Foreign Trade

Trade in agricultural products

Under the Association Agreement, Turkey's agricultural exports to the Community have been treated as imports from a third country, and subjected to the Common Customs Tariff. The Community from the beginning granted tariff concessions on imports of agricultural products from Turkey, although the major impediment to entry always consisted of the non-tariff barriers. Turkey's responsibility during the transitional stage was to take the necessary steps to close the gap between its agricultural policy and that of the Community's CAP.

The first concessions concerning Turkey's agricultural exports were made by the Ankara Agreement. The Annexed Protocol to the agreement provided low tariffs for unprocessed tobacco, raisins, dried figs and hazelnuts. By Association Council decisions of January 1967, February 1967 and February 1969 the list was later enlarged to include sea and fresh-water products, certain citrus fruits and wine.

Turkey has always been a net exporter of agricultural products, although the number and quantity of commodities traded and the range of destinations have been relatively limited. This mainly stemmed from the orientation of the agricultural policy to securing self-sufficiency rather than international trading.

The major changes in Turkey's agricultural export development took place during the post-1980 period. First of all, the relative importance of agricultural exports in total exports declined; second, both the number of commodities traded and the range of destinations increased; and, latterly, there was an increasing share of agricultural exports in processed form. In line with development, the relative importance of agricultural exports in total exports to the Community declined from 48.9 per cent in 1980 to 26.8 per cent in 1986.

Turkey's agricultural exports to the Community constituted almost 40 per cent of total agricultural exports, while agricultural imports from the EC represented 35 per cent of total agricultural imports. The main agricultural exports to the Community were fresh vegetables and fruits (around 50 per cent of total agricultural exports), nuts, tobacco and processed food, while the main imports from the Community were cereals, vegetable fats and oil, live animals, and prepared foodstuffs (around 36 per cent of total agricultural exports). Turkey's main agricultural export market has been Germany (around 35 per cent) and the main import country, France (around 20 per cent).

A study indicates that, during the first half of the 1980s, exports of both animal and crop products exhibited a negative competitiveness effect.[17] We will not repeat here the reasons for this which stem from the Turkish structural adjustment programme not favouring agriculture. In addition, the import-restrictive character of the CAP and the Community's application of tariff exemptions for many Mediterranean products within the framework of its Global Mediterranean Policy were other reasons which explain why Turkey's average export growth rate for agricultural products has been below the world average.

The concessions provided were broadened by Association Council decisions during 1975–8 and took final form by Decision No: 1/80. This foresaw the gradual elimination of duties by January 1987 on primary agricultural products having a regulated market in the EC but not on processed ones (see Appendix Table I). For the latter there are tariff reductions but variable levies, while other additional duties remain applicable.

The implementation of this decision did not bring any fundamental change in the volume of Turkey's agricultural exports since it was essentially the non-tariff barriers which impeded the free entry of agricultural products to the Community. Concessionary quotas still existed for hazelnuts, (25.000 tons), tomato paste (8.500 tons), processed tomatoes (8.000 tons) and apricot pulp (90 tons), as well as a seasonal calendar for tariff exemptions for fruit and vegetables and, of course, price regulations were applied to a number of products.

In a future hypothetical case involving the elimination of non-tariff barriers to trade, agricultural exports to the Community are only expected to increase in those products where Community self-sufficiency is low, and this is limited. The self-sufficiency rate of the Community in a large number of products in which Turkish agriculture may be competitive is already 100 per cent or above. For example, there is very little possibility of expanding exports of fresh fruits and vegetables following the full membership of other Mediterranean countries, particularly Spain. In light of these facts one may conclude that even if Turkey succeeds in expanding agricultural exports to the Community, these are unlikely to be substantial. In contrast, unless

Turkey succeeds in expanding production to meet the rapid increase in demand due to population growth and the growth in per capita income, imports of such basic foodstuff as livestock products, in which self-sufficiency is questionable, can expect a substantial increase.

The Commission demands progress in securing preferential tariff treatment for the EC in certain Turkish agricultural imports. Since the necessary measures have not been activated yet, the issue will be taken up in future meetings concerning the further liberalization of agricultural trade.

The Southeastern Anatolian Project in Turkey, which will be completed in the first decade of the twenty-first century, will supply irrigation water to the vast plains in the region and is expected to lead to a significant increase in local agricultural production, especially for cereals, cotton, oilseeds and fresh fruits and vegetables. The result will be a rise in the agricultural exportable surplus by several fold; assuming no reduction in CAP protectionism, this factor could become the major strain in relations.

Trade in industrial products

The conditions for the formation of a customs union in industrial products were based on the difference between the economic development level of the partners. On the part of the EC, all tariffs on Turkish exports of industrial goods were to be abolished as of January 1973 with the coming into effect of the Additional Protocol. However, the Community abolished the tariffs as early as September 1971 by the Annexed Agreement. An exception was provided for imports of sensitive products: cotton yarn, cotton fabrics, carpets and oil products.

In return, Turkey would eliminate tariffs and other duties and taxes on imports of industrial goods by the end of the transition period in two stages. For 55 per cent of the imports in the reference year (1967), the customs tariffs and other duties would be eliminated in twelve years and for the remaining 45 per cent in twenty-two years. The complete adoption of the Common Customs Tariff was also expected to take place at the end of the transition period. (See Appendix Table J).

To eliminate the quantitative restrictions, 35 per cent of the imports in the reference year were to be liberalized and consolidated in favour of the EC. For products whose importation was not liberalized, the setting of special quotas favouring the Community was stipulated. The rate of liberalization was expected to reach 80 per cent at the end of the eighteenth year and 100 per cent at the end of the transition period.

The main industrial item in the foreign trade of the EC is machinery and motor vehicles, constituting almost one-half of exports and imports. Textiles and clothing, iron and steel, which are the main export categories of Turkey, although constituting around 5 per cent of the total EC imports, have been subject to strict protectionist measures. This must be evaluated in view of the fact that these are the sensitive sectors going through restructuring in Europe, plus the fact that the dominant characteristic of EC trade is the high ratio of inter-EC trade in both exports and imports. Three-fourths of this trade is comprised of industrial products, while EC trade with third countries is heavily orientated towards the industrialized world, with only around 20 per cent towards the developing countries. The inclusion of Mediterranean countries as full members had a trade-diverting impact, as can be shown with the Portuguese case, where textiles, clothing and footwear account for nearly 40 per cent of it exports.

When we examine in detail Turkey–EC trade in industrial goods, non-electrical and electrical machinery and motor vehicles constitute over 35 per cent of imports from the EC. Textiles (31.6 per cent) and clothing (20.4 per cent) make up almost 52 per cent of the exports while iron and steel (11.8 per cent), non-electrical (21.9 per cent) and electrical machinery (9.5 per cent), motor vehicles (6.3 per cent) and chemical products (13.3 per cent) are the main import items from the Community.

Textiles and ready-made garments had been a sensitive issue in Turkey's trade relations with the Community. Compared with other Third World suppliers, the Turkish textile industry was a latecomer in the European market and was not considered a real competitor until the late 1980s. Since then, the Community has tried to limit the further expansion of Turkish textile and clothing exports, at first by imposing quantitative restrictions on T-shirts (commencing on 27 July 1982) and later increasing them to include six categories of textile items until 1986. Although subject to quantative restrictions, the export value of Turkish textiles and ready-made garments increased from $298 million (1980) to $3,009 million (1990), comprising around 44 per cent of total exports.

The Turkish government was initially resolute in insisting on the application of Articles 24 and 22 of the Additional Protocol, instead of reaching an agreement on export quotas. According to Article 24, the Community pledges to remove all quantitative restrictions on industrial exports, which also include textiles and clothing. Article 22 foresees that the Community does not impose any new quantitative restrictions or similar measures on imports after the signing of the Protocol. Therefore, it was the Association of Turkish Exporters who finally concluded Voluntary Restraint Arrangements with the Commission on supplies of textile items in categories considered sensitive. The Turkish government acted as a supervisor. This was subsequently followed by further agreements covering more categories.

Turkey's proposal for early liberalization of the textile and ready-made garments sector, reciprocally with the EC, was officially presented to the Commission on 26 November 1990, but was not supported. The counter-proposal by the Commission included the establishment of a joint working group on all matters of the customs union.

Another trouble spot involving Turkey's industrial exports has been the dumping and subsidy investigations, conducted under the framework of Council Directives No. 2423/88/EEC and 2424/88/ECSC. Turkey has taken the first place among third countries in anti-dumping investigations initiated against her exports. The obligation to consult the governing bodies of the Association prior to opening a case concerning unfair trade practices (Additional Protocol, Article 47) has been overlooked by the Commission. In the period 1979–91, ten of the nineteen different investigations initiated against Turkish products concerned textiles.

As a conclusion one can say that Turkey's industrial export increases to the EC during the 1980s depended on the general increase in EC trade and on the competitiveness of Turkey's export products, which rested highly on the export promotion policies applied during the 1980s. The elimination of some basic incentives, such as tax rebates, have exerted a negative effect on further export increases. Coupled with this is the fact that major export items to the EC in the 1980s were relatively labour-intensive products based mainly on agricultural inputs, in which comparative advantage lay in low real wages, an abundance of unskilled labour and deterioration of agriculture's terms of trade. As wages began to increase in real terms, beginning in 1988, agricultural support prices could not be suppressed any longer and this took place at a time when export incentives were gradually reduced. Given the current structure and technology level of industry, further expansion in EC markets did not seem to be feasible. Thus in the 1990s, Turkish policy-makers face the task of redirecting the export promotion policy from production to the final stage, in view of technological changes which completely alter comparative advantages, as well as the policy changes in the EC connected with the Single Market.

EC direct investment in Turkey

Following the liberalization of legislation on foreign investment within the framework of the outward-orientated programme since 1980, significant developments have been witnessed in the fields of foreign-capital inflow and foreign investment. Over 50 per cent of the foreign capital in Turkey has come from the Community and over two-thirds of the foreign firms in Turkey originate from Community members.

Policy-makers in Turkey believed that close ties with the EC would be viewed as a symbol of a guarantee provided to foreign investors concerning the security of democracy and the free-enterprise system. Capital inflows also depend on economic development in the host country, coupled with macroeconomic stability as well as the favourable international economic environment in orienting the investment to a particular country: Turkey lacked all these factors at the beginning of the 1980s.

The Iranian Islamic Revolution had frightened many Western investors and made them reluctant to invest in another Muslim country. Western Europe was also trying to recover from the second oil crisis, experiencing slow growth of around 1.5 per cent in the period 1981–5,[18] and when growth gained momentum in the second half of the 1980s investments were directed towards Spain and Portugal, then new members of the Community.

The domestic macroeconomic instability of Turkey also adversely affected European investors at the beginning of the 1980s. The share of EC members in the total number of foreign firms investing in Turkey which was 56 per cent in 1979, dropped to around 32.7 per cent (1985), not only on account of the reasons cited above but also as a result of the increase in the share of oil-rich countries. The share of Community members later rose to

39.8 per cent in 1990, due to reasons originating both from the domestic economy and also the international environment.

OECD countries account for the great majority of foreign investment in Turkey, nearly $1.74 billion in 1991, representing almost 90 per cent of total foreign investment, of which the EC countries accounted for $1.02 billion. The share of the EC in OECD foreign investment in Turkey has declined to around 58 per cent from its peak of about 77 per cent in 1990, and 70 per cent in 1989 as the dissolution of the Soviet Union and the market orientation of Eastern Europe began to divert the attention of European investors to these new outlets. In 1991 five Community members accounted for half of the total foreign investment in Turkey:

United Kingdom 16 per cent;
Germany 10 per cent;
Netherlands 9 per cent;
France 8 per cent;
Italy 7 per cent.

The United Kingdom stands out as the country which invested heavily in Turkey post-1980, due to Polly Peck investments, whose founder was a Turkish-Cypriot. Germany, France, the Netherlands and Italy were the other member countries which had invested considerably (Table 5.8). In contrast, the Mediterranean countries of the Community have a very small share in total foreign investment. (See Appendix Table K).

The major investing countries of the EC with respect to the number of firms are Germany (343 firms), the United Kingdom (156 firms) and the Netherlands (80 firms). The number of firms of EC origin increased more than twelve-fold (from 58 firms to 722 firms) during the last decade, while the number of non-EC firms increased over fifteen times (from 69 firms to 1,090 firms) (See Appendix Table K). The foreign capital invested by major countries in rank order was the United Kingdom (16.35 per cent), Germany (10.40 per cent), the Netherlands (9.43 per cent) and France (7.40 per cent).[19]

As with other foreign investors, post-1980 trade liberalization reforms reduced the relative attractiveness of manufacturing for EC investors. However, in certain branches, such as agro-industry, foreign investment acted as an engine for growth. In this field alone, there were thirty-five firms of EC origin at the end of 1990.

The textile and ready-made garment sector is an area where cooperation has been at a minimum level between Turkey and the Community. After the investments realized by British firms in 1952, it was not until the post-1980 period that thirteen firms of German, British, French and Italian origin invested in Turkey. However, most of the machinery and inputs used in these investments were still imported from the EC countries.

The electronics industry, Grundig, Philips, Schaub-Lorenz, Telefunken and Imperial became the most favoured brand names in production. Nearly one-half of imported electronic items came from EC countries, and switchboards of European origin had a significant share in the communications market. The defence industry had also concluded large-scale contracts with

Table 5.8 Foreign direct-investment permits by country (%)

	1986	1987	1988	1989	1990	1991
OECD countries	53.8	77.7	86.0	87.8	90.1	91.3
EEC countries	28.9	37.5	46.5	61.7	70.0	53.7
Germany	12.4	11.9	11.4	8.2	7.7	9.8
Belgium-Luxembourg	4.9	1.1	0.9	2.3	1.2	2.1
Denmark	1.3	0.4	0.1	2.1	0.9	0.2
France	2.3	3.9	8.9	17.1	36.7	12.8
Netherlands	0.7	2.4	4.8	6.7	3.9	14.6
United Kingdom	6.0	13.4	15.2	19.0	15.7	3.6
Ireland	0.0	0.0	0.0	0.1	0.0	0.0
Italy	1.3	4.0	4.8	5.7	3.3	10.0
Greece	0.0	0.0	0.1	0.0	0.0	0.1
Spain	0.0	0.3	0.3	0.3	0.5	0.4
Portugal	—	—	—	—	—	0.0
Other OECD countries	24.9	40.2	39.5	26.1	20.2	37.6
USA	6.7	9.2	16.0	8.9	6.6	23.9
Japan	0.7	8.4	8.1	4.9	5.6	2.8
Switzerland	14.6	20.2	13.0	10.7	6.1	5.5
Austria	0.2	0.2	0.6	0.6	0.4	0.4
Others	2.6	2.2	1.7	1.1	1.4	5.0
Islamic countries	26.6	6.6	6.2	7.1	3.1	5.6
Middle-East countries	25.1	6.0	5.7	5.4	2.4	4.7
North-African countries	0.1	0.1	0.0	0.3	0.5	0.9
Other Islamic countries	1.5	0.5	0.5	1.4	0.2	0.0
Other countries	19.6	15.7	7.8	5.1	6.8	2.7
Total	100.0	100.0	100.0	100.0	100.0	100.0

Source: State Planning Organization

companies from the EC countries. A substantial part of the investments in the Turkish energy sector was realized through credits provided by EC countries, and certain investment contracts have been awarded to companies from the EC.

The service sectors prefered by the EC investors have been tourism, banking and insurance. The share of tourism in total foreign investment was around 16 per cent, of which 33 per cent was of EC origin. When one considers that nearly one-half of the tourists visiting Turkey are from the Community, this percentage seems a natural consequence. Joint promotion activities were also being carried out in third countries through the European Travel Agency. The number of EC bank branches and subsidiaries operating in Turkey had reached 22 in 1990. Their advanced banking know-how has been helpful in transforming the financial sector from inefficient intermediaries towards modern and dynamic institutions offering diverse services.

EC firms also favoured the insurance sector which, under the recent changes in insurance regulations,[20] allowed them to operate with a minimum of formalities and to release without delay the sums deposited exceeding those required to constitute technical reserves.

Turkey also began to implement project schemes under the build–operate–transfer model. This allows an international consortium bidding on a project to design the project, raise and secure funding for the construction, own, manage and maintain the project in exchange for the host government's guarantees to take the products of the plant over a given period. At the end of the term, when all the project's loans have been repaid, and equity capital (not less than 15 per cent of total investment cost) has been repatriated, ownership of the project would be transferred to the host government without charge. Several projects have been initiated within this model.[21]

Turkey's initiatives in Europe

Turkish workers have been living mainly in Germany and the Netherlands with a population of over 2 million including spouses and children. Having a strong tendency to stay, they have invested in over 50 different sectors, ranging from video-cassettes, computer systems to tailors specialized in alterations. Initially, such investments were related to job creation consisting of self and family employed ventures, but today the number of locals and foreigners employed by these initiatives is steadily increasing. Although the capital invested in the initiatives is from remittances, affecting adversely the foreign exchange earnings of Turkey, they provide a remarkable example of Turkish people's integration in the Community.[22]

Conclusion

Any evaluation of the Community's reaction to Turkey's accession should be based on the two official documents, namely the Commission's 'Opinion Record on Turkey's Request' and 'The Cooperation Package'. The basic idea behind these documents can be summarized in two points. The first is that although the EC considers Turkey eligible for full membership, it does not give priority to Turkey's accession in the short- or medium-term, and does not even plan to start negotiations for adhesion in the foreseeable future. The second point is that the EC accepts its fundamental interest in pursuing a closer relationship with Turkey in political, social and economic fields and suggests the reactivation of the Association Agreement, mainly under the proposed measures in four areas: the completion of the customs union, the resumption and intensification of financial cooperation, the promotion of industrial and technological cooperation and the strengthening of political and cultural links. The specific proposals by the Commission emphasized the establishment of a customs union for industrial products by the end of 1995, and closer cooperation in certain sectors including industry, agriculture, financial services, transport, environment, energy, science and technology. The conclusion of the Fourth Financial Protocol, which has almost became the symbol of favourable relations, had already encountered a Greek veto.

The nature of events after the Turkish application, including dramatic changes in Eastern Europe and the Soviet Union, diverted European interest away from Turkey. This was compounded by the Community moving toward the Single European Market, which had the tacit implications that Turkey was going to be kept on the periphery of European integration rather than being incorporated as a full member in the foreseeable future. The accession of Greece in 1981, followed by Portugal and Spain in 1986, has already created substantial economic losses for Turkey, particularly trade-diverting effects encompassing agricultural products and textile exports. The Turkish view was that only full membership can put Turkey on an equal footing with the other three Mediterranean countries.

The belief concerning the loss of Turkey's strategic importance in the region was reversed by the Gulf Crisis. Under the given set of relations with the Community, Turkey's new role in the region implied closer cooperation with the United States, with the possible danger of distancing itself from the EC. Improvement in relations with the Balkan countries and the newly established Turkic Republics, the Black Sea Economic Cooperation Project (with Bulgaria, Romania, Russia, Moldavia, Georgia, Ukraine, Armenia and Azerbaijan as potential members), and the reactivation and enlargement of the Economic Cooperation Organization (ECO) which currently includes Turkey, Iran and Pakistan are important steps in this connection.

Thus by the early 1990s, new opportunities had emerged and Turkey's outward orientation had to undergo a shift in regional targets in order to be sustainable and to provide a new horizon to the already established expansion in the Middle East and North Africa in the 1980s. However, this has not stopped Turkey trying to intensify its links with Western Europe and signing a protocol with EFTA as the first step to a free-trade agreement.

The Community has been the main trading partner of Turkey, and one can safely assume that it will maintain this position in the 1990s. Turkey's relations with a vast number of countries under the Black Sea Economic Cooperation Region project, ECO and its intensifying ties with the East-Asian countries through the Turkic Republics will help Turkey to diversify its export market, thereby reducing its vulnerability. Reconstruction and policy reforms in the countries torn by the Gulf War will increase their growth rate and will reactivate Turkey's trade relations with them.

These new markets are all the more important in the case of Turkey's agricultural and textile exports which face strict Community protectionist measures. In addition these neighbouring countries are likely to sustain their position as net agricultural importers over the coming decade and will reduce the foreign market constraints on agricultural goods. But should Turkey continue toward the formation of a customs union in industrial products despite the Community's restrictions on the entry of Turkey's agricultural products? This question will become more critical when new technological changes increase the exportable surplus and the impacts of Southeastern Anatolian Project are felt. The Community, under the incentives provided by the CAP, might also grow into a major exporter of agricultural products, mainly food items.

The formation of a customs union in industrial products with the Community, and the adoption of the Common External Tariff, will put Turkey in an awkward situation in which imports are increasing while export receipts from agriculture will be constrained. Thus the nature of agricultural trade relations can be expected to play a crucial role in the formation of a customs union in industrial products. If the CAP is sustained in its present form and the Community is enlarged by new members, Turkey will lose by not having market access for its potential increase in exportable agricultural surplus in the coming decade.

In the case of the customs union for industrial products, imports from the Community may explode as they gain in competitivity *vis-à-vis* domestic products as well as third-country products upon the dismantling of tariff and import taxes. And the adoption of the Common Customs Tariff might worsen the picture, since all third countries which enjoy tariff concessions in the Community market will gain a competitive edge in the Turkish market without giving any concessions in return.

The Association Agreement is based on mutual obligations: Turkey's obligation being to take concrete steps towards the customs union, whereas the EC's is, among others, to provide financial aid to support Turkey's efforts. At the beginning of the 1990s there are all the signs that Turkey is willing to progress towards its ultimate target, while the EC refrains from fulfilling its obligations in the areas of financial aid, free movement of labour and in the elimination of non-tariff barriers to Turkish export products. The existence of quantitative restrictions imposed by the EC on textiles and clothing items of Turkish origin is considered to be one of the most controversial issues in achieving the objectives of a customs union. Turkey's proposal concerning the early and full liberalization of the textile trade reciprocally with the EC was officially presented to the Commission by a *note-verbale* on 26 November 1990. The general proposal on the mutual abolition of tariff and non-tariff barriers was not supported by the Commission, which, as a counter proposal, proposed the establishment of a joint working group on all matters of the customs union.

The disparity between Turkey and other Mediterranean countries in receiving financial aid is striking. From 1964 to 1992, Turkey as an associate member received a sum of ECU 827 million as financial aid from the Community. This represented an annual average of ECU 30 million, whereas other Mediterranean countries, which had only signed commercial agreements with the EC, had received far more. The percentage share of Community aid to GDP has been 0.10 per cent for Turkey while for the former Yugoslavia and Tunisia, respectively, 1.25 per cent and 0.40 per cent. The figure for Portugal is 3.2 per cent while for Greece it is 2.7 per cent. It is an important fact that no Mediterranean member state has been asked to establish a full customs union with the Community without receiving financial aid. Will or should Turkey complete this stage without financial assistance is a critical question that has to be answered.

In contrast, bilateral financial relations with Europe along with increasing trade, investment and even credits have improved in the 1980s and have contributed to the de facto integration of the Turkish economy to the Community. Turkey has received about $7 billion bilateral credits both from European financial institutions and from individual member states. Thus the provisions concerning financial cooperation in the 'cooperation package' contain more symbolic weight, but nonetheless are important.

The early 1990s brings to a close a very important stage in European moves towards a Single European Market. At the same time, European integration has been extended to other countries with the signing of Association Agreements with Hungary, Poland and Czechoslovakia. It is expected that most of the EFTA countries will also become members of the Community by mid-decade. Austria, Finland and Sweden have already expressed their intention to join the EC. Although the timetable is still uncertain, what is certain is that Turkey's efforts to intensify relations with the Community will have to search for a place on the agenda which confronts the Community. The talk of an enlarged Community operating at different levels of integration raises the question as to whether Turkey is likely to be given a place in the second tier with limited participation in the policy-making process.

The deepening of European economic integration will be a positive and welcome contribution to the world economy as long as the process liberalizes trade with the rest of the world. If liberalization within Europe comes at the expense of third-country interests, then the result will be increased barriers to non-European trade and investment. The Uruguay Round of the GATT talks is expected to support the acceptance of progressive reductions in protectionism.

Turkey, during the 1980s, implemented a wide range of reforms, including the liberalization of international trade, the relaxation of the tariff system, the deregulation of the financial sector and foreign-investment regulations. The success story on this front was expected to enhance Turkey's possibility of accession to the EC, and the government in office applied for full membership in April 1987. The 1990s will be a period to pursue this transformation uninterrupted, and to consolidate with fine tuning what has already been achieved. Further liberalization of the economy by reducing the weight of the public sector through privatization and the deepening of financial markets will be steps in the de facto integration of the Turkish economy with that of the Community. Turkey, being on the axis originating from the Far East reaching to the Mediterranean Basin, the Middle East and Europe, will continue to play a relevant role in trade relations. This should pave the way to full membership in the EC which is that country's explicitly articulated goal.

Notes

1. For a detailed analysis of income distribution after 1980 see G. Kazgan, *Income Distribution in Turkey. Yesterday and Today*, Studies in Development (Istan-

bul: Middle East Business and Banking Publication, 1991); also C. Balkir, 'The Economic Liberalization Programme and its Distributional Impact: The Turkish Case after 1980', (paper presented to the symposium on Economic Liberalization and its Social and Political Effects in the Middle East, Exeter, 26–8 September 1991).

2. 1985 figures, UN, *1986 International Trade Statistics Yearbook*, p. 1,185.

 SITC 001 live animals (Turkey's share — 4.16 per cent)
 SITC 057 fruits and shelled fruits, fresh or dried fruits (Turkey's share — 4.30 per cent)
 SITC 121 tobacco (Turkey's share — 7.82 per cent)
 SITC 278 other raw materials (Turkey's share — 4.71 per cent)

3. Export incentives can be listed as follows: Tax rebates on exports; payments from Export subsidy and Price Stabilization Fund; low-cost export re-discount credit; exemption from taxes, duties and fees; advance payment of tax rebate on exports; exemption from the value-added tax (VAT) on exports; exemption from corporate and income tax; incentives to freight; imported goods exempt from customs duty; retaining and utilizing abroad foreign exchange earned from exports; allocation of global amounts of exchange for imports; importation of goods and packaging materials under the temporary admission regime; sales and deliveries considered as exports benefiting from incentives; Eximbank pre- and post-shipment credits.

4. See M. Celasun and D. Rodrik 'Debt, adjustment and growth: Turkey' in *Developing Country Debt and Economic Performance*, (J.D. Sachs and M.S. Collins (eds)), Chicago: The University of Chicago Press, 1989, p. 729.

5. Concerning Turkish Eximbank's export credit strategy see P. Lasonde and H. Kozanoglu, *A review of Turkish Eximbank's Export Credit Strategies*, Ankara: Eximbank mimeo, 1989.

6. For an elaboration on this subject, see Selim Ilkin 'Exporters: Favoured Dependency' in M. Heper (ed.), *Strong State and Economic Interest groups — The Post-1980 Turkish Experience*, New York: Walter de Gruyter, 1991, pp. 89–98.

7. G. Kazgan (ed.), *Prospects for Turkey's Accession to the Community with Special Reference to Competitivity*, Istanbul: SIAR mimeo, 1987, p. 14.

8. For calculation of rates of protection see S. Togan, H. Olgun and H. Akder, *Report on Developments in External Economic Relations of Turkey*, Istanbul: Turktrade Publication, 1987, p. 22.

9. G. Kazgan, op. cit. p.16.

10. For discussions on foreign capital during those years see YASED (Association for the Coordination of Foreign Capital), *Application of Foreign Capital in Various Countries*, Istanbul: YASED Publication, 1984 and YASED, *Selected Opinions on Foreign Capital*, Istanbul: YASED Publication, 1983.

11. Various decrees and directives have been issued in order to clarify and simplify procedures and provide additional incentives to foreign capital. The Foreign Capital Decree No. 10353, the Financial Leasing Statute No. 3226, Law for the Encouragement of Tourism (Law 2634), Free Trade Zone Law No. 3218 and the establishment of a Foreign Capital Directorate within the framework of Prime Minister's Office were the main steps taken.

12. SPO calculations show that under the subsectoral breakdown of foreign invest- ment, the share of sectors with comparative advantage was 29.2 per cent in 1985, dropping to 13.3 per cent, while the share of net importer sectors rose from 62.5 per cent to 69.3 per cent.

13. H. Akder, 'Constant Market Share Analysis of Changes in Turkey's Exports to

the EC (1981–85)', Yapi Kredi Economic Review, 1, No. 2, Istanbul: Yapi Kredi Publication, 1987, pp. 33–42.
14. The main studies conducted in Turkey during the 1980s on the competitivity of the Turkish economy were:

   — Economic Development Foundation — IKV *Avrupa Topluluga (AET) Karsisinda Turk Sanayiinin Durumu*, pub. no. 13, Istanbul, 1985.
   — G. Kazgan (ed.), *Prospects for Turkey's Accession to the Community with Special Reference to Competitivity*, Istanbul: SIAR mimeo, 1987.
   — G. Kazgan (ed.), *Manufacturing Survey with Special Reference to Turkey's Integration with the EC*, Istanbul: SIAR mimeo, 1988.
   — SPO, *Turk Sanayiinin AT Sanayii Karsisinda Rekabet Imkanlari*, ÖIK, Raporu, pub. no. 2,141, Ankara, 1988.

15. F. Senses and Yamada, *Stabilization and Structural Adjustment Program in Turkey*, Tokyo: Institute of Developing Economies, ORP series 88, 1990.
16. G. Kazgan (ed.), *Prospects for Turkey's Accession to the Community*, op. cit., p. 76.
17. Op. cit. p. 176.
18. A.M. Williams, *The European Community*, Oxford: Basil Blackwell Ltd, 1991, p. 80.
19. For a detailed analysis see *Economic Report on Turkey — EC Integration*, Ankara: SPO, Report prepared for the 34th session of the Turkey–EC Joint Parliamentary Committee.
20. Insurance Supervisory Law No: 7397 as amended by Law No: 3379 dated 11 June 1987; the Regulation regarding Principles of Operation of Insurance and Reinsurance Intermediaries, dated 21 August 1988.
21. The projects are the Akkuyu nuclear power plant, thermal power projects, the Ankara Metro, Istanbul Airport and World Trade Centre, Birecik Hydroelectric Power plant and Izmit Water Supply project.
22. See *Economic Report on Turkey–EC Integration*, op. cit, and F. Sen, *Turks in the Federal Republic of Germany – Achievements, Problems, Expectations*, Zentrum Für Türkeistudien, Bonn, 1987.

References

Akder, H., 1987, 'Constant Market Share Analysis of Changes in Turkey's Exports to the EC (1981–1985)', *Yapi Kredi Economic Review*, 1, (2): 33–42.
Balkir, C., 1988, *Structural Adjustment of Turkish Agriculture and Industry in the Light of Turkey's Accession to EC*, Harvard University Conference, The Political Economy of Turkey in the 1980s.
Balkir, C., forthcoming, 'Trade Strategy in the 80's' in A. Eralp, M. Tünay, B. Yesilda (eds), *Socioeconomic Transformation of Turkey in the 1980's*, New York: Praeger Publishers.
Baysan, T. and C. Blitzer, 1990, 'Turkey's Trade Liberalization in the 1980s and Prospects for its Sustainability' in *The Political Economy of Turkey*, T. Aricanli and D. Rodrik (eds), 9–36, London: The Macmillan Press Ltd.
Celasun, M. and D. Rodrik, 1989, 'Debt, Adjustment, and Growth: Turkey' in *Developing Country Debt and Economic Performance*, J.D. Sachs and M.S. Collins (eds), 617–820, Chicago and London: The University of Chicago Press.
Central Bank, Bulletins.
Conway, P., 1988, 'The Record on Private Investment in Turkey' in *The Political*

Economy of Turkey, T. Aricanli and D. Rodrik (eds), 78–97, London: The Macmillan Press Ltd.

Dervis, K., and S. Robinson, 1978, *The Foreign Exchange Gap, Growth and Industrial Strategy in Turkey*, 1973–83, World Bank Staff Working paper no. 306, Washington DC.

Erdilek, A., 1986, 'Turkey's new open-door policy for direct foreign investment: A critical analysis of problems and prospects', *METU Studies in Development*, 13 (1/2): 171–91, Ankara..

Ersel H. and A. Temel, 1984, 'Turkiye'nin Dissatim Basarisinin Degerlendirilmesi', *Toplum ve Bilim*, No. 27, Ankara.

Güran, N., 1990a, *Disa Acilma Surecinde Turkiye Ekonomisinin Rekabet Gucu*, SPO Publication No. 2231-AET b: 24, Ankara.

Güran, N., 1990b, *Turkiye-Avrupa Toplulugu Iliskileri*, SPO Publication No. 2230-AET b: 23, Ankara.

Ibrahimhakkioglu, N., 1986, *Planli Donemde Ihracati Tesvik Politikasi*, Ankara: IGEME Yayini.

Kazgan, G., 1987, *Prospects for Turkey's Accession to the Community*, Istanbul, mimeo.

Kazgan, G., 1988, *Summary Report of the Manufacturing Survey with Special Reference to Turkey's Integration with the EC*, mimeo.

Kazgan, G., 1991, *Studies in Economic Development*, Istanbul: Middle East Business and Banking Publication.

Krueger, A.O., 1974, *Foreign Trade Regimes and Economic Development: Turkey*, New York: Columbia University Press for the NBER.

Lasonde, P. and H. Kozanoglu, 1989, *A Review of Turkish Eximbank's Export Credit Strategies*, Ankara, mimeo.

Milanovic, B. 1986, *Export Incentives and Turkish Manufactured Exports, 1980–1984*, World Bank Staff Paper No. 768, Washington DC.

NCM Associates Ltd, 1989, *Some Practical Measures used by Turkish Business to Manage Under High Interest, Inflation and Devaluation of the Turkish Lira*, Izmir, mimeo.

SPO, 1990, *1980' den 1990' a Makroekonomik Politikalar-Türkiye Ekonomisindeki Gelismelerin Analizi ve Bazi Degerlendirmeler*, Ankara: SPO Publication.

State Planning Organization (SPO), various statistics.

Sen, F., 1987, *Turks in the Federal Republic of Germany – Achievements, Problems, Expectations*, Zentrum Für Turkeistudien, Bonn.

Senses, F., 1983, 'An assessment of Turkey's liberalization attempts since 1980 against the background of her stabilization program', *METU Studies in Development*, 10 (3): 271–321.

Togan, S., H. Olgun, and H. Adker, 1987, *Report on Development in External Economic Relations of Turkey*, Istanbul: Turktrade.

Turkish Eximbank, bulletins.

Under Secretariat of Treasury and Foreign Trade, various statistics.

World Bank, 1982, *Turkey: Industrialization and Trade Strategy*, Washington DC.

World Bank, 1988, *Turkey–Country Economic Memorandum Towards Sustainable Growth*, Report N. 7378-Tu, Washington DC.

World Bank, 1989, *Country Report: Turkey 1988*, Washington DC.

Yagci, F., 1984, *Protection and incentives in Turkish Manufacturing*, World Bank Staff Working Paper No. 660, Washington DC.

Yased (Association for the Coordination of Foreign Capital), 1983, *Selected Opinions on Foreign Capital*, Istanbul.

Yased, 1984, *Application of Foreign Capital in Various Countries*, Istanbul.

Statistical appendix

Table A Exports by countries, 1980–90 (%)

Countries	1980	1981	1982	1983	1984	1985	1986	1987	1988	1989	1990
I. OECD Countries	57.7	48.1	44.5	48.2	52.4	51.6	57.6	63.2	57.5	61.7	67.9
EC countries	44.7	33.3	31.4	36.1	38.3	40.3	43.8	47.8	43.7	46.5	53.1
Other OECD countries	13.1	14.9	13.1	12.1	13.2	11.3	1.7	15.5	13.8	15.2	14.8
II. Islamic countries	22.5	42.0	48.2	46.1	42.0	42.8	35.0	30.3	30.3	24.7	19.3
III. East-European countries	17.7	7.5	5.8	4.3	3.7	4.2	4.2	3.3	5.2	8.9	7.6
IV. Other countries	2.0	2.4	1.5	1.5	5.6	1.4	3.3	3.2	7.0	4.7	5.3
Total	100.0	100.0	100.0	100.0	100.0	100.0	100.0	100.0	100.0	100.0	100.0

Source: SPO, *Main Economic Indicators*, various issues

Table B Exports by sector, 1980–90 (%)

Sectors	1980	1981	1982	1983	1984	1985	1986	1987	1988	1989	1990
I. Agriculture and livestock	57.44	47.19	37.26	32.83	24.52	21.61	25.29	18.18	20.08	18.29	18.43
Crops	52.75	40.88	29.58	25.92	19.37	18.11	20.88	14.57	17.05	15.35	16.22
Cotton	11.09	7.40	5.01	3.43	2.36	2.13	1.86	0.20	1.21	1.15	1.05
Tobacco	8.03	8.40	6.06	4.15	3.03	4.15	3.62	3.08	2.28	4.14	2.86
Hazelnuts	13.57	6.42	4.19	4.29	4.27	3.21	5.07	3.83	3.08	2.29	3.41
Raisins	4.48	2.77	1.75	1.25	0.87	0.94	1.38	1.06	1.20	1.40	1.17
Others	15.59	15.89	12.42	12.79	8.84	7.68	8.81	6.39	9.28	6.36	7.73
Livestock Products	3.72	5.49	6.78	6.32	4.53	3.07	3.83	3.05	2.45	2.39	1.68
Fishery Products	0.78	0.57	0.42	0.35	0.28	0.26	0.53	0.44	0.44	0.45	0.43
Forestry	0.20	0.26	0.49	0.24	0.33	0.16	0.18	0.12	0.13	0.11	0.10
II. Mining and quarry products	6.56	4.11	3.05	3.30	3.36	3.06	3.31	2.67	3.23	3.55	2.56
III. Industrial products	35.99	48.70	59.68	63.87	72.12	75.33	71.40	79.15	76.69	78.17	79.02
Processed agricultural products	7.20	8.75	9.89	11.69	11.33	8.13	8.94	9.36	7.59	7.90	7.08
Petroleum products	1.32	2.28	5.99	4.06	5.73	4.67	2.39	2.28	2.84	2.19	2.15
Other industrial products	27.47	37.67	43.81	48.12	55.06	62.53	60.07	67.51	66.26	68.09	69.79
Cement	1.36	4.22	3.60	1.41	0.79	0.55	0.36	0.07	0.06	0.29	0.59
Chemicals	2.61	1.99	2.57	2.10	2.42	3.34	4.70	5.17	6.30	6.66	4.77
Rubber and plastic	0.55	1.53	1.05	1.34	1.37	1.36	1.88	2.53	3.02	2.69	1.75
Hides and leather products	1.70	1.75	1.94	3.35	5.62	6.09	4.63	7.08	4.41	5.20	5.79
Forestry products	0.15	0.42	0.58	0.26	0.33	1.33	0.69	0.31	0.19	0.14	0.17
Textiles	14.58	17.07	18.38	22.68	26.29	22.49	24.82	26.57	27.45	30.18	31.64
Glass and ceramics	1.23	2.17	1.81	1.89	2.05	2.38	2.12	2.01	2.00	2.22	2.51

Iron and steel	1.16	2.13	6.30	7.11	8.08	12.17	10.78	8.36	12.50	11.60	12.50
Non-ferrous metal	0.63	0.63	0.78	1.38	1.20	1.45	1.49	1.32	l.94	2.29	1.95
Metal products	0.28	0.43	0.48	0.34	0.23	0.91	0.81	1.05	0.44	0.20	0.21
Machinery	0.75	1.38	2.01	1.79	1.66	4.75	2.72	6.68	2.86	1.68	1.58
Electrical appliances	0.40	0.55	1.31	1.20	1.40	1.49	1.74	2.88	2.52	2.01	3.25
Motor vehicles	1.73	2.50	1.92	2.21	1.89	1.84	1.11	1.08	1.01	1.33	1.54
Others	0.35	0.90	1.08	1.06	1.75	2.38	2.23	2.41	1.58	1.60	1.53
Total	100.00	100.00	100.00	100.00	100.00	100.00	100.00	100.00	100.00	100.00	100.00

Source: State Institute of Statistics, Turkey

Table C Imports by sector, 1980–90 (%)

Sectors	1980	1981	1982	1983	1984	1985	1986	1987	1988	1989
I. Agriculture and livestock	0.65	1.40	1.99	1.56	3.88	3.31	4.12	5.33	3.48	6.61
II. Mining and quarry products	39.14	38.93	42.28	38.92	33.88	31.97	19.32	21.43	19.96	18.41
III. Industrial products	60.21	59.67	55.72	63.96	62.24	64.72	76.56	73.04	76.56	74.98
Processed agricultural products	3.83	2.58	2.00	2.32	4.03	4.30	4.32	5.08	5.15	5.35
Petroleum products	11.50	6.95	2.50	4.78	2.45	2.56	1.80	1.73	2.39	2.79
Other industrial products	44.88	50.14	51.23	56.85	55.76	57.87	70.45	66.23	69.01	66.49
Cement	0.00	0.00	0.01	0.00	0.01	0.01	0.02	0.35	0.35	0.07
Chemicals	14.20	13.45	l0.11	13.05	12.46	11.41	12.80	13.68	13.84	13.35
Rubber and plastic	2.31	2.69	2.68	2.85	3.33	3.02	3.35	3.45	3.66	3.08
Hides and leather products	0.00	0.01	0.00	0.02	0.05	0.14	0.23	0.52	0.36	0.46
Forestry products	0.03	0.03	0.07	0.03	0.04	0.07	0.05	0.05	0.06	0.06
Textiles	1.01	0.88	1.17	1.11	1.09	1.29	1.45	1.44	1.81	1.88
Glass and ceramics	0.45	0.45	0.39	0.65	0.58	0.55	0.86	0.83	0.98	0.80
Iron and steel	5.71	6.79	6.70	7.65	8.01	9.34	9.26	10.86	11.55	14.07
Non-ferrous metal	1.10	1.58	1.39	2.21	2.05	1.97	2.07	2.95	2.87	2.67
Metal products	0.29	0.25	0.43	0.38	0.32	0.33	0.46	0.39	0.43	0.36
Machinery	11.01	13.96	14.97	16.39	15.04	13.67	20.75	17.34	16.74	13.88
Electrical appliances	3.54	3.82	4.28	4.54	5.33	5.85	8.03	6.64	7.50	6.52
Motor vehicles	3.30	4.30	6.92	5.61	4.81	7.17	6.91	3.88	4.81	5.01
Others	1.92	1.94	2.12	2.36	2.63	3.05	4.20	3.85	4.04	4.28
Total	100.00	100.00	100.00	100.00	100.00	100.00	100.00	100.00	100.00	100.00

Source: State Institute of Statistics, Turkey

Table D Imports by countries, 1980–90 (%)

Countries	1980	1981	1982	1983	1984	1985	1986	1987	1988	1989	1990
I. OECD countries	45.3	47.9	50.1	48.5	51.7	56.1	65.8	63.8	64.4	62.9	63.8
EC countries	29.8	29.5	29.0	30.1	30.8	34.3	41.1	40.0	41.1	38.4	41.8
Other OECD countries	15.5	18.4	21.1	18.5	20.8	21.8	24.7	23.8	23.3	24.5	21.9
II. Islamic countries	41.4	40.3	43.0	40.1	36.3	33.0	19.3	22.3	20.5	18.6	17.7
III. East-European countries	10.5	9.5	4.8	8.7	8.8	5.8	7.9	6.8	7.7	9.5	10.1
IV. Other countries	2.8	2.3	2.0	2.7	3.2	5.1	7.1	7.1	7.4	9.1	8.5
Total	100.0	100.0	100.0	100.0	100.0	100.0	100.0	100.0	100.0	100.0	100.0

Source: SPO, Main *Economic Indicators*, various issues

Table E Timetable for customs tariff reductions in the Additional Protocol

	Products for which tariffs will be eliminated in 12 years			Products for which tariffs will be eliminated in 22 years	
	Reduction (%)			Reduction (%)	
	Annual	Total		Annual	Total
1/1/1973	10	10	1/1/1973	5	5
1/1/1974	—	10	1/1/1974	—	5
1/1/1975	—	10	1/1/1975	—	5
1/1/1976	10	20	1/1/1976	5	10
1/1/1977	—	20	1/1/1977	—	10
1/1/1978	10	30	1/1/1978	—	10
1/1/1979	10	40	1/1/1979	5	15
1/1/1980	10	50	1/1/1980	—	15
1/1/1981	10	60	1/1/1981	—	15
1/1/1982	10	70	1/1/1982	—	15
1/1/1983	10	80	1/1/1983	5	20
1/1/1984	10	90	1/1/1984	—	20
1/1/1985	10	100	1/1/1985	10	30
			1/1/1986	10	40
			1/1/1987	—	40
			1/1/1988	10	50
			1/1/1989	—	50
			1/1/1990	10	60
			1/1/1991	10	70
			1/1/1992	—	70
			1/1/1993	10	80
			1/1/1994	10	90
			1/1/1995	10	100

Table F Export/import ratio, 1981–90

	Total trade	Trade with the EC
1981	53	65
1982	65	77
1983	62	80
1984	66	86
1985	70	86
1986	67	78
1987	72	92
1988	81	87
1989	74	89
1990	58	74

Source: Undersecretary of Treasury and Foreign Trade, Turkey

Table G Turkey–EC foreign trade, 1967–90

Years	Exports to EC (Mil. US$)	Share in total exports (%)	Imports from the EC (Mil. US$)	Share in total imports (%)	Foreign trade volume (Mil. US$)	Share in Turkey's total trade (%)
1967	234.1	44.82	333.7	48.74	567.8	47.05
1968	225.5	45.44	392.9	51.46	618.5	49.09
1969	266.7	49.69	393.0	49.05	659.7	49.31
1970[1]	294.4	50.04	426.9	45.06	721.4	46.97
1971[2]	329.4	48.69	581.5	49.67	910.9	49.31
1972	428.0	48.37	851.0	54.47	1279.1	52.26
1973[3]	652.1	49.51	1160.9	55.65	1813.1	53.27
1974	761.0	49.67	1747.6	46.26	2508.6	47.25
1975	644.6	46.01	2377.9	50.18	3022.5	49.23
1976	1016.5	51.86	2411.4	47.02	3428.0	48.36
1977	896.5	51.15	2558.9	44.15	3455.4	45.77
1978	1127.2	49.26	1930.7	41.98	3057.9	44.40
1979	1131.5	50.04	1941.8	38.30	3073.3	41.93
1980[4]	1299.7	44.66	2360.3	29.84	3660.0	33.83
1981[5]	1564.0	33.26	2632.4	29.47	4196.5	30.78
1982	1801.6	31.35	2565.6	29.02	4367.4	29.94
1983	2066.3	36.07	2775.4	30.05	4841.7	32.36
1984	2780.4	38.98	3314.3	30.81	6094.8	34.07
1985	3204.0	40.26	3895.1	34.34	7099.1	36.78
1986[6]	3263.1	43.76	4564.9	41.11	7828.1	42.17
1987	4867.7	47.77	5665.8	40.02	10533.6	43.26
1988	5098.3	43.72	5895.1	41.12	10993.4	42.29
1989	5407.8	46.52	6055.2	38.34	11463.0	41.81
1990	6892.8	53.19	9328.3	41.83	16221.1	46.00

[1] Additional Protocol signed
[2] Directives of the Additional Protocol concerning trade have been put into effect by the Annexed Protocol
[3] Additional Protocol put into effect. England, Ireland and Denmark joined the Community
[4] 24 January 1980 Austerity Measures
[5] Greece joins the Community
[6] Spain and Portugal join the Community

Source: Undersecretary of Treasury and Foreign Trade, EC and Turkey, Ankara, 1991

Table H Timetable for customs union

	12-Year List				22-Year List			
	Customs Tariff		Adoption of Com. Customs Tariff		Customs Tariff		Adoption of Com. Customs Tariff	
	Reduction rate (%)		Reduction rate (%)		Reduction rate (%)		Reduction rate (%)	
	Annual	Total	Annual	Total	Annual	Total	Annual	Total
1988	10	30	—	—	10	20	—	—
1989	10	40	20	20	10	30	20	20
1990	10	50	—	20	10	40	—	20
1991	10	60	20	40	10	50	—	20
1992	10	70	—	40	10	60	20	40

Source: SPO

Table I Timetable for customs tariff reductions for agricultural products

Date	Reduction (%)	Cumulative Reduction (%)
1/1/1981	30	30
1/1/1983	30	60
1/1/1985	20	80
1/1/1987	20	100

Source: SPO

Table J Timetable for the adoption of common customs tariff

	Products for which tariffs will be eliminated in 12 years			Products for which tariffs will be eliminated in 22 years	
	Reduction (%)			Reduction (%)	
	Annual	Total		Annual	Total
1/1/1973	—	—	1/1/1973	—	—
1/1/1974	—	—	1/1/1974	—	—
1/1/1975	—	—	1/1/1975	—	—
1/1/1976	—	—	1/1/1976	—	—
1/1/1977	20	20	1/1/1977	—	—
1/1/1978	—	20	1/1/1978	—	—
1/1/1979	—	20	1/1/1979	—	—
1/1/1980	20	40	1/1/1980	—	—
1/1/1981	—	40	1/1/1981	—	—
1/1/1982	20	60	1/1/1982	—	—
1/1/1983	—	60	1/1/1983	20	—
1/1/1984	—	60	1/1/1984	—	—
1/1/1985	40	100	1/1/1985	—	20
			1/1/1986	—	20
			1/1/1987	—	20
			1/1/1988	30	20
			1/1/1989	—	50
			1/1/1990	—	50
			1/1/1991	20	50
			1/1/1992	—	70
			1/1/1993	—	70
			1/1/1994	—	70
			1/1/1995	30	100

Source: Additional Protocol

Table K Foreign firms of EC origin

Countries	1981	1982	1983	1984	1985	1986	1987	1988	1989	1990
EC countries	58	67	75	100	145	200	284	383	556	722
West Germany	28	37	40	47	59	92	131	167	233	307
Belgium	2	2	3	3	6	7	12	13	20	21
Denmark	4	4	4	4	6	7	8	8	9	12
France	6	6	6	6	7	9	16	28	52	81
Netherlands	6	6	6	10	18	23	30	42	59	72
United Kingdom	5	5	8	21	34	44	60	85	117	148
Italy	5	5	6	7	11	11	15	23	40	50
Luxembourg	2	2	2	2	4	5	7	9	11	13
Spain						1	2	4	6	8
Greece						1	3	4	9	10
Non-EEC countries	69	103	110	167	267	412	555	726	927	1,090
Total	127	170	185	267	421	612	839	1,109	1,483	1,812

Source: YASED

6
The human tie: international labour migration

Ayşe Kadıoğlu

The person in transition is 'both-and' or 'neither-nor' and indeed simultaneously. His identity becomes blurred and indeterminable. This situation renders some urgency to the problem of determining the indeterminable.
Niklas Luhmann (cited in Tibi, Bassam, 1990, *Islam and the Cultural Accommodation of Social Change*, Boulder Westview Press).

An overview of the 'migratory chain'[1]

In the post-1945 period, labour emigration from the European South to the industrially developed countries of Northern and Western Europe emerged as a popular remedy for resolving problems of development and underdevelopment in the labour-receiving and labour-sending societies respectively. Labour emigration from Turkey to the Federal Republic of Germany should be viewed as part of this general movement of labour from the less-developed European South. These migratory flows were mostly government-regulated and involved bilateral agreements between these two groups of countries.

The first agreement regarding emigration from Turkey was made between the Turkish Ministry of Foreign Affairs and the Ministry of Labour of Schleswig-Holstein in 1957. This led to the arrival of twelve craftsmen with their families at Kiel on April 1957.[2] The early 1960s signify the initiation of the period of planned economic development in Turkey. With the establishment of the State Planning Organization (*Devlet Planlama Teşkilatı*) and the initiation of development plans, labour emigration from Turkey became a government-coordinated act and thus acquired a role within the Five-Year Plans. The involvement of the government in this issue, through signing bilateral agreements with various North- and Western-

European countries, led to a sudden outflow of emigration from Turkey. Turkish government officials signed such bilateral agreements with the government of the Federal Republic of Germany in 1961, with Austria, the Netherlands and Belgium in 1964, with France in 1967 and Australia in 1968.

Despite the significance of such bilateral agreements between Turkish government officials and the governments of various other European countries, the number of Turkish workers entering the Federal Republic of Germany was visibly higher. For instance, in 1961 100 per cent of the Turkish workers officially dispatched by the Turkish Institute of Employment (İş ve İşçi Bulma Kurumu) to Europe were sent to the Federal Republic of Germany.[3] The same figure was 99 per cent in 1962, 77 per cent in 1963, 85 per cent in 1967 and 80 per cent in 1972.[4] Table 6.1 presents an overview of the destinations of the Turkish workers sent abroad by the Institute of Employment, during the official recruitment period, through bilateral agreements.

With the closing of the European borders, the destinations of the Turkish emigrants have changed considerably. In the course of the 1980s, while the numbers of the emigrants have decreased to a great extent, the dominant destination has been the Arab countries.[5] By 1990, emigration figures from Turkey were considerably lower compared to the influx of Bulgarian nationals of Turkish origin. In 1990 (from the beginning of January to the end of June), the number of workers sent through official channels was 29,604 with 27,248 going to Arab countries.[6] The number of Bulgarian nationals entering Turkey by 15 August 1990, on the other hand, was 352,958.[7] Moreover, recent figures of return migration from both European and Arab countries are significantly higher than the emigration rates.[8]

In 1961, the construction of the Berlin Wall brought an end to the flow of labourers from the German Democratic Republic to West Germany. This situation increased the West German government's motivation in engaging in bilateral contracts to import additional workers. The first bilateral agreement was signed in 1955 with the Italian government and involved the importation of labourers in the construction and agricultural sectors. Additional bilateral agreements were signed throughout the 1960s; with Greece and Spain in 1960, Turkey in 1961, Portugal in 1965, Tunisia in 1965, Morocco in 1963 and 1966, and Yugoslavia in 1968.

The 1961 agreement signed between the Federal Republic of Germany and Turkey contained specific provisions governing the recruitment of Turkish workers for employment in the Federal Republic of Germany. All the requests for labour were made by the officially recognised host government or employer association representatives to the Turkish Institute of Employment. These requests were usually made by the German Federal Labour Office (Bundesanstalt für Arbeit) and its liaison office in Istanbul. They were either 'nominative' (naming a specific individual) or 'anonymous' (calling for groups of workers for various employment opportunities). The Turkish Institute of Employment was able to use some judgement over whom they sent in the latter case. Between January 1965 and December 1975, 33.8 per cent of all Turkish workers who were sent abroad were sent

Table 6.1 Turkish workers sent abroad through the Institute of Employment by year and country of destination

Host country	1961–6	1967	1968	1969	1970	1971	1972	1973	1974	31 Jan–June 1975
Fed. Rep. Germany	168,891	7,199	41,409	98,142	96,936	65,684	65,875	103,753	1,228	237
France	88	–	–	191	9,036	7,897	10,610	17,544	10,577	19
Austria	4,973	1,043	673	973	10,622	4,620	4,472	7,083	2,501	197
Switzerland	504	215	97	183	1,598	1,342	1,312	1,109	770	90
Netherlands	6,598	48	875	3,404	4,843	4,853	744	1,994	1,503	22
Australia	–	–	107	970	1,186	879	640	886	1,138	189
Belgium	13,917	–	–	–	431	583	113	265	555	39
United Kingdom	8	–	–	4	536	1,289	82	116	133	64
Others	16	442	43	108	4,360	1,295	1,381	3,030	1,826	1,128
Total	195,095	8,947	43,204	103,975	129,575	88,442	85,229	135,820	20,211	1,965

Source: Abadan-Unat, Nermin et al, 1976, *Migration and Development : A Study of the Effects of International Labour Migration on Boğazlıyan District*, Ajans-Türk Press, Ankara, p. 11

through nominative requests.[9] The prospective migrants were subjected to an initial screening by the Institute of Employment officials, eliminating those with criminal records, applicants who were denied passports for political reasons, and illiterate, ill and elderly candidates. After the first selection, the candidates were sent to the German liaison office where they were subjected to medical tests by German doctors and skills tests by the employers.[10]

Labour migration from Turkey to the Federal Republic of Germany increased throughout the 1960s and early 1970s until the imposition of an immigration ban in November 1973. This suspended all former recruitment agreements except for the original European Community Treaty concerning the freedom of movement of labour.

The European Community (EC) was established by the Treaty of Rome, signed by the representatives of the original six member states in 1957. It was a full decade after the conclusion of the Treaty of Rome before the EC was able to implement full freedom of labour within its boundaries. Since 1968, a worker from any EC member state has been able to accept employment in any other member country without the necessity of obtaining a work permit or arranging employment in advance of entering the host country.[11] These provisions still apply to the first ten member states of the EC, and will be extended to Spain and Portugal in January 1993.[12] The November 1973 restrictions imposed by the Federal German government applied predominantly to workers from the non-EC countries. The Turkish application for membership of the EC is still pending.

The decisions concerning the November 1973 ban were taken exclusively by the Federal German government's Ministry of Labour, as a response to the staggering unemployment problems which were expected to worsen as a result of the energy crisis. Neither the Bundestag nor the governments of the countries of emigration were consulted. In other words, it became evident that the terms of the former bilateral agreements were limited in accordance with the demands formulated by the governments of the labour-importing countries.

In the initial period of labour migration (1957–73), the number of foreign workers in the Federal Republic of Germany constantly increased except for a brief recession period, 1966–7. This recession led to the discharge of about 70,000 Turkish workers.[13] This period was a dress rehearsal of what would take place in the late 1970s. By 1973, the number of employed immigrant workers in the Federal Republic of Germany was 2,595,000, whereas the figure was down to 1,932,600 in 1976.[14] The number of non-national wage and salary earners amounted to 1,557,000 in 1987 out of which 68.9 per cent were from non-EC countries.[15] Turks have constituted the largest group of foreigners residing and working in the Federal Republic of Germany since 1970. In 1982, Turks constituted 1,580,000 of the total resident foreign population of 4,667,000.[16] Moreover, of the 2,038,000 foreign workers in 1982, 1,580,000 were Turkish.[17]

In the 1957–73 period, the majority of the recruited workers were single men who had left their families behind.[18] The November 1973 ban did not lead to a sudden halt of immigration to the Federal Republic of Germany.

Rather, the composition of the workers changed as more women and children began to participate in the emigration process as a result of family reunification policies. The proportion of Turkish emigrant women in the total flow of Turkish emigrants was only 15.6 per cent between 1961–67.[19] By the end of 1986, 32.2 per cent of all foreigners in the Federal Republic of Germany were females over 16 years of age and 22.7 per cent were children under 16 years of age.[20]

An overview of the 'migratory chain' between Turkey and the Federal Republic of Germany needs to refer to return migration as well as to initial emigration and to the changing composition of the migrant population in the host society over the years. The return movement of the migrants to their home societies is a process as old as that of emigration itself. Yet, it has become more significant in the 1980s due to the fact that first-generation migrants reached retirement age, while certain policies followed by the host society governments were geared towards encouraging return. An overview of return surveys indicates an increase in the rate of return of Turkish migrants from the Federal Republic of Germany in 1967, 1976, and 1984.[21] In 1967, the number of workers claiming to return permanently was 17,000, which was unusually high compared to the 1970, 1971 and 1972 figures of 4,756, 5,695 and 4,624 respectively.[22] The unusually high return rate in 1967 can be explained by the economic recession which led to the unemployment of many foreign workers in the labour markets of the receiving countries.

The increase in return rates in 1976 can be explained by the adoption of discriminatory policies by the Federal German government regarding family reunification, as well as the unleashing of the practice of prohibiting the settlement of migrants in the so-called 'congested' or 'overburdened' areas, in which the proportion of foreigners exceeded 12 per cent of the total population.[23] Accordingly, foreign workers wishing to bring their families would have to move if they were living in a congested area where the ban was in effect. This would mean a change of jobs in most cases. Yet, those workers who had not been in the Federal Republic of Germany for at least three years were constrained from changing jobs, thus restricting the area where they were free to look for housing. Ironically, workers were able to reside for at least one year in the Federal Republic of Germany, and to have access to adequate housing, prior to applying for family reunification.[24] The practice of prohibiting entry into congested areas remained in effect between April 1975 and April 1977. Such circular restrictions seem to have become a way of life for migrants and their families. The reason for the sudden increase in return rates in 1984 may be accounted for by the introduction in 1983 of the return bonus scheme, ie the payment of premiums to returnees, in the Federal Republic of Germany. Accordingly, a premium was offered to unemployed migrants, and to those who no longer worked full time in factories, provided that they agreed to return home with their spouses and their minor children, and did not re-enter the host society as wage-earners.[25]

In the post-1973 period, with the increasing emigration of families to the host societies, the labour migration of the post-war period acquired a new feature. By the beginning of the 1980s, it had become clear that the 'guestworkers' — who were expected to work in the host societies for a couple of years and then return home — were 'here for good'.[26] Hence, the earlier perspectives of policy-makers in the host societies regarding the guestworker phenomenon had to be re-evaluated. It proved harder to re-establish contact between the early theoretical assumptions of immigration policies and the reality of permanent immigrant settlement in the Federal Republic of Germany. This was largely due to the German government's historically ingrained determination that Germany is *kein Einwanderungsland* (not a country of immigration). In what follows, I will elaborate on the shift in the *problematique* of the post-war guestworker phenomenon, as this was expressed in policy-making circles and academic studies, by emphasizing the various stages of the cross-national movement.

The shifting *problematique* of the guestworker phenomenon

When emigration from the less developed countries of the European South to the industrially developed countries of North and Western Europe was unleashed via bilateral agreements in the 1960s, the attentions of both policy-makers and researchers were focused on the beneficial implications for both the labour-receiving and labour-sending societies. Labour migration was viewed as a policy indicator of a convenient coincidence of interests between these two groups of countries.

Early analyses of labour migration have emphasized the relationship between labour migration and development. Most of these were based on the Lewis model of development, with unlimited supplies of labour.[27] According to this model, the economy consists of two sectors: a traditional, rural subsistence sector characterized by zero or low productivity and a modern, urban industrial sector characterized by high productivity into which labour from the subsistence sector is gradually transferred. The presence of redundant labour in the traditional sector, and its transferability to the modern sector, can result in higher profits without a change in wage rates. This process can continue for as long as there is an unlimited supply of labour. Lewis's model, and its later extensions, have become the widely accepted theory of development in many Third World countries with surplus labour.[28] The relationship between migration and socio-economic development has been emphasized in the literature as a result of widespread acceptance of Lewis's model. One such analysis, for instance, maintains that: 'Migration consists of a variety of movements that can be described in the aggregate as an evolutionary and development-fostering process operating in time and space to correct rural–urban, inter-urban and inter-regional imbalances.[29]

During the 1960s, there was widespread belief in the benefits of international labour migration. In a classical study, assessing the role of labour supply in Europe's post-war growth, Kindleberger pointed to the favourable effects of foreign-labour-generated growth strategies in the short run: 'In the country of immigration, short-run elasticity of the labour supply has a favourable impact on wages (holding them down), on profits (holding them up), on investment and growth, and on price stability.'[30] The favourable impact of labour migration on price stability was due to the tendency of foreign workers to send their earnings to their home countries, in the form of remittances, rather than spending them on consumption in the host country.

These early studies of the labour migration phenomenon shared a common analytical framework in that they presented strikingly ahistorical analyses of migration and development. This was a manifestation of the particular paradigm of socio-economic development in which they were firmly embedded. Accordingly, international labour migration was believed to overcome traditional imbalances by correcting the skewed distribution of factors of production. The overall migration process, then, was viewed as beneficial for the receiving countries as well as the sending countries in a world leading towards a gradual convergence in levels of economic growth and social well-being.

In the Turkish context, the planners of the 1960s saw in external migration an indispensable solution to the chronic double problem of unemployment and foreign-exchange crisis. For this reason policies encouraging external labour migration were adopted by all the existing political parties at that time; this policy appeared to be one almost above politics, despite pronounced party differences on other matters. External labour migration seemed, undoubtedly, the only way to manage the deteriorating economic and political climate in a peripheral economy. The planners of this period went as far as to write policies into the official Five-Year Development Plans which were dependent on workers' remittances. The role of remittances in temporarily alleviating foreign-exchange crises was more clearly seen by the time of the second and third Five-Year Development Plans (1968–72 and 1973–77, respectively). As a result, remittances were built into the balance-of-payments projections.

Workers' remittances represented 14 per cent of the foreign currency earned by Turkey in 1964.[31] The same figure was close to 70 per cent at the beginning of the 1970s.[32] Table 6.2 presents an overview of the amount of Turkish workers' remittances between 1964–74. In 1973, Turkey's total exports amounted to $1,317 million whereas total imports amounted to $2,086 million.[33] Workers' remittances, which amounted to $1,183 million in this year, not only covered the balance-of-payments deficit but also created a $154 million surplus for the Turkish economy.[34]

The significance of the workers' remittances for the functioning of the Turkish economy was nowhere better expressed than in a statement by President Turgut Özal in 1969, when he was the Undersecretary for Planning: 'Remittances come to our aid like a lottery, a God-send. The money received from the OECD consortium is $100–110 million per year, whereas $130 million enter this country annually from workers' remittances.'[35]

The benefits to be derived by the sending and receiving societies were not only economic. In addition to the remittances of the migrants, which were

Table 6.2 Turkish emigrants' remittances, 1964–74

Year	1964	1965	1966	1967	1968	1969	1970	1971	1972	1973	1974
Total ($'000s)	8,112	69,777	115,333	93,030	107,318	140,612	273,120	471,362	740,155	1,182,362	1,426,211
Average yearly remittance per worker (in $)		438	598	543	525	486	617	8,971	1,209	1,638	1,762

Source: Abadan-Unat, Nermin et al., 1976, Migration and Development : A Study of the Effects of International Labour Migration on Boğazlıyan District, Ajans-Türk Press, Ankara, p. 101

viewed as instrumental in restoring the balance of payments and overcoming the foreign-exchange crises in the sending societies, social and political benefits were also expected from the migration process. Acquisition of technical skills, and Western attitudes while abroad, were viewed as assets, while repatriates themselves were considered to be agents of change. In the receiving societies, the presence of guestworkers ready and willing to accept jobs that are at the bottom of the labour market was expected to contribute to the ascendance of the indigenous workers on the social and economic scale. Politically, international labour migration was expected to alleviate political pressures that could arise from excessive unemployment in the urban centres of the sending societies.[36] In the receiving societies, international labour migration had the political function of creating a split between immigrant and indigenous workers along national and racial lines, hence weakening the labour movements as a whole. Whereas in periods of growth, the economic function was important, at times of recession it was primarily the political significance of the migrant workers that justified their existence in the receiving societies. In a study of the Maghribin workers in France, one author sums up the view that was evidently shared by employers in many other industrially developed countries: 'The French bourgeoisie would not have bothered to attract or to import them if they were not socially, politically, and economically profitable.'[37]

The impact of labour migration on intra-country regional imbalances has been studied extensively within the Turkish context.[38] In order to assess this impact, one needs to look first of all at where the returnees settle. Many factors, such as the structure of the return setting, pre-migration occupations, and levels of education seem to influence the resettlement patterns. One study which evaluates such multi-faceted dimensions of resettlement concludes that the propensity to live in urban centres upon return is higher.[39] The two areas that attract the largest percentages, Marmara and the Central Anatolian regions (28.0 per cent and 27.8 per cent, respectively), are the most developed regions in Turkey; whereas the least-developed region, the south-east, attracts only 0.9 per cent of the returnees.[40] It is obvious that the initial relief of the overpopulated areas by external migration, as advocated by the balanced growth model, is offset by the over-concentration of the returnees in large urban centres located in the western part of Turkey.

The second dimension of the impact of external migration on regional disparities is studied by examining the nature and direction of returnees' investments, and the activities involving the utilization of their savings. Many return surveys in the Turkish context have focused on this dimension.[41] A review of the existing return surveys points to the existence of two types of investments: individual/family ventures and participatory investments. The latter, which were encouraged by the government, involved the Workers' Joint Stock Corporations (WJSCs) and the Village Development Cooperatives (VDCs). By the end of the 1980s, it became clear that both types of participatory investments had failed in redressing regional imbalances and providing sources of employment for the returnees.[42]

The nature and the extent of the individual/family ventures, on the other hand, differed from one region to the other. Nevertheless, it is possible to observe a tendency towards non-productive areas such as speculation in urban property, the purchase of consumer durables and of land/vehicles for commercial use. The State Planning Organization's 1971 survey, for instance, reports that about two-fifths of the returnees, in the sample studied, channelled their investments towards purchasing a house or a building plot.[43]

Many returnees to the rural areas had spent their savings on purchasing a field or an orchard. The second most popular item on the returnees' agenda was consumer durables. Another return survey reports that 59 per cent of returnees' investments went into housing and building plots, followed by agricultural land (11 per cent), vehicles and industrial development (9 per cent), and business premises (7 per cent).[44] A more recent return survey reports that 85.2 per cent of returnees have acquired real estate such as houses and plots of land.[45] It is obvious that whatever the impact of such individual/family ventures on the lifestyles of the returnees, they do not imply socio-economic development on a larger scale. Yet, the houses that were built by the returnees in their villages, for instance, are quite visibly different from the houses of the locals who have never participated in the migration experience. They are usually larger, have more rooms, and are equipped with many types of durable household goods that modern consumer markets offer such as telephones, televisions, videos, washing machines etc. As one author who has studied return migration to Spain put it, 'economic development appears only skindeep'.[46] The resulting scheme has been called 'cosmetic development', ie a superficial facelift with no fundamental change in socio-economic structures.[47]

In the early period of post-war labour migration, academic anlayses and government policies emphasized the economic, political, and social benefits of this phenomenon. I have already pointed out that the migration process was regulated via bilateral governmental contracts. These contracts entailed the recruitment of *temporary* workers in most cases, indicating that they were expected to go back to their home societies at times of unemployment. In other words, they were viewed as *Konjonkturpuffer* or shock absorbers, regulating the ups and downs of the economy. It is obvious that the provisions of various government regulations display very different characteristics. The principle of the temporariness of the labourers, in other words the rotation principle, was more pronounced in some cases than others. This principle was nowhere better articulated than in the widespread use in Germany since 1942 of the term *gastarbeiter* or guestworker.[48]

In the mid-1970s, many labour-receiving societies started the imposition of immigration bans, preventing further arrivals of foreign labourers. In Switzerland, where foreigners comprised 15.9 per cent of the population by 1970, the Federal Council and the parliament responded by introducing a global ceiling on the number of foreign citizens in the country.[49] It was decided that the foreign population would not be allowed to become larger and would be reduced if possible. In the Federal Republic of Germany, the immigration ban came in November 1973, while in France it was imposed in July 1974 after Giscard d'Estaing took office.

The control of Commonwealth immigration was largely enhanced in Britain via the 1971 Immigration Act and later by the British Nationality Act which was introduced by the Conservative government and took effect in 1983.[50]

In the course of the 1970s, it is possible to observe two simultaneous processes which eventually led to such recruitment bans and the gradual elaboration of a new perspective. The latter shifted the *problematique* of labour migration towards focusing on cultural clashes arising from the continuing presence of foreigners in the host societies: in other words, problems of integration. The first process involves the gradual ending of the temporary migrant phenomenon and the de facto emergence of ethnic minorities who were 'here for good'.[51] The rhetorical attachment to the rotation principle still continued at the governmental level. In conjunction with their virtual permanence, the initial attractiveness of the migrant workers as sources of cheap labour faded when the accumulated social costs began to soar. Host society governments found themselves having to respond to some of the immediate material concerns of these foreign families, such as housing, in order to prevent further urban decay and socio-political tension. Thus, the guestworker phenomenon became more or less permanent and the successive German governments found themselves trapped between adherence to the rotation principle, along with the view of *kein Einwanderungsland*, and the reality of a so-called guestworker population who did not plan to return home. What had in reality become permanent, ethnic minorities were still being referred to as 'guestworkers'.

The second process, that was unleashed in the 1970s, involves the increasing political importance of such issues as pollution and destruction of the environment. The increasing focus of the political parties on the detrimental effects of industrial growth has paved the way to the internationalization of production which led to a decreasing need for further employment of guestworkers.

These two processes, that is the increasing cost of employing foreign workers in terms of welfare state provisions and the restrictions placed on government policies by environmentalist groups, seem to favour a new international economic system in which the export of jobs is preferred to the importation of workers. This 'new international division of labour' involved the internationalization of production, which brought about substantial changes to the peripheral economies, along with internationally created jobs.[52] It is obvious that the further importation of foreign workers to the industrially-developed countries of Northern and Western Europe had become an anachronism in this new international division of labour. Hence, it is possible to observe a shift in the *problematique* regarding labour migration. Accordingly, both in academic studies and governmental concerns there is an increasing tendency to emphasize the problems of the integration of culturally different migrants into the host societies. In other words, by the mid-1970s, the foreign workers who were once viewed as the instrumental *Konjonkturpuffer* were increasingly being referred to as the 'traditional', 'Muslim' intruders whose presence in the host societies is reluctantly tolerated. This novel definition of the guestworkers was evident in the statements of political party officials in the Federal Republic of Germany by the early

1980s. In what follows, I will elaborate on such a shift in the *problematique* of labour migration in the German context. I will also demonstrate the impossibility of the integration *problematique* and unravel the significance of adopting what I call a 'government policies' approach in understanding labour migration.

The impossibility of the integration *problematique*: the lessons of the German experience

In 1982 the leader of a CDU/CSU parliamentary group made the following remarks:

> . . . Since Turks are different from Germans in culture and mentality, and want to stay different, it is only natural that they seek the proximity of their fellows in Germany. That means that Turkish quarters, also known as ghettos, are developing in our cities. That could only be prevented by force, not by social security benefits or persuasion . . . We have no reason to let critics at home and abroad accuse us of racism, when we insist that the German Federal Republic must not become a country of immigration. Anyone who disregards this natural and justified feeling of our fellow citizens is preparing the way for the extreme right . . . The question of reasonable and humane rotation must be reconsidered.[53]

In June 1983, the CDU chairman in his address to the CDU Annual Conference maintained that Germany should retain its cultural identity against the Oriental and Muslim culture of foreign groups.[54]

I believe the most important aspect of the above statements is the emphasis laid on the cultural differences between Turks and Germans, which are viewed as 'irreconcilable'. These and similar views constitute the crux of what I call the integration *problematique*. The adoption of such a colonial perspective regarding guestworkers inevitably paves the way to restrictive governmental policies. In November 1981, for instance, a CDU resolution in the Bundestag stated that: 'The role of the German Federal Republic as a national unitary state and as part of a divided nation does not permit the commencement of an irreversible development to a multiethnic state.'[55]

Once the migrants are defined as a 'traditional', anomic group, the integration *problematique* becomes impossible to resolve. When the most important implication of the prolonged stay of guestworkers is defined as the generation of irreconcilable differences between the culturally different Turks and the Germans, then the only logical policy implication would be the adoption of assimilationist policies. Yet, a survey of the history of citizenship and immigration policies in Germany reveals an opposite trend.

German admission-to-citizenship policy has always been based on the blood principle (*jus sanguinis*). The reason why such an exclusionary principle is adopted in Germany can be traced back to the distinct path it has followed towards nation-statehood. Accordingly, the German idea of a nation evolved as a cultural, linguistic, and racial phenomenon — as a

Volksgemeinschaft.[56] As a result, German citizenship included all persons of German descent regardless of political boundaries. As one author puts it: 'The German citizenship recognized by the Federal Republic is the legal expression of a basic political commitment to German national unity.'[57] Hence, the Basic Law refers to 'Germans' not to 'German citizens'. 'Germans' is a more inclusive category, including all German citizens plus certain categories of ethnic German refugees and expellees and their spouses and descendants.[58]

Since the adoption of assimilationist policies is incompatible with such a Volk-centred conception of nationhood, it is possible to argue that what makes the German notion of citizenship so peculiar is exactly its opposite nature, ie non-assimilationism. The adoption of such a citizenship notion is evidently the reason why German governments have always favoured applying the rotation principle to the immigration of non-Germans. I believe that herein lies the impossibility of the integration *problematique*. It is this historically ingrained non-assimilationism that makes the focus on the irreconcilable cultural, ethnic, and religious differences between the Germans and the guestworkers virtually irrelevant. German policy-makers employ a non-assimilationist rhetoric regarding citizenship and immigration, together with an emphasis on ethnicity, culture and a religion-based integration *problematique*. In other words, these different attributes of migrants are identified as the source of the problem in a society that does not have a tradition of adopting deliberate policies of making people similar, ie assimilationism. When both dimensions are juxtaposed, the problem seems impossible to resolve. I believe that German citizenship and immigration policies pose a more immediate barrier confronting the integration of guestworkers as full members into this society when compared to *their* 'traditional' attributes. Therefore, a 'government policies' ' approach that unravels such political barriers seems to offer promising avenues in grappling with the problems generated by the prolonged residence of guestworkers in Germany.

It is obvious that German policy-makers quite often found themselves trapped with exclusionary citizenship and immigration policies in a society that had become home to a de facto permanent ethnic minority. Hence, a full integration of these ethnic minorities challenges the very foundations of German notions of nationhood. I believe the adoption of a rhetoric of irreconcilable cultural, ethnic, and religious differences provides the policy-makers with an easy escape from this dilemma.

By the 1980s, the policy debates regarding immigration issues in the Federal Republic of Germany had shifted from acknowledging the presence of guestworkers to virtually rejecting them and encouraging repatriation. The Social Democratic Party's (SPD) commissioner on immigrant issues, for instance, issued a memorandum in 1979 highlighting the government view at the time. This view seemed like a real attempt to come to grips with the guestworker phenomenon: future policy towards foreign employees and their families living in the Federal Republic was to be based on the assumption that a development had taken place which could no longer be reversed. The majority of those concerned were no longer guestworkers but immigrants, for whom return to their countries of origin was, for various reasons, no longer a viable option.[59]

By 1983, the Social Democrats had become aware of the fact that the adoption of this view of the guestworkers had cost them dearly in electoral terms. In fact, SPD leaders began to fear a loss of popular support as a result of growing racism in the Federal Republic of Germany. This probably led Willy Brandt, the late chairman of the SPD, to say that: 'We cannot cope with any further immigration.'[60] By 1982, the SPD Prime Minister of Hesse was arguing that: 'The Federal Republic of Germany is not a country of immigration, the limits of our endurance have been reached . . . I regard the further immigration of Turks to the Federal Republic as impossible.'[61]

A CDU election leaflet distributed in the autumn of 1982, during the state elections in Hesse, on the other hand, promised to reduce the number of foreigners by a million over the next five years.[62] The same leaflet contained arguments for banning the further immigration of families from non-EC countries.

By 1989, the immigration issue in the Federal Republic of Germany was overtly politicized. The politicization of this issue was crystallized in the increasing election scores of the political parties that had gathered around anti-immigration and anti-immigrant themes.[63] Moreover, it was possible to observe a trend on the part of the traditional conservative parties to discard their anti-discriminatory stances, at a time when the activities of the overtly racist parties have acquired some momentum in all the major labour-receiving societies. The position of the new ethnic minorities in the labour markets of the host societies will be shaped according to how the new political cleavages in these societies, related to the prolonged residence of guestworkers, are expressed. It will, first of all, be a function of how strong a resistance will develop in these societies against this unequal and unjustifiable treatment of migrants. Second, the positions of the old and established political parties regarding this phenomenon will play a crucial role in shaping these cleavages. They will either exacerbate these cleavages by institutionalizing discrimination or manage them. The latter approach is, to a large extent, conditioned by a view of the guestworker phenomenon that goes beyond an integration *problematique* and acknowledges the presence of permanent ethnic minorities. The approaches of the established political parties, on the other hand, will be shaped by the strength and the bases of social support for the overtly racist and nativist parties in future years.

The guestworker phenomenon in Germany has acquired a renewed significance today with the unification of the Federal Republic of Germany and the German Democratic Republic. Since the opening of the Iron Curtain, thousands of people of German descent have flooded into the labour markets of the Federal Republic of Germany. These new population movements are likely to pose a threat to the already fragile position of the Turks and other non-German migrants in Germany. Since unification, two important policy decisions have been taken by the German government regarding resident non-Germans. The first policy decision was taken by the Constitutional Court on 31 October 1990. It involved voting rights and the right to be elected to local parliaments on the part of foreigners. Accordingly, such rights as were being enjoyed by foreigners, in certain states such as Hamburg and Schleswig-Holstein, have been abolished by a unilateral decision.[64] This development clearly indicates a step backwards as far as the political participation of non-Germans is concerned. The second policy decision, which was recently passed by the Bundestag, and has been in force since 1 January 1991, is the new Foreigners Law (*Almanya Federal Cumhuriyeti Yabancılar Yasası*). The new Foreigners Law indicates a clear trend towards facilitating deportation, especially for those foreigners who are recipients of social aid for themselves or for their families.[65] These policy decisions signal a trend on the part of the post-unification German government towards further exclusionary policies regarding the political status of foreigners in Germany. These developments point to the importance of adopting a government-policies' *problematique* in approaching the guestworker phenomenon. There is no doubt that further emphasis on the integration problems of the migrants, that stem from their cultural differences, paves the way to the identification of an insoluble problem if not an easy escape for the policy-makers.

Notes

1. 'Migratory Chain' is a term coined by the Organization for Economic Co-operation and Development (OECD) in a 1978 publication referring to the totality of the various phases of the migration phenomenon such as the initial emigration, stay abroad, and return: OECD, 1978, *The Migratory Chain*, Paris.
2. Abadan-Unat, Nermin *et al.* (eds), 1976a, *Migration and Development: A Study of the Effects of International Labour Migration on Boğazlıyan District*, Ajans-Turk Press, Ankara, p. 27.
3. Paine, Suzanne, 1974, *Exporting Workers: The Turkish Case*, Cambridge University Press, London, p. 58.
4. Ibid.
5. Devlet Planlama Teskilati, *Altinci Bes Yillik Kalkinma Plani (1990–1994), 1990 Yili Programi*, Ankara, p. 360.
6. SOPEMI–OECD, 1991, *Continuous Reporting System On Migration, 1990*, Paris, p. 69.
7. Ibid.
8. In 1988, for instance, while there were 137,800 returnees to Turkey, only 53,021 persons emigrated through official channels, SOPEMI–OECD, 1989, *Continuous Reporting System On Migration, 1989*, Paris, p. 53.
9. Rist, Ray C., 1978, *Guestworkers in Germany: The Prospects for Pluralism*, Praeger, New York, p. 61.
10. This selection process is most dramatically displayed in photographs in Berger, John and Jean Mohr, 1987, *Yedinci Adam: Avrupa'daki Gocmen İşçilerin Oykusu*, Ankara, V Yayinlari. See also; Yucel, Ersan A., 1987, 'Turkish Migrant Workers in the Federal Republic of Germany: A Case Study', in Hans Buechler and Judith-Maria Buechler (eds), *Migrants in Europe: The Role of Family, Labour and Politics*, New York, Greenwood Press.
11. Rist, 1978, p. 24.
12. International Labour Organization (ILO), Regular Budget, Technical

Cooperation Programme, Informal Consultation Meeting on Migrants from non-EEC countries in the Single European Market after 1992, Geneva, 27–8 April, 1989, Informal Summary Record.

13. Abadan-Unat Nermin et al. (eds), 1976b, Turkish Workers in Europe, 1960–1975: A Socio-economic Reappraisal, Leiden, E.J. Brill, p. 15.
14. Rist, 1978, p. 62.
15. ILO, 1989, p. 32.
16. Esser, Hartmut and Hermann Korte, 1985, 'Federal Republic of Germany', in Tomas Hammar (ed.), European Immigration Policy, Cambridge University Press, London, p. 171.
17. Ibid.
18. Mehrlander, Ursula, 1979, 'Federal Republic of Germany', in Kubat Daniel et al. (eds), The Politics of Migration Policies, Center for Migration Studies, New York, pp. 147–148.
19. Abadan-Unat et al., 1976b, p. 12a.
20. SOPEMI–OECD, 1988, Continuous Reporting System On Migration, 1987, Paris, p. 35.
21. See, for instance: Paine, 1974,; Gokdere, Ahmet Y., 1978, Yabanci Ülkelere Isqucu Akimi ve Turk Ekonomisi Uzerine Etkileri, Turkiye Is Bankasi Kültür Yayinlari; Demircioglu, M., 1984, Ankara, 'Federal Almanya'dan Kesin Dünüs Yapan Isgucu', Amme Idaresi Dergisi, 7, No. 2; Penninx, Rinus, 1986, 'International Migration in Western Europe Since 1973: Developments, Mechanisms and Controls', International Migration Review, 20, No.4, Winter, pp. 951–72.
22. Devlet Istatistik Enstitusu, Turizm Istatistikleri, 1967, 1970, 1971, 1972, cited in Gokdere, 1978, p. 99.
23. Mehrlander, 1979, p. 152.
24. Rist, 1978, p. 81.
25. Penninx, 1986, p. 966.
26. Castles, Stephen et al., 1984, Here for Good: Western Europe's New Ethnic Minorities, Pluto Press, London and Sydney.
27. Lewis, Arthur, 1954, 'Economic Development with Unlimited Supplies of Labour', The Manchester School of Economic and Social Studies, May.
28. See, for instance: Fei, J.C. and G. Ranis, 1961, 'A Theory of Economic Development', The American Economic Review, September.
29. Spengler, Joseph J. and George C. Myers, 1977, 'Migration and Socioeconomic Development: Today and Yesterday', in Alan A. Brown and Egon Neuberger, Internal Migration: A Comparative Perspective, New York, Academic Press, p. 11.
30. Kindleberger, C.P., 1967, Europe's Postwar Growth: The Role of Labour Supply, Harvard University Press, Cambridge, p. 200.
31. Kubat, 1979, p. 253.
32. Ibid.
33. Gokdere, 1978, p. 49.
34. Ibid.
35. Cited in Adler, Stephen, 1981, A Turkish Conundrum: Emigration, Politics and Development, 1961–1980, Migration for Employment Project, World Employment Programme Research, Working Paper (WEP 2-26/WP52), ILO, Geneva, p. 47.
36. The author has conducted several personal interviews with Turkish migrants who returned home. In the course of these interviews, one returnee said that if the emigration possibility (even if it was only a dream for some people) was absent, the unemployed marginalities could constitute a serious threat to politi-

cal stability in Turkey. Such statements point to the system-maintenance role of emigration.

37. Bennoune, Mahfoud, 1975, 'Maghribin Workers in France, *MERIP Reports*, no. 34, January, pp. 1–30, esp. 5.

38. One of the most informative texts is by Keles, Rusen, 1985, 'The Effects of External Migration on Regional Development in Turkey', Ray Hudson and Jim Lewis (eds), *Uneven Development in Southern Europe: Studies of Accumulation, Class, Migration and the State,*: London Methuen. See also, Toepfer, Helmuth, 1985, 'The Economic Impact of Returned Emigrants in Trabzon, Turkey', in Hudson and Lewis (eds), 1985, London, New York; Abadan-Unat *et al.*, 1976a.

39. Keleş, Ibid, p. 64.

40. Ibid.

41. See, Keyder, Caglar and Ayhan Aksu-Koc, 1988, *External Labour Migration From Turkey and Its Impact: An Evaluation of the Literature*, International Development Research Centre (IDRC), Manuscript Report, 185e, for a review of the return surveys in the Turkish context.

42. See, for instance; Abadan-Unat *et al.* (eds), 1976a; Penninx, Rinus and H. Van Renselaar, 1978, *A Fortune In Small-Change*, The Hague:REMPLOD; Adler, Stephen, 1981; Gitmez, Ali, 1983, *Yurtdışına işçi Göğü ve Geri Dönuşler*, Alan Yayincilik, Istanbul; Keyder and Aksu-Koc, 1988; for an assessment of the WJSCs and the VDCs.

43. The results of the State Planning Organization's 1971 survey are reported in Paine, 1974. See, esp. pp. 118–19.

44. Toepfer, 1985.

45. Central Bank of the Republic of Turkey, 1986, *Savings Tendencies of Turkish Citizens Working in West Germany and of Those Already Returned Home Permanently*; a more detailed report is given in the Turkish version, Turkiye Cumhuriyet Merkez Bankasi, *Yurt Disindaki Vatandaslarimizin Tasarruf Egilimleri Arastirmasi-II: Yurda Kesin Donenler*.

46. Rhoades, Robert E., 1978b, 'Intra-European Return Migration and Rural Development: Lessons from the Spanish Case', *Human Organization*, 37, No. 2, Summer, pp. 136–47. esp. 142.

47. Ibid., p. 144.

48. Despite the fact that, at the societal level, there was a semantic shift from *Fremdarbeiter* (foreign workers) to *Gastarbeiter* (guestworkers) in the post-war period, the word '*Gastarbeiter*' was already being used in the official literature of the Nazis as early as 1942; on this issue, see: Rhoades, Robert E., 1978a, 'Foreign Labour and German Industrial Capitalism, 1871–1978: The Evolution of a Migratory System', *American Ethnologist*, 5, No.3, August, pp. 553–73.

49. Hammar, Tomas (ed.), 1985, *European Immigration Policy: A Comparative Study*, Cambridge: Cambridge University Press.

50. For an overview of the phases of immigration policies in these countries, refer to ibid.

51. The expression 'here for good' is used *á la* Castles *et al.*, 1984.

52. Frobel, F. *et al.*, 1980, *The New International Division of Labour: Structural Unemployment in Industrialized Countries and Industrialization in Developing Countries*, Cambridge: Cambridge University Press, London.

53. Cited in Castles *et al.*, 1984, p. 208.

54. Cited in Edye, Dave, 1987, *Immigrant Labour and Government Policy: The Case of the Federal Republic of Germany and France*, Aldershot, Hants: Gower, p. 42.

55. Cited in Castles, Stephen, 1985, 'The Guests Who Stayed: The Debate on "Foreigners" Policy' in the German Federal Republic', *International Migration Review*, 19, No.3, Fall, pp. 517–34, esp. p. 528.

56. Brubaker argues that this peculiar evolution of the German idea of a nation has stemmed from the development of a national feeling before the nation-state. This temporal distance between the emergence of nationalist yearnings and the formation of a nation-state has led to the evolution of a 'particularist, organic, and Volk-centered' conception of nationhood in Germany: Brubaker, William Rogers, 1989, *Immigration and the Politics of Citizenship in Europe and North America*, Lanham, New York, London, The German Marshall Fund of the United States and the University Press of America, p. 8.

57. Hailbronner, Kay, 1989, 'Citizenship and Nationhood in Germany', in Brubaker, 1989, p. 73.

58. Ibid.

59. Cited in Castles *et al.*, 1984, p. 80.

60. Cited in ibid., p. 209.

61. Cited in ibid., pp. 209–210.

62. Ibid., p. 208.

63. On 30 January 1989, The Republikaner led by an ex-SS sergeant received 7.5 per cent of the votes in West Berlin legislative elections after pursuing a campaign structured around a 'Turks Out' theme. On 12 March 1989, the National Democratic Party (NDP) with a similar campaign took 6.6 per cent of the votes in municipal elections in Frankfurt that led to a crushing defeat for the CDU: *Wall Street Journal* 13 February 1989; *The Boston Globe*, 13 March 1989.

64. *Günes*, 1 November 1990.

65. Almanya Federal Cumhuriyeti Yabancılar Yasası (New Foreigners Law in the Federal Republic of Germany), Turkish Ministry of Labour and Social Security.

Part Three
Political and cultural relationships

7

Turkey and Greece: a difficult Aegean relationship

Şükrü S. Gürel

Differences and problems between Turkey and Greece include sovereignty and control over the sea and airspace, rights over the Aegean continental shelf, and minority issues. These problems and differences have deepened and proliferated over time, despite the facts that the two countries have not been at war since the 1920s, have gone through several periods of close political cooperation since then, and have been allies since 1952.

The main aim of this chapter is to provide an overview and general assessment of the relations between the two countries from the perspective of Turkey's relationship with Europe. It will be argued that the differences and problems between Turkey and Greece cannot be reconciled in the short term. Thus, it will be assumed that, rather than looking for simple, magical formulations for reconciliation, we should try to formulate a general framework for conciliation.

Living history and current distrust

The main obstacle preventing solution to these problems or even serious negotiation between Turkey and Greece seems to be the distrust created by a living history. First of all, Turkey and Greece have shaped their 'nation-state' identities through struggle against and interactions with each other. For example, it is almost impossible in even a glimpse of modern Greek history to exclude the 'Turkish factor'. Every part of the present Greek territory has been under Turkish rule for at least four hundred years. Modern Greece emerged as an independent nation-state at the end of a national independence struggle against Turkish rule.[1]

In return, Turkey achieved nation-state status within the post-First World War international system, leaving behind its feudal–imperial Ottoman identity, only at the end of an armed struggle against occupying Greek forces. Turkish people refer to this as their 'war of national liberation', whereas the Greeks still recall the 1919–22 period as the years of 'catastrophe'.[2]

The fact that both nations have achieved their nation-state status through armed struggle against each other has undoubtedly been important in shaping Turkish–Greek relations. Moreover, this fact also contributed to the complex identity problems of Turkish and Greek peoples. Greece and Turkey — but at present probably Turkey rather than Greece — unable to find a modern identity and therefore a role in the world, have felt insecure in the West and the East. 'Greece and Turkey . . . in various ways, deny their Ottoman past — a past that still lingers in the present. But to deny the past is to deny themselves — hence the identity problem which bedevils their relationships'. (Groom, 1986: 380). On top of a denied common past, the two peoples, in order to hold on to the best defined part of their identity — their nationhood — have to continue recalling their 'national liberation struggles'. This not only brushes a shared past to the dusty, dark corners of past history, but also brings the conflicts and clashes to the fore, making them a living part of history. Hence, only distrust is nourished.

As Richard Clogg (1980: 141) writes:

. . .But even if a Greek–Turkish rapprochement is achieved at official level, the changing of the popular attitudes, reciprocal stereotypes and mutual fears that underlie the present antagonism will be a much more protracted and difficult process. Until such a radical transformation in mutual images and perceptions takes place then we are likely to see a recurrent pattern of suspicion and crisis in relations between the two countries.

Above all, the interactions between the two peoples have created and recreated serious humanitarian issues. From 1830 until 1922, Greece pursued a foreign policy aimed at territorial gains from the Ottoman Empire. During this period, Thessaly (1881), Macedonia, Southern Epirus, several Aegean islands, and Crete (1912–13) were taken from the Ottomans. This process not only resulted in territorial transfers, but also created refugees and immigrants: the Turkish populations living in these territories were forced to emigrate. This Greek policy reached its peak in 1919–22, when Greece, with some outside encouragement, tried to occupy Anatolia. This adventure, once again, created human agony. The Treaty of Lausanne, signed in 1923, permanently defined the frontiers between the two states, and the only change in the Aegean territorial status quo since then has been the Greek annexation of the Dodecanese, detached from Italy by the Treaty of Paris in 1947. In addition to the Peace Treaty, a concomitant convention was also signed in Lausanne which provided for a compulsory exchange of Turkish nationals of the Greek Orthodox religion settled in Turkish territory, and of Greek nationals of the Moslem religion established in Greek territory. This convention was implemented in a very short period of time and more than a million Greeks from Turkey moved to Greece, and over half a million Turks went to Turkey from Greece.

Then, between 1955 and 1974, the Cyprus problem not only resulted in human misery in Cyprus by creating demographic dislocation on both sides in 1963 and 1974 but also led to policy changes towards and maltreatment of the remnants of Greek and Turkish minorities in both countries.

Objective research and logic clearly indicate that perceptions of threats on the two sides of the Aegean cannot be considered as symmetrical.[3] It is only logical to find that the Greek people regard Turkey — with its past, its territorial and demographic scale — threatening, while the vast majority of the Turkish people do not place as much importance on a Greek threat. But distrust created by a living history is mutual and perpetual.

Anyone dealing with Turkish–Greek relations cannot proceed without taking into account this feeling of distrust on both sides. In order to overcome this psychological barrier it is essential for both sides to commit themselves to long-term efforts. We have not witnessed such efforts up to the present.[4] But even if such efforts were forthcoming they would not be sufficient to provide harmony. Again in Clogg's (1980: 143) words:

> The pattern of ethnic conflict in the modern world does not hold out much hope that palliative steps . . . can have much effect in modifying a deeply entrenched collective memory of past wrongs real or imagined. Moreover it would be simplistic to seek to reduce the present Greek–Turkish impasse to a question of the mutual misperceptions that each country has of the other.

In this writer's view only a long-term gradually rising level of cooperation can cure the open wounds of living history.

Competition — a rule; cooperation — an exception

Cooperation is easier to preach than to practice in Turkish–Greek relations. Even at first glance the patterns of relations between the two countries show that competition and rivalry have been the dominant themes. The two states, with social, political and economic similarities (Özkale, 1992: 25–6), have been constantly seeking similar roles in the international system. Could they pursue the same goals in harmony? Perhaps they could if the living history shared had not kept bringing differences and problems to the present and thus had not been nourishing the drive for competition and rivalry.

The history of relations between the two countries reveals two basic periods of cooperation between Turkey and Greece: the 1930s and the first half of the 1950s. During the former period, the two countries mutually perceived an Italian threat and were encouraged by Britain to cooperate. Thus, during the 1930s Turkey and Greece settled their major disputes, signed several agreements, and the improved climate in relations culminated in the close cooperation of the two states for the creation of the Balkan *Entente* in 1934. During the latter period, the first half of the 1950s, they cooperated because they both felt threatened by the Soviet Union and at the same time were both encouraged to cooperate by the West, mainly by the United States. Between 1950 and 1955, Turkey and Greece agreed to set aside several problems, found places in NATO, and thus were drawn into close cooperation.[5] If it were possible to deduce definite rules concerning the bilateral relations of states by evaluating historical evidence, we could summarize thus: Turkey and Greece can/could only develop their relations in harmony when and only when they mutually perceive(d) a threat and are/were at the same time encouraged by an extra-regional power dominant in the region to cooperate against this threat.

Although the Cyprus conflict emerged during the second half of the 1950s and was aggravated after 1963, and the problems and differences related to the Aegean emerged and proliferated rapidly after 1973, Turkey and Greece could at least live together with these problems within the framework of the Western Alliance. But, as cold war conditions began to change during the 1960s, the 'Western connection' with its negative aspects and limitations began to be underlined and questioned in both countries.

During the 1960s and 1970s, first Turkey and then Greece (belatedly the latter because of the 1967–74 military rule) became aware of the strictly global role they had assumed during the cold war period. With *détente* between the two political and military blocs, global roles and 'responsibilities' could no longer comprise the whole of Turkish and Greek foreign and security policies. Both countries became aware that they should also emphasize a regional identity and, if they did, they should also change their attitudes towards the regional states, the Soviet Union and the Third World. But the same process also contributed to the surfacing of differences between the two countries. This regional restraint and the relatively easier task of assuming global roles in the Western Alliance were in decline. Both Turkey and Greece gradually became aware that they should pursue foreign policies based on their 'national interests'. These would be separate from, but not necessarily in conflict with, the global interests of the alliance to which they belonged. As far as their bilateral relations were concerned, their Western ties were a guarantee to keep their mutual conflict in check, and the Western world was still a competition ground.

The impact of external factors

The 'Western Question' in Greece and Turkey had been present long before Arnold Toynbee wrote his incisive book,[6] and has continued to make an impact on the domestic and foreign affairs of both countries since then. The two, but especially Greece, have been sensitive to external influences in formulating their foreign policies, and their place and role in the international system has had an exceptional influence on their domestic politics.

During the nineteenth century, the Ottoman Empire, while trying to outmanoeuvre the great-power policies aligned against it within the context of the 'Eastern Question', had at the same time tried to overcome societal obstacles to adopting Western institutions and to modernization following the Western example. When the modern Turkish nation-state was founded on the ashes of the Ottoman Empire, which in fact was brought to its end by a coalition of Western powers, Turkey began to strive for development on

Western lines. After the Second World War, Turkey, while adopting a cold war stance, opted for a transformation of its political life within the framework of a new multiparty parliamentary system.

The birth of the Greek state was in large part a by-product of great power policies. 'From its very birth the new Greek state was acutely aware of its dependence on the protecting powers — Britain, France and Russia' (Couloumbis, 1980: 21). Indeed, Greece not only owed her independence to the great powers, but also built her irredentist foreign policy on great power protection and favour. 'As Russian influence waned in the late-nineteenth century, Great Britain and France continued to support or tolerate Greek aspirations' (Dimitras,1985: 135). Those Greek aspirations were to reconstitute a greater Greece incorporating the lands and peoples of the former Byzantine Empire which, in fact, lay almost totally within the Ottoman boundaries. 'From the very beginning, the young kingdom undertook strenuous diplomatic activity aimed at achieving this goal. In its foreign office, departmental divisions were established corresponding to the provinces of the Ottoman Empire to be liberated, notably Macedonia, Thessaly, Epirus and Crete' (Psomiades, 1968: 18).

The great powers supported Greece in various ways. They handed territory to Greece on the diplomatic level — as in the case of the annexation of Thessaly and Epirus in 1881. They checked the Ottomans in time to prevent disasters for Greece in the conflicts it had provoked, as, for example in 1898. They also actively supported Greece against Turkey during armed conflicts in 1912–13 and 1919–22.

Although Greece could muster great power, influence and protection to support her foreign-policy aims, the great powers in return began to control both domestic political developments and the foreign-policy initiatives of Greece. Greek financial and military dependence on the great powers prepared the ground for great-power intervention. Even the first political organizations in Greece in the 1830s and 1840s were referred to by the great powers' names. (Couloumbis, 1980: 22).

Even so, there are certain elements of Greek culture and identity which are not easily compatible with a Western orientation. 'The first is the Greek Orthodox church's official doctrine of anti-westernism, which dates to the East–West schism that split Christianity beginning in 1054' (Dimitras, 1985: 135). Another is the resentment against frequently experienced foreign interference in the affairs of a small state. Further, Western intervention and influence combined and became part of the major themes of nineteenth and twentieth Century Greek politics: the cultural division between Westernizers and traditionalists, the political polarization between the republicans (Venizelists) and the royalists, followed by a schism between communists and anti-communists, and frequent and long-lasting intervention of the military in politics (Couloumbis, 1980: 22–4). There is no need to comment on the combination of Western influences with the differences between the Westernizers and the traditionalists or with the conflict between the communists and the anti-communists. But it should be noted that Venizelos was restored to power with foreign intervention in 1917, and it should also be remembered that United States' support for the

Colonels between 1967 and 1974 has been criticized both in Greece and the United States.

Turkey, after 1923, was able to minimize great-power influence with autarchic policies pursued within a multipolar European international system. But, starting from 1947, Turkey's cold war stance and her increasing financial and military dependence on the West — particularly the United States — facilitated Western influence on her foreign and domestic politics.

Both Turkey and Greece began to find new avenues for their foreign relations, as cold war conditions faded. Again, while the conflicting interests of the two countries came to the surface, the Western Alliance, which could hitherto silence and hold differences in balance, had grown weaker in this regard. The West, particularly the United States, began to find it very difficult to continue its role as the honest broker between Turkey and Greece. Any Western step or initiative regarding Turkish–Greek relations began to be perceived as unfriendly on both sides of the Aegean.

The constitution adopted in 1961 had laid down the necessary foundations for the formation of a pluralistic society in Turkey. Internal changes, combined with the impact of new international developments, had culminated in a wide public debate on Turkish foreign relations as well as on dormant domestic issues such as Westernization versus traditionalism or socialism. Turkish people were openly questioning their identity and debating their 'national interests', which were not necessarily identical with the global interests of the Western Alliance.

Turkish public opinion regarded the 'Greek Question' as a component of the general Western question which Turkey had traditionally faced. The West had been on Greece's side traditionally, but the Turkish people had at least hoped to have the Western factor neutralized after the 1950s. However, in 1964 the Johnson letter, clearly underlined the American attitude to Turkey. At the time of the 1963–4 Cyprus crisis, the Turkish government was seriously considering military intervention. President Johnson bluntly told the Turkish Prime Minister he was not entitled to use US-supplied equipment for this purpose, and that Turkey could not rely on NATO's assistance should the intervention trigger Soviet aggression. Then again in 1975 the American arms embargo, and currently the attitudes of the European Community and of the United States have all been regarded as indications of the continuing traditional stance of the West. Changes and nuances witnessed in Turkish foreign policy since 1964 and the continuous search for a 'new national security concept' since 1978[7] are mainly due to Western attitudes vis-à-vis Turkish–Greek differences, together with changes in the international order.

Despite all the changes experienced in Greece and Turkey in their relations with the West, one aspect remained untouched: the West has always been and still is regarded as a reference point in Turkish–Greek relations. Both sides have always been careful to explain and complain to the West about their bilateral problems and to take a position which is more likely to be favoured by the West. Greece undoubtedly has been the more active party in this regard and, probably because of its perceptions of threats, regarded its NATO membership as a protection against Turkey. Shortly after pulling out of NATO's military wing in its disappointment over the United States' attitudes during the Cyprus crisis of 1974, Greece began to search for re-entry. In 1980 the new military rulers of Turkey, facing isolation in Western Europe, and susceptible to American inducements, gave their consent to the 'Rogers Agreement'. This facilitated the return of Greece to NATO's military wing but not an improvement in Turkish–Greek relations. Although the two sides had agreed to start negotiations based on an interim solution to the airspace dispute in the Aegean, these were never implemented. When Papandreou came to power in Greece in 1981, he did not leave NATO as promised during the election campaign but chose to deny and shelve the 'Rogers Agreement'.[8]

During the 1980s Greece tried to use her power and influence within the alliance to diminish Turkey's importance and influence.[9] On the European platform Greece has done the same. Following its membership of the European Community in 1981, being aware of the advantages of acting against a country under military rule, it used all the democratic platforms against its isolated rival, until Turkey restored democratic institutions in the second half of the 1980s.

On the other hand, taking the West as a reference point in bilateral relations also resulted in mutual attempts to use bilateral problems and confrontations as a leverage in gaining better advantages in the Western world. For example, Papandreou, in the first half of the 1980s aggrandized the bilateral problems and Greece's threat perceptions in order to draw more support from the West and to consolidate Greece's position. Papandreou frequently repeated the slogan that the threats confronting Greece are 'from the East and not from the North' (Coufoudakis, 1985: 214). Özal, on the other hand, taking a different path, seemingly overlooked and undermined bilateral problems as if they could be solved overnight, perhaps in order to create a favourable image of himself and Turkey in the eyes of the West.

In short, Western influence on the bilateral relations of Greece and Turkey is evident, and the salience of external factors in shaping the domestic and foreign policies of the two countries is comparable, if not identical.

Current problem areas

Several problems and conflicts between the two countries will be touched upon in this part of the chapter, but there will only be a general assessment of these rather than a detailed analysis.

The Aegean problems

The equilibrium established in the Aegean by the Lausanne Treaty of 1923 seemed to satisfy both states until the early 1970s. Since then, however, differences between Turkey and Greece over the Aegean have developed into a conflict. These problems and differences have deepened and proliferated to form a web of interrelated disputes. As Bahcheli (1990a: 129) states, the 'essence of the Aegean dispute is the overlapping Greek and Turkish national interests in the area. The Greeks view the Aegean as a Greek sea ... Turks consider that, as an Aegean nation, Turkey is entitled to an equitable share of the resources in the Aegean.'

MILITARIZATION OF THE AEGEAN ISLANDS OF NON-MILITARY STATUS[10]

Accordlng to the Lausanne Treaty, and the Paris Treaty of 1947, Greece had agreed to keep only security forces and not armed forces on the following Aegean islands under its sovereignty: islands situated at the entry of the Çanakkale Straits (Lemnos, Samothrace and adjacent islands), the central Aegean islands (Mitylene, Khios, Samos and Ikaria), and the Dodecanese (Rhodes, Stompalya, Khalki, Skarpanto, Khasos, Piskopis, Misiros, Kalimnos, Leros, Patmos, Sombeki, Kos and Meis). According to its treaty obligations Greece is also required not to fortify these islands. Greece started to militarize the islands after 1964 and has attempted to include at least one of them, Lemnos, in NATO plans and exercises. The final aim appears to be to achieve a total abolition of its obligations to the non-military status of these islands (Ronzitti, 1982: 106).

It is beyond the scope and purpose of this chapter to take a close look at the conflicting legal arguments of Greece and Turkey. Greece, putting forward different claims regarding different islands, has tried to become totally free of its obligations. Without going into detail, it suffices to state that Greek legal arguments boil down to these points: conditions have changed since the international instruments laid down the non-military status of the islands (*rebus sic stantibus*); the Montreux Convention of 1936 has lifted the demilitarized status of the islands situated at the entry of the Çanakkale Straits (Dardanelles); since Turkey is not a signatory of the Paris Treaty of 1947, Greece has no obligation towards Turkey to keep the Dodecanese demilitarized; Greece perceives a 'Turkish threat' and therefore can militarize the islands according to Article 51 of the United Nations Charter.

Turkish legal arguments, in turn, can be briefly stated as follows: all the treaties governing the status of the Eastern Aegean islands attach, as a permanent condition to Greek sovereignty, demilitarization; there have not been any essential changes in conditions to support Greek claims; the Paris Treaty of 1947 has put forward an objective status which is valid even for non-signatories; the Montreux Convention of 1936 has not changed the non-military status of Lemnos and the adjacent islands; Greek allegations that the islands have been militarized as a defensive measure against a 'Turkish threat' constitute a gross distortion of the sequence of developments, since it is Turkey that has felt the need to take defensive measures in the face of violations by Greece of its obligation to keep the islands demilitarized.

Greek efforts to consolidate and further the militarization of the islands have continued, even after the start of negotiations and the process of reducing conventional forces in Europe (CFE). Valinakis (1991: 20–1) explains:

> Turkey seemed to fear that Greece intended to use the CFE process and provisions as a new legal basis justifying the defensive measures Athens had taken after 1974 in these islands. The Turkish Foreign Minister K. Alptemocin told a press conference a few days after the Paris summit, that the CFE treaty did not change 'the status of demilitarization of the Eastern Aegean islands.' Replying to these statements, the Greek Foreign Minister clarified that Greece had declared its military forces and weapons systems 'for the entire country', in accordance with international treaties. . .

In spite of such general statements, it seems that the Greek government refrained from declaring regular and permanently stationed units in all the Eastern Aegean islands. However, since helicopters and (up to 600) ACVs in use by paramilitary units do not count under the CFE ceilings, there is a possibility, in the foreseeable future, for Greece to enlarge its potential in these two weapon categories in this zone, should it so wish.

DELIMITATION OF THE CONTINENTAL SHELF[11]

The solution of Turkish–Greek problems regarding the Aegean is closely related to the continental shelf issue. A solution of this problem could also lead to the solution of other difficulties. There are two levels of conflict regarding this issue: the first is the conflict over the essence of delimitation, while at the second level there are conflicting views over ways of solving the delimitation problem. While Turkey is in favour of solving this problem via bilateral negotiations, Greece is trying to take the problem to international forums and jurisdiction bodies. Consequently, the problem has been taken to the International Court of Justice by Greece. However, the Court took a 'non-jurisdiction' decision in 1978.

Greece's basic legal arguments on the continental shelf issue can be summarized as follows:

1. The islands facing Turkey constitute an integral part of Greece and the Greek land must be considered as a whole without detaching these islands from continental Greece.
2. Islands also have continental shelves, as confirmed by the Law of the Sea Agreement of 1982. Therefore, the islands must be considered under the same conditions as the mainland when determining the continental shelf borders.
3. The delimitation of the continental shelf borders between Turkish and Greek islands must be based on the equidistance principle by taking their closest coast to Turkey into account.

On the other hand, Turkey has put forward the following legal arguments:

1. Natural prolongation is fundamental in delimiting the continental shelf. The islands which are located on the natural prolongation of a land mass do not have continental shelves of their own.

2. Greece wishes the delimitation of the continental shelf to be based on the islands closest to Turkey. However, the 1982 UN Law of the Sea Convention not only disallows the consolidation of the islands with mainland Greece, but also forbids consideration of the islands as benefiting from the 'archipelago regime' and the mainland, following the principle of unconditional equality as an idea originating from the 'national integrity' principle.
3. In determining the continental shelf borders between a group of islands and the huge land mass facing them, no rule of law or logic can justify that they should be treated on an equal basis. Delimitation should be effected in accordance with equitable principles. In order to assure that the principle of equity is not disregarded, the importance of the semi-closed characteristic of the Aegean, its natural resources, security requirements of the parties, and transportation routes in the Aegean have to be taken into consideration for both parties.
4. The Treaty of Lausanne of 1923 has set a balance between Turkey and Greece, and this should be considered in the delimitation of the Aegean continental shelf. This balance requires that both countries utilize the Aegean on an equitable basis.

In view of its peculiar geographic features, the Aegean has a number of distinctive aspects. Settlement of the continental shelf issue is bound to be a complicated task requiring delicate political decisions which can only be worked out through bilateral negotiations. This issue has led to tensions between Turkey and Greece. Greece made recourse to the UN Security Council and the International Court of Justice, while Turkey has consistently called for bilateral negotiations.

The UN Security Council in Resolution 395 adopted 25 August 1976, called upon Turkey and Greece to resume direct negotiations in order to reach mutually acceptable solutions. The International Court of Justice, in turn, deliberated on the issue upon the application of Greece, for nearly two and a half years between the summer of 1976 and December 1978, but it rejected Greece's argument that Turkey was bound to submit to the jurisdiction of the Court. In the meantime, however, 'both Greece and Turkey had reached a form of *modus vivendi* by agreeing (in the Bern Declaration of November 11, 1976) to adopt a set of procedures for bilateral negotiations and to refrain from any exploration in areas outside their respective territorial waters' (Bahcheli 1990a: 137).

In order to reach an agreement based on mutual consent with regard to the delimitation of the Aegean continental shelf, as well as other related Aegean issues, Turkey and Greece started negotiations. Several meetings were held between prime ministers, ministers of foreign affairs and secretaries general of the ministries of foreign affairs up to 1981. However, Greece terminated the negotiating process with Turkey in 1981 and started seismic and related activities and planned drilling operations in the disputed areas of the Aegean continental shelf in 1987. These activities led to the March 1987 crisis between Turkey and Greece. This crisis over the continental shelf issue was, in Turkey's view, the culmination of unilateral actions perpetrated by Greece on the Aegean continental shelf, beyond its territorial waters. However, the crisis was averted and a new process of negotiations was started. But talks between prime ministers, ministers, and officials have yielded no tangible results on the major issues.

THE TERRITORIAL WATERS[12]

In 1923, when the Lausanne Treaty was signed, Turkish and Greek territorial waters only extended three nautical miles. However, in 1936 Greece unilaterally extended its territorial waters to six miles; Turkey later extended *its* territorial waters to six miles. Now, Greece possesses 43.68 per cent of the Aegean Sea. and Turkey 7.47 per cent, while the remaining 48.85 per cent is high seas (see Figure 7.1a).

Greece has declared an intention to extend its territorial waters to twelve miles, in which case 73 per cent of the Aegean will become Greek and only 19 per cent will remain as high seas (Figure 7.1b). This would not only obstruct Turkish transportation lines, but also place the disputed continental shelf under Greek sovereignty. In the light of these consequences, Turkey opposes Greece's intentions.

ISSUES OF AIRSPACE COMMAND AND CONTROL[13]

International law and the Chicago Convention of 1944 require that the breadth of national airspace corresponds to the breadth of territorial sea. But Greece claims to have an airspace of ten miles regardless of her territorial sea of six miles. The Greek claim is based on a Royal Decree of 1931. Greece only made this claim internationally known in 1975 mentioning the 1931 decree in an aeronautical information publication, and Turkey immediately objected.

The Greek claim to have an airspace of ten miles has been the source of frequent disturbance between the two states and also between Greece and other NATO allies. Greece alleges that Turkish and allied military aircraft violate its national airspace during training flights and exercises. But Turkish and allied military airforces argue that they are using the international airspace of the Aegean without entering the recognized six-mile Greek national airspace.

The six-mile breadth of national airspace is taken as a basis for NATO exercises as well. The only exception was the joint NATO exercises planned for October 1991. When the NATO command decided not to include the international airspace of the Aegean in exercise plans, Turkey declined to participate. Although the NATO command declared that the exercise plans by no means implied acceptance of Greek claims over the airspace of the Aegean, the Turkish decision remained unchanged (*Milliyet*, 15 October 1991).

In addition to its claim to a ten-mile national airspace, Greece also has complicated disputes with Turkey regarding the Istanbul/Athens FIR (Flight Information Region), international flight routes, terminal areas, and such military flight issues as early-warning borders and command and control areas.

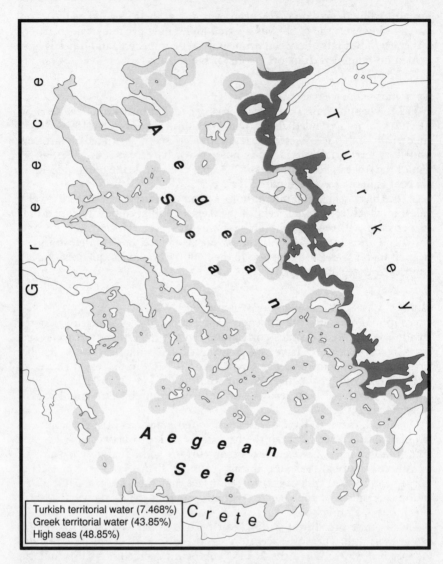

Turkish territorial water (7.468%)
Greek territorial water (43.85%)
High seas (48.85%)

Figure 7.1a The present territorial waters of Turkey and Greece in the Aegean sea (six miles each)

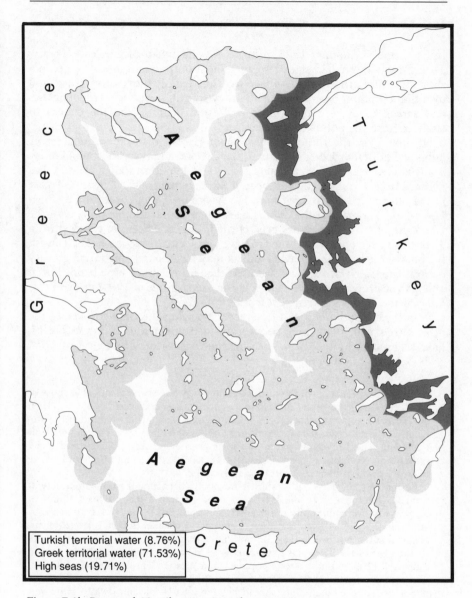

Figure 7.1b Proposed 12-mile extension of territorial waters

Violations of the human rights of the Turkish minority in Greece[14]

In Lausanne, in January 1923, prior to the enactment of the Peace Treaty, Turkey and Greece had signed an agreement on population exchange. In a short time more than a million Greeks from Turkey moved to Greece, and over half a million people went to Turkey from Greece, but both countries had agreed to exempt the Turks of Western Thrace and the Greeks of Istanbul from the population exchange.

Helsinki Watch, an international human-rights organization, in a report published in March 1992, states that 'the Greek community in Istanbul today is dwindling, elderly and frightened . . . Greek population in Turkey has declined from about 110,000 at the time of the signing of the Lausanne Treaty in 1923 to about 2,500 today'. Since 1955, with the growth of tension between Greece and Turkey over the Cyprus question, an unfavourable climate for the Greek minority in Turkey has been created. Greeks who were expelled from Turkey were the ones who elected to have Greek citizenship instead of Turkish (Helsinki Watch, 1992: 9), while others may have found emigration an easy option. The Greek citizens who were expelled from Turkey were banned from selling their property in Turkey by a government decree in 1964; this ban was lifted by the Turkish government in 1989.

Since 1923, both Turkey and Greece, asserting the right to oversee the other's treatment of their respective kinsmen under the Lausanne Treaty, have accused each other of mistreating these minorities.

As Bahcheli (1990b: 60–1) writes:

> Many of the grievances of the Turkish community have been identical to those of the Greeks in Turkey, but the fortunes of each of these communities has also been governed by important socio-economic differences as well as patterns of settlement. For instance, as a community, the Greeks of Istanbul were much better off than their Turkish counterparts, and their grievances were political and social rather than economic . . . The Greeks of Turkey have been an urban and visible minority through their concentration in Istanbul.
>
> By contrast, the Turks of Western Thrace have been a poor rural community of farmers concentrated in the least developed area of Greece. The mobility of members of this community has been sharply curtailed by high levels of illiteracy and the lack of skills other than farming. Consequently, in relative terms, emigration has not been as easy an option for them as for the Greeks of Istanbul. At the time of the Treaty of Lausanne in 1923, the population of Turks was an estimated 120,000 out of a total population in Western Thrace of about 190,000. Given an average yearly birthrate of 28 per 1000, some sources estimate that the population of the community should have trebled by the mid-1980s. However, due to a high rate of emigration, the number of Thracian Turks has remained virtually unchanged over the past sixty years.

Turkey considers that the Greek government has been mistreating the Turkish minority following rising tensions between the two countries, especially since the mid-1960s. In addition to the Greek Constitution, the Greek government's obligations to protect and guarantee the rights of the Turkish minority have been established by international treaties and agreements which include: The Treaty of Lausanne, the 1968 Protocol between Turkey and Greece, the European Convention for the Protection of Human Rights and Fundamental Freedoms, the Helsinki Final Act, and the 1989 Concluding Act of the Vienna Follow-up Meeting to the Conference on Security and Cooperation in Europe.

Helsinki Watch, in a report published in 1990, has identified Greek violations of the human rights of the Turkish minority. According to this report, the Turkish minority in Western Thrace has suffered from significant human rights abuses over the years (Helsinki Watch, 1990).

Ethnic Turks can be stripped of their citizenship by an administrative decree, without a hearing. The threat of stripping citizenship from ethnic Turks who leave the country temporarily clearly affects their freedom of movement. The Greek government also inhibits Turkish Greeks' freedom of movement by seizing their passports. In addition, their freedom of movement is inhibited by the Greek government's declaration of much of Western Thrace as a restricted military area. The Greek government also denies the existence of a Turkish minority within its borders, thus denying ethnic identity. The Turkish minority in Western Thrace continues to experience degrading treatment in the form of continued harassment by police. In spite of supposed national and international protection, the rights of free expression of the Turkish minority in Western Thrace are frequently violated. The Greek government has also violated international guarantees concerning the religious freedom of the Turkish minority in three ways: by denying permission to repair or rebuild old mosques or to build new ones; by denying the right to choose the muftis, who are the chief religious officers, and by efforts to control the Turkish minority's wakfs (charitable foundations).

The Cyprus conflict[15]

It is hard to assess the history of, and the present, Cyprus problem by looking at it as a conflict between Turkey and Greece. There are many levels at which this problem manifests itself. Undoubtedly, it essentially is a conflict between the two peoples of the island and the focal point should be at this intra-community level in order to assess the core of the issue. But, undoubtedly, the issue is much more complex. The national affiliations of the two peoples of the island with two states of the international community, ie Greece and Turkey, bring the question to another platform. The involvement of Greece and Turkey in the conflict, and the particular strategic position of the island itself, have elevated the issue to another league, where extra-regional powers lead. Thus, the Cyprus conflict has gone beyond the relatively limited dimensions of an issue between two national communities, and has gained a regional and international dimension.

The island of Cyprus was part of the Ottoman Empire from 1571 until 1878. Since 1571, the population of the island has been composed of two national communities: Orthodox Greeks in majority and Moslem Turks in minority. The Ottoman Turks, upon destroying the Venetian feudal structure, began to settle Turkish peasants on the lands of the dispossessed Venetian aristocracy (Inalcik, 1969). In time, Turkish villages and quarters came to be dispersed over the whole of the island and this remained a firm fact until the population uprootings of 1963–4 and 1974–5.

The ailing Ottoman Empire consented to Cyprus being temporarily occupied and administered by Britain at a time when the latter power was looking for a 'place of arms' close to the vital vein of her empire, which she could not any more trust to Ottoman protection. But the change of administration, caused by the Convention of 1878, proved to be the basis of British colonial rule over the island until 1960.

Cyprus lacks the experience of an anti-colonial struggle in which the two communities of the island acted together. Until the present, conditions for the formulation of a common Cypriot consciousness have been absent. A common political front against the colonial power could have been formed if the two communities had been able to unite against economic exploitation in the form of imposed taxes and a flow of revenue from the island to British stockholders. In fact, there are a few examples of common political action in this direction, but these did not alter the general trend.

Greek Cypriots, under the leadership of their Church, aimed at achieving 'enosis', union with Greece. The Turkish Cypriots would not take part in this movement, since it would have consolidated a minority position for the Turkish Cypriots irreversibly. Besides, Turkey and Greece had become competitors if not rivals after the truce in 1923.

During colonial rule the two communities also fell apart in the labour movement which gained momentum in the second half of the 1940s. In addition, the leftist Greek Cypriot political party, AKEL, could not — and did not try to — attract Turkish Cypriots: first, because of strong anticommunist feelings, the politically organized Turkish Cypriots had been in harmony with the policies adopted in mainland Turkey. Second, AKEL, from the beginning, chose to include 'enosis' in its programme as an ultimate aim, for it was seemingly the only way of competing with its main political adversary, the Church. Besides, in the early 1950s, the Soviet Union had at least encouraged if not ordered AKEL to take an enosist stand, for the Cyprus problem provided an opportunity to encourage the disruption of the south-eastern flank of the Western Alliance.

The Cyprus question was brought to the international scene by Greece in 1954 when it took the problem to the United Nations. In return, Britain tightened its grip on the island and tried to deal with the enosists, now united around a subversive organization supported by Greece. Britain also invited Turkey to take part. Cyprus was of vital strategic importance for Turkey, which considered it could not accept enosis on the island because it felt responsible for the fate of the Turkish Cypriots. Therefore Turkey willingly became involved.

In 1960 Cyprus became an independent republic.[16] Unlike most other colonies which became independent states upon proclamation by the former colonial government, the Colony of Cyprus achieved its independence through the promulgation of three multilateral treaties. The basic articles of the 1960 Constitution were first set out in the Zurich Agreement of 1959, between Greece and Turkey. Representatives of the two communities initialed this agreement. These basic articles determined the structure of the government of the republic, including the manner in which power would be shared by the two communities. Then in 1960 the three multilateral treaties, ie the Treaty of Establishment, the Treaty of Guarantee and the Treaty of Alliance were signed. Each treaty was signed by representatives of Britain, Greece, Turkey, and, for the Republic of Cyprus, by both communities' representatives. The Treaty of Establishment provided that the Republic of Cyprus would have sovereignty over the territory of the former colony, with the exception of two British military bases. In the Treaty of Guarantee, Britain, Greece and Turkey pledged to guarantee the independence, territorial integrity, and security of the Republic of Cyprus, and the state of affairs established by the Constitution. Finally, the Treaty of Alliance was signed by Turkey and Greece with the Republic of Cyprus represented by the two communities' representatives.

The Constitution of Cyprus came into force on the same day as the three treaties and incorporated all of these international agreements. In Article 181, the Constitution declares that the Treaties of Guarantee and Alliance 'shall have constitutional force', and Article 182 provides that the Basic Articles, derived from the Zurich Agreement, 'cannot, in any way, be amended'. Article 185 prohibited total or partial union with any other state. In short, the Republic of Cyprus was born as a result of a compromise between the two communities of the island and the three powers concerned. But developments after 1960 proved that the compromise was far short of a permanent solution.

The Constitution perpetuated both the equality of the two communities and their obligation to share sovereignty. According to the Constitution, the president of the Republic would be a Greek Cypriot, and the vice-president would be a Turkish Cypriot, and they were to be elected separately by their respective communities. Each had veto power. The Council of Ministers, the House of Representatives, the judiciary, the military, and the civil service were also divided between the two communities in agreed proportions. In short, the Constitution gave the two communities extraordinary checks on each other's authority at the federal level (Leigh, 1990: 47–8).

The Constitution also gave the two communities extensive powers of self-government. The two communities were to elect a Greek-Cypriot and a Turkish-Cypriot Communal Chamber, and these Chambers had full legislative power concerning matters of religion, education, personal status, and municipal institutions and affairs. In addition, separately governed municipalities of the two communities were created in the five largest towns of the island.

Unfortunately, this carefully balanced regime lasted only for three years. On 30 November 1963, Archbishop Makarios, the Greek Cypriot President of the Republic, proposed to the Guarantor powers thirteen amendments to the Cypriot Constitution. This proposal was refused by Turkey since it clearly aimed at eliminating the carefully created balance of power between the two communities so as to favour majority (Greek-Cypriot) rule. Armed violence and civil disorder broke out in Cyprus.

During the course of the crisis, the Turkish members of the House of Representatives, members of government, and civil servants were forced from their offices. Thus, the government of the Republic of Cyprus became a Greek-Cypriot administration. Thereafter, the Greek-Cypriot members of this administration, claiming to act in legitimate exercise of their offices, enacted all thirteen amendments. They argued that the Turkish Cypriots could now be readmitted as partners in the administration if they accepted the amendments passed. (Leigh, 1990: 49) But, the Turkish Cypriots never again participated in this administration which had become the administration of the Greek Cypriots.

As Monroe Leigh (1990: 50) states:

> From 1964 until the present, the Greek Cypriot regime has claimed to be the legitimate government of the Republic of Cyprus, with sovereign right over the whole Island and all of its inhabitants. There is no legal basis in international law for such a claim. The formation of a regime founded on the unilateral usurpation of rights specifically reserved to the Turkish Cypriot people contravenes the plain language and obvious intent of the Treaty of Guarantee, the Zurich Agreement and the 1960 Constitution. The Greek Cypriot regime is neither the government of the 'Republic of Cyprus' originally recognized by the community of nations in 1960 nor the legitimate successor of that government. The Greek Cypriot regime therefore had in 1964 and has today no right under international law to claim that it speaks for the Turkish Cypriot community or that it wields the sovereign powers that devolved upon the Republic of Cyprus in 1960.

From the end of 1963, the Turkish Cypriots began to be pushed back into their enclaves and began to suffer under the embargo imposed upon them by the Greek Cypriot administration.[17] The Turkish community began to govern itself with legislative, judicial and administrative organs, and parallel administrations of the two communities emerged.

During the second half of the 1960s, differences between Greece and the Greek-Cypriot administration of Makarios developed. Subversive activities against Makarios were started by the Greek governments which replaced the Papandreou Centre Coalition. Grivas was easily able to reorganize EOKA on the island, and the Greek military force stationed in Cyprus became the other instrument of subversion. The differences between Greece and the Greek Cypriots became even deeper after the Colonels took power in Greece.

In 1974, backed by Greek troops stationed in Cyprus, Sampson overthrew the regime of Archbishop Makarios with a *coup d'état*. The Turkish-Cypriot community found itself spread around the island, albeit in separate quarters and enclaves, with very limited self defence capability. There was an imminent threat to the well-being and even the existence of the Turkish community. Turkish Prime Minister Bülent Ecevit tried to find a concerted solution with Britain. But this and other attempts to find a peaceful way to reconstitute the state of affairs, envisaged by international treaties and the Constitution, failed. Turkey intervened militarily, basing this action on Turkey's rights as a guarantor power. As a result, not only did the Sampson regime collapse but so did that of the Colonels in Greece. A movement of population took place and, by 1975, the two communities on the island were physically regrouped into geographically contiguous zones.

After 1974, the Greek-Cypriot regime used its international status to the full to campaign for a return to pre-1974 conditions. This campaign was backed up with an economic blockade of the Turkish-Cypriot community. The Turkish-Cypriot administration, on the other hand, declared that a final solution to the problem could only be found in a new form of partnership government, ie federation. It renamed itself and became the Turkish Federated State of Cyprus, waiting for the Greeks to form their 'Federated' state. During the 1970s inter-communal talks were held, but no substantial results were achieved and the talks were dead-locked by the end of the decade.

The inter-communal talks were resumed in 1980, but lost their momentum in a short time. On 15 November 1983, the Turkish Cypriots declared independence and took the name of the Turkish Republic of Northern Cyprus. In the declaration, the Turkish Cypriots stated that their final aim was to achieve partnership with the Greek Cypriots within a federal framework.

The two parties met in 1984 for 'proximity talks' under the chairmanship of the UN Secretary General, Perez de Cuellar. This process culminated in high-level talks between the two leaders — Denktash and Kyprianou, together with de Cuellar — in New York in January 1985. Prior to the meeting, the secretary-general had prepared a document which he submitted to be sanctioned by both leaders. Denktash declared that he was willing to sign, but Kyprianou refused to do so. A major chance of a breakthrough had been missed.

By March 1986, the Secretary General had prepared a Draft Framework Agreement; once again Denktash was willing to sign, but the Greek Cypriot leader Kyprianou refused. Soon after, Vasiliou was elected to Kyprianou's office. Starting from September 1988, until the summer of 1989, Vasiliou and Denktash held bilateral talks. But the course of developments in 1989 had already made it clear that the talks between the two Cypriot leaders would not lead to a positive outcome — unless the two leaders agreed on the essentials of a substantially new framework of analysis of the Cyprus problem.

On 11 October 1989, by submitting a new document to the UN Secretary General, the Turkish-Cypriot side declared that the problem must now be addressed within a new framework and that 'a new pattern of relationships' between the two sides in Cyprus must be established. According to the Turkish-Cypriot proposals, in order to attain a realistic, just, and lasting solution, it was a prerequisite to reach a common understanding regarding the basic aspect of the problem: both parties should agree on the political equality of the two Cypriot peoples; the self determination rights of the two peoples; the mutual acceptance of the existence of the separate cultural, religious and national identities of the two peoples of the island.

Then, in February 1990, within the framework of the UN Secretary General's initiatives, the two leaders, Denktash and Vasiliou, met in New

York, but Vasiliou was uneasy about the Turkish proposals, and the meeting adjourned without any concrete result. This unsuccessful attempt at a breakthrough was followed in March 1990 by UN Security Council Resolution 649. This emphasized the political equality of the two sides and at the same time defined the good offices mission of the secretary-general.

From March, until the summer of 1990, the interested parties took no further steps, awaiting the outcome of domestic political developments within the Turkish Republic of Northern Cyprus (TNRC). President Denktash, facing international criticism which blamed him for the failure of solution-finding efforts, decided to hold early presidential and parliamentary elections in the TRNC; he was re-elected with a vast majority.

Starting in June, the Greek-Cypriot government tried to 'warm up' the issue. The newly elected government in Greece, the Mitsotakis government, sought to help the Greek-Cypriot administration by trying to place the issue back on the international platform and by trying to establish a linkage between Turkish–European Community relations and the Cyprus problem.

The Greek-Cypriot application for EC membership and the Turkish and Turkish-Cypriot reactions to this move are elaborated below. One point must be mentioned here: the EC, by linking the Cyprus issue with Turkey's relations with the Community, and by deciding to give serious consideration to Greek-Cypriot application, has probably not helped the overall situation in Cyprus. The EC has thus shown its willingness to ignore the legal arguments put forward by the Turkish Cypriots and to deny the political reality on the island. After all, the Greek-Cypriot administration does not represent the Turkish-Cypriot people, and the EC seems to apply a different standard to the Turkish Cypriots, compared, for example, to its attitude *vis-à-vis* self-determination within the former Yugoslavia.

The EC's attitude towards the Cyprus question also does not help the negotiating process within the UN Secretary General's good-offices' framework. The UN Security Council with its resolutions 649 (12 March 1990), 716 (11 October 1991), and 750 (10 April 1992), and the UN Secretary General (with his reports dated 19 December 1991 and 3 April 1992) have stated that a solution to the Cyprus problem should be based on the political equality of the two communities within a bi-zonal federal framework, safeguarded by international guarantees. The only 'hot' issues remaining are the ones related to the rotating presidency and the territorial ratio of the two zones of the federal state to be created.

The new Greek government, confounding initial Turkish hopes, has not changed the basic attitude of previous Greek governments: Mitsotakis has also shown that he regards a Cyprus settlement to be a prerequisite for discussing other issues with Turkey. But if the Greek and Greek-Cyriot governments will not begin to regard TRNC as a separate political entity, a solution to the problem seems improbable. Since Mitsotakis took power, the Greek government has not accepted the Turkish proposal to hold a 'quadripartite conference' on Cyprus — with the participation of Turkey, Greece, and the representatives of the two parties of the island. Instead, it has continued with efforts to reach a solution by exerting international pressure on the Turkish side.

The present situation

When the New Democracy Party won the elections and Mitsotakis came to power in Greece in spring 1990, new hopes for fresh approaches to Turkish–Greek relations began to be expressed by many observers. After all, there had been no progress in bilateral relations of the two countries for ten months since the 'Davos Spirit' between Özal and Papandreou had vanished, following the political instability in Greece caused by political scandals involving Papandreou and the eventual fall of his government. Furthermore, violations of the human rights of the Turkish minority in Western Thrace had stirred the Turkish public. Besides, the Cyprus question had proved to be in an impasse after an unsuccessful summit meeting between the Greek and Turkish-Cypriot leaders in New York. Mitsotakis, in this atmosphere, tried to carry hopes high by declaring that he intended to start a 'serious dialogue' with Turkey and that he was ready to visit Ankara for this purpose. (*Cumhuriyet*, 18 April 1990)

Mitsotakis, and his Turkish counterpart Akbulut, met in London on 6 July 1990 when they were attending a NATO summit. The two prime ministers agreed to hold meetings at foreign-minister level in September and continue the dialogue. But it was evident that Mitsotakis was now approaching the idea of a visit to Ankara more cautiously, and the two politicians were adopting a policy of 'wait and see'. The possibility of another Turkish–Greek summit in 1990 would depend upon political developments in both countries. (*Cumhuriyet*, 7 July 1990) The enthusiasm to revive the 'Davos Spirit' was somewhat muted and developments following the London summit further indicated that a Turkish–Greek dialogue at a high political level would not be very easy to start in the near future.

Officials from the Turkish foreign ministry commented that a summit meeting between Turkish and Greek leaders 'could not be held in the short run', and said they 'did not expect that a visit to Ankara by Mitsotakis could be realized in 1990' (*Cumhuriyet*, 13 July 1990). These comments revealed the cautious approach on the Turkish side. From the end of June, several steps taken by Greece and attitudes revealed by the West had also revived suspicion and distrust in the Turkish public.

Since the mid-1980s it was well known that Greece would constitute one of the main obstacles to Turkish membership of the European Community (Catsiapis, 1989: 109–16). Several officials of the Community had already implied on numerous occasions that the EC members would not give their consent to Turkish membership unless Turkish–Greek differences were resolved and a political solution was reached in Cyprus. But this EC attitude was not explicit at the highest political level until very recently. Community leaders, at the June 1990 Dublin summit meeting, adopted a common attitude by declaring that they saw the future of EC relations with Turkey being tied to Turkish attitudes on Cyprus. (*Cumhuriyet*, 28–9 June 1990) A Turkish official, on the first of July, criticized EC attitudes over Cyprus and stated that 'this untimely and negative development meant that the EC has become a party sharing responsibility with Greeks and the Greek Cypriots in contributing to the formation of a dead-end in Cyprus' (*Cumhuriyet*, 1 July 1990).

Then, during the first week of July, the Greek-Cypriot government applied for European Community membership. Turkish-Cypriot leader Denktash responded by declaring that this application did not represent his peoples' will, and that this step would make the resumption of negotiations on the Cyprus issue impossible (*Milliyet*, 7 July 1990). Turkish responses were formulated when the premier and the foreign minister of the Turkish Republic of Northern Cyprus visited Ankara during the third week of July. After bilateral talks, a document was signed and Turkey pledged to give full support to the TRNC. The document also included the mutual expression of intent not to require passports from the nationals of the two countries in visits to each other. Moreover, letters were sent by the Turkish foreign minister to the UN Secretary General and to the current EC chairman, attaching a document indicating Turkish concerns over the possible adverse effects of the Greek-Cypriot application. (*Newspot*, 28 July 1990)

The new American–Greek Defence Cooperation Agreement (DCA) signed on 8 July 1990 turned Turkish attention to American attitudes over Turkish–Greek differences. According to Turkish press reports, a clause in the DCA stated that the signatories guaranteed each others' 'sovereignty, independence and territorial integrity' against 'armed aggression or threats'. This caused deep concern in Turkey. The opposition, almost all the political parties and the press, agreed that, in the new DCA, the United States was standing behind Greece and opposing Turkey. After all, it was asked, what purpose could this guarantee serve while the NATO Treaty was still effective if it were not against Turkey? Consensus in Turkey was that this could only mean American acceptance of the Greek claim that Turkey posed a threat against it. Furthermore, Greek government officials interpreted the DCA in the same manner. Seeking parliamentary ratification, they declared that the new DCA was 'a guarantee against Turkish threat' (*Cumhuriyet*, 9–11 July 1990; *Hürriyet*, 12 July 1990). Turkey expressed its concern officially. Although American Secretary of Defense Cheney, while visiting Ankara, and President Bush, by telephone and in a letter to the Turkish president, stated that the United States would not sign any document with clauses favouring one ally over the other, they fell far short of satisfying the Turkish public (*Cumhuriyet*, 11 and 30 July 1990).

During the summer of 1990, up to the start of the Gulf Crisis in August, an increasing sensitivity and concern was evident in Turkey over relations with Greece, particularly related to the 'new' attitudes of the external actors. This was mainly due to changes in the international environment and to Turkey's concerns that these changes would result in a radical shift in its role and position in the international system. As many Turks perceived, on the other hand, Greece could feel very comfortable in the present process of reconstruction of the international system, and the Greek leaders could be thinking that the time was ripe for an all-out diplomatic offensive on Cyprus and bilateral relations with Turkey. After all, Greece was part of Europe and a European era in international relations seemed to be opening. In contrast, Turkey, for several reasons — including very serious internal ones — was far from being an immediate candidate for integration with Europe. Besides, on another front, the New Democracy government had erased the image created by PASOK in American eyes.

In Turkey, this pessimistic atmosphere related to Western attitudes over Turkish–Greek relations and Cyprus seemed to fade away from the first week of August 1990. The Gulf Crisis not only revealed the limits of the security achieved by the West with the end of the cold war and the disintegration of the Eastern political and military bloc but also underlined Turkey's unique place in the region and its importance for the Western world.

When the crisis broke, many in the West had predicted that Turkey would choose a low profile and would not take a risky position against Iraq. Some thought that Turkey was not 'likely to risk direct confrontation with Iraq by unilaterally cutting off the Iraqi pipelines that passed through its territory' (*International Herald Tribune*, 6 August 1990: 4). Indeed, Turkey could have taken a cautious attitude, leaving open the taps of the 1,300-kilometres twin pipeline which carried 1.5 million barrels of Iraqi oil a day to the Turkish Mediterranean terminals. But within hours of the UN Security Council vote on 6 August 1990 to impose an economic embargo on Iraq, Turkey declared that it had banned the loading of Iraqi oil at its Mediterranean terminals, effectively blocking more than half of potential Iraqi exports. The Turkish government spokesman said that Turkey had taken this step in compliance with the UN Security Council resolution. In addition, Turkey stopped all trade with Iraq and froze all Iraqi and Kuwaiti assets in Turkey (*International Herald Tribune*, 8 August 1990). Since Iraq owed Turkey about 750 million dollars in trade debts, and Turkish-Iraqi trade amounted to $2 billion a year, Turkey's losses by siding with the West were not confined within the limits of the $300 million annual fee Turkey had been receiving for piping Iraqi oil.[18]

Turkey's role within Western efforts to put heavy pressure on Iraq was crucial, and it was duly recognized as such by Western public opinion. Turkey's prestige began to rise in the Western world for 'coming through for the US — and the West in general — unhesitatingly and at great cost and danger to itself' (*International Herald Tribune*, 25–6 August 1990: 4). People in the West began to feel that 'Ankara should be recompensed for lost sales (and lost opportunities), given firm international security guarantees, and rewarded politically for solidarity with its NATO allies and with the European Community — which Turkey, of course, wishes to join' (*International Herald Tribune*, 9 August 1990: 4). The crisis had not only underlined Western security interests in Turkey, but also had emphasized that security should be incorporated with mutual economic and political interests.

In September 1990, the United States and the European Community began to consider extending compensatory aid and loans to those countries most affected by the crisis, including Turkey. The sudden change in international climate in favour of Turkey seemed to worry the Greek government. Prime Minister Mitsotakis, in a letter to the EC Commission President Delors, stated that Greece's losses because of the Gulf Crisis amounted to

$1.5 billion and that the EC members should consider Greece as one of the recipients of compensatory aid. In addition, according to Turkish press reports, Greece categorically objected when the EC began to discuss giving such aid to Turkey (*Cumhuriyet*, 7 and 19 September 1990). Greek Foreign Minister Samaras also took an initiative and wrote a letter to his American counterpart, James Baker, stating that the 7:10 'rule'[19] had to be observed when the additional American aid to Turkey is considered, so that extra assistance be given to Greece as well (*Cumhuriyet*, 19 and 26 September 1990).

When Turkish President Özal visited the United States at the end of September 1990, he obtained President Bush's vague and general promises for political and economic support and cooperation (*Cumhuriyet*, 26–7 September 1990). This seemed short of the expectations of the Turkish government which had extended the Turkish–American Defence and Economic Cooperation Agreement (DECA) for another year without even renegotiating its terms; had reached an understanding with the United States to expand 'military and intelligence cooperation'; and had recently overcome firm opposition in the Turkish Parliament to assume the power to declare war and to send troops abroad (*International Herald Tribune*, 11–13 August 1990).

But Turkish disappointment on the European front undoubtedly deepened when the EC decided to consider seriously the Greek–Cypriot application for membership. As stated above, the Turkish government had already expressed its concern over this matter. In addition, UN Secretary General Perez de Cuellar, with a press statement on 11 September 1990, reminded the EC that a final solution to the problem required a comprehensive agreement between the two Cypriot leaders. Also referring to UN Security Council Resolution 649, de Cuellar stated that he wished the EC would consider the Greek-Cypriot application within the general framework of the Cyprus question. (*Cumhuriyet*, 12–13 September 1990). However, neither the Turkish warning, nor the de Cuellar reminder seemed to have an effect on the EC, and EC Ministers decided on 17 September to start normal procedures for considering the Greek Cypriot application (*Milliyet*, 18 September 1990). Turkish and Turkish–Cypriot governments expressed their regret and disappointment over the EC decision and it was announced that the Turkish Prime Minister would visit TRNC in October 1990 (*Milliyet*, 19 September 1990).

Thus, in September 1990, the time was not ripe to start a fresh Turkish–Greek dialogue. Nevertheless, Greek and Turkish delegations met in Ankara as scheduled. But neither side had high expectations and the meeting ended without any achievements (*Milliyet*, 21 September 1990). On 27 September 1990, Turkish and Greek foreign ministers met in New York, where they were attending the United Nations General Assembly meeting. They were only able to agree to plan a meeting for their undersecretaries before the end of 1990 and did not mention any plans for high-level contact in the near or distant future (*Cumhuriyet*, 28 September 1990).

In the meantime a change of government had also taken place in Turkey. The new Turkish prime minister, Yılmaz, sent a letter to his Greek counterpart and expressed his wish to resume dialogue. There were even press reports about the possibility of enacting a 'non-aggression pact' between the two states. But violations of the human rights of the Turkish minority during the summer of 1991 once again wiped out optimism. Confiscation of Turkish lands in Western Thrace, mistreatment of the members of the Turkish minority by the Greek government, and violent incidents in the region created tension.

When Greece became a member of the Western European Union, now commonly regarded as the defence organization of the EC, and Turkey obtained only associate membership, members of the Greek government did not fail to declare this a victory over Turkey. According to their view, Greece had obtained another safeguard against 'the Turkish threat' (*Milliyet*, 3, 4, 9 December 1991).

On the other hand, the Turkish government did not block the way for the participation of Greece in the Black Sea Economic Cooperation Project (BSEC), which was born essentially through Turkish initiative and comprised all the Black Sea states. Turkish Prime Minister Demirel, meeting in Davos with his Greek counterpart, Mitsotakis, on 1 February 1992, declared Turkey's support for Greek participation in the BSEC. In the joint communiqué issued after their meeting, the two prime ministers also expressed 'their readiness to conclude an agreement on friendship, good-neighbourliness and cooperation between the two countries'. But in the following months no concrete step was taken towards this end.

During 1991 and 1992 Greece did not hide its exasperation in the face of new developments in the region. Greece made efforts to prevent the EC from recognizing Macedonia, since it denies ethnic identity to the Macedonian minority within its borders. The government of Greece seems to be worried about recent developments in the region, since the new regional balances might work in favour of Turkey: after all Turkey has solved its differences with Bulgaria and has already established close ties with the newly independent states of the region with the help of historical and cultural ties. In the near future, Greece may face further difficulties in balancing the new facts of the new international regional order with its traditional rivalry with Turkey.

Conclusion

There is a widely shared belief that Turkish–Greek differences will not be resolved in the foreseeable future and that the two nations will learn to live with bilateral problems (Birand, 1989: 7–12). This writer can be neither optimistic about the immediate future, nor about the long term, unless a new vision shared by both sides gains prominence over unilateral short-term aims. If the best achievement of the two sides in their efforts to reach a solution remains frequently repeated but futile summit talks, one cannot be optimistic. Responsible people on both sides should now start thinking about ways of overcoming the stalemate and making future dialogue different from that of the past.

There must be alternatives to the pursuit of short-term unilateral interests. For the long run, the decision-makers on both sides can choose to continue with the stalemate, with all its possible consequences. Alternatively, they can choose harmony and cooperation as a long-term target now, and deal with the differences and problems with such a target in mind.

Both countries have much to gain from future regional harmony and cooperation. The change in the international environment indicates that both sides will live through an era in which their regional roles will be emphasized. Regional stability is a prerequisite for fruitful cooperation in the Balkans and the eastern Mediterranean. In return, a stable and harmonious Balkan region is a requirement for an enlarged but stable Europe (Sander, 1990: 27). Balkan cooperation cannot be achieved without the participation of Turkey and Greece. Turkey, through Balkan cooperation, would gain a room in a possible 'Common European House', and could also satisfy her security needs. Greece, on the other hand, should see that cooperation in the region will be fruitful and give it security as well.

For some outside observers Cyprus seems to be the key in Turkish–Greek relations. Cyprus is a very important issue affecting the bilateral relations of the two states, but it cannot be treated solely as a problem between Turkey and Greece. After all, the Cyprus question has its own dynamics and it is much more complex than being just a bilateral problem. Therefore, to deal with Turkish–Greek differences in one basket, including the Cyprus issue will, in this writer's view, result in another futile attempt. Further, it is unrealistic to assume that under external pressure Turkey would give up its support for the Turkish–Cypriot people. Therefore, a settlement in Cyprus cannot be regarded as a prerequisite for the start of Turkish–Greek negotiations on bilateral issues.

If Turkey and Greece in the near future can agree to start a negotiation process, problems and differences in-between should be divided among several baskets. The disputes over the Aegean and the ones related to the minorities could be put in separate baskets. A third could include confidence-building measures. The two states could start negotiations by opening the third basket first.

As an initial step towards confidence building, the two states could adapt for their use in the Aegean the 1972 American-Soviet Agreement on the prevention of incidents on and over the high seas (Haas, 1979: 23–29). Then, they could proceed to further measures. Turkey could abolish its Fourth Army and Greece, for its part, could demilitarize its islands facing Turkey. They could go further and Greece could agree to the implementation of the 1980 'Rogers Agreement' and, at the same time, come to an understanding with Turkey on the civil-aviation issues. For its part, Turkey could stop engaging in military manoeuvres in the region, unless Greece also participates. More suggestions for initial steps to melt the ice in bilateral relations are possible. On a parallel track, the two states could start right away with cooperation over environmental issues and continue with efforts to increase communication and understanding between their peoples in order to correct misperceptions on both sides.

Turkish Prime Minister Demirel, on 1 June 1992, declared that 'Turkey is willing to hold talks with Greece for the signature of a friendship agreement'. According to Demirel, the Cyprus issue should not block the road for the establishment of friendly relations between the two countries. Demirel added that, 'the Cyprus question can only be solved by the two peoples of the island, and not by Greece and Turkey'. In reply, Greek Prime Minister Mitsotakis stated that, 'in order to reach an understanding with Turkey and to sign a friendship agreement, Greece has to see some substantial development towards solution in Cyprus' (*Cumhuriyet*, 2 June 1992). Therefore, there seems to be no change in the basic attitudes of the two countries, as of June 1992.

Greece has the option to use its EC membership against Turkey, especially in Cyprus, and seems to wish a solution to the problem within a European framework. But it should be noted that without Turkish-Cypriot consent, the whole of Cyprus will not be able to join the EC. Therefore, the EC needs to take the political reality of the island into account and approach Greco–Turkish differences and the Cyprus issue from a new perspective. After all, the integration of only the Greek part of Cyprus with the EC will not be an achievement towards regional harmony. On the other hand, a positive European approach towards Turkey and the TRNC will undoubtedly help to eliminate regional differences within a broader framework of integration.

Notes

1. For a general assessment of modern Greek history, see: Clogg, R. (1989) and Stavrianos, L.S. (1958).
2. See, R. Jensen, P.K. (1979).
3. P.E. Dimitras (1985: 137) writes that 'more than 90 percent of Greeks believe that Turkey threatens Greece'. A survey of public opinion in 1986 indicated that 63 per cent of the Greeks questioned, 'did not trust the Turks at all'. See, Catsiapis, J (1989: 116). Further, T.A. Couloumbis (1980: 42) writes that, 'since 1974 the Greek political world has been proceeding more with consensus than polarization type politics — especially given the near-universal perception of a Turkish threat'.
4. Perhaps, the 1987 bilateral decision to review the reciprocal images emphasized in text-books and private efforts to increase communication and understanding between the two nations like the Abdi Ipekci Foundation can be developed.
5. R. Clogg (1980: 130) notes that 'there was even vague and heady talk of the possibilities of a Greek–Turkish customs union'.
6. A. Toynbee, (1922).
7. See, Boll, M.M. (1979: 609–32).
8. For the PASOK attitude towards the Rogers Agreement', see Coufoudakis, V. (1985: 212).
9. For Papandreou's policy *vis-à-vis* NATO, see Coufoudakis, V. (1985: 210–14) and Spourdalakis, M. (1988: 233–6).
10. On this issue, see Pazarci, H. (1986a: 29–16) and (1986 b); and also see

Ronzitti, N. (1985: 101–116).
11. See: Pazarci, H. (1982) and Karl, D.E. (1977: 642–73).
12. For the development of the continental shelf issue, see Bahcheli, T. (1990a: 130–41) and Pazarci, H. (1986c: 19–34).
13. See Pazarci, H. (1986c).
14. See Oran, B. (1986), Bahcheli, T. (1990b) and Ahmet, S. (1989).
15. Most of the arguments on the history of the Cyprus conflict in this chapter are based on Gürel, Ş.S. (1985) and (1984).
16. Evaluations of the nature of the 1960 Constitution and 1959 and 1960 international agreements are mainly based on Lauterpacht, E. (1990) and Leigh, M. (1990).
17. See TRNC (1985).
18. See *International Herald Tribune*, 25–6 August 1990, p. 4. In September, a World Bank official, in an interview with a Turkish journalist, predicted that the Gulf Crisis would 'hit the Turkish economy very hard.' See *Cumhuriyet*, 16 September 1990. Again, in September, Turkey refused an Iraqi offer of free oil. See *Cumhuriyet*, 19 September 1990.
19. Since the end of the American arms embargo on Turkey in 1978 the American government gives aid to Greece and Turkey in a 7:10 ratio.

References

Ahmet, S. (1989), 'Grievances and Requests of the Turkish–Moslem Minority Living in Western Thrace, Greece', *Turkish Review Quarterly Digest*, 3, No. 15, 37–44.

Bahcheli, T. (1990a), *Greek-Turkish Relations Since 1955*, San Francisco, Boulder; London, Westview Press.

Bahcheli, T. (1990b), 'The Grievances of the Turkish Community in Western Thrace and Greek–Turkish Relations', in E. Manisali (ed.), *Turkey and the Balkans*, Istanbul, The Middle East Business and Banking Magazine Publications, 59–69.

Birand, M. (1989), 'Önsöz', in S. Vaner (ed.), *Türk–Yunan Uyuşmazlığı*, (Turkish/Greek Dispute), Istanbul, Metis, 7–12.

Boll, M.M. (1979), 'Turkey's New National Security Concept: What it means for NATO', *Orbis*, 23, No. 3, 609–32.

Catsiapis, J. (1989), 'L'attitude de la Grèce face a la demande d'adhesion de la Turquie aux CE', *CEMOTI*, 8; 109–11.

Clogg, R. (1979), *A Short History of Modern Greece*, Cambridge, Cambridge University Press.

Clogg, R. (1980), 'The Troubled Alliance: Greece and Turkey', in R. Clogg (ed.), *Greece in the 1980s*, New York, St. Martin's Press, 123–49.

Coufoudakis, V. (1985), 'Greek–Turkish Relations, 1973–1983: The View from Athens', *International Security*, 9, No. 4, 185–217.

Couloumbis, T.A. (1980), 'Defining Greek Foreign Policy Objectives', in T.A. Couloumbis and J.O. Iatrides (eds), *Greek–American Relations. A Critical Review*, New York, Pella Publishing Co., 21–47.

Dimitras, P.E. (1985). 'Greece: A New Danger', *Foreign Policy*, 19, 134–50.

Groom, A.J.R. (1986), 'Cyprus: Back in the Doldrums', *The Round Table*, 300, 362–83.

Gürel, Ş.S. (1984), 'The Cyprus Conflict : An Interpretation and an Evaluation of Prospects for Settlement', *Fehmi Yavuz'a Armağan*, Ankara, SBF Yay., 483–90.

Gürel, Ş.S. (1985), *Kıbrıs Tarihi, 1878–1960*, (History of Cyprus, 1878–1960), 2 Vols, Istanbul, Kaynak Yayınları.

Haas, R. (1979), 'Confidence-building Measures and Arms Control', in *The Future of Arms Control*, Adelphi Paper 149, 23–9.

Helsinki Watch (1990), *Destroying Ethnic Identity — The Turks of Greece*, New York and Washington, DC, A Helsinki Watch Report.

Helsinki Watch (1992), *Denying Human Rights and Ethnic Identity — The Greeks of Turkey*, New York and Washington, DC, A Helsinki Watch Report.

Inalcik, H. (1969), *Ottoman Policy and Administration in Cyprus after the Conquest*, Ankara, DTCF YayInlari.

Jensen, P.K. (1979), 'The Greco–Turkish War, 1920–1922', *International Journal of Middle East Studies*, 10, No. 4, 553–65.

Karl, D.E. (1977), 'Islands and the Delimitation of the Continental Shelf: A Framework for Analysis', *American Journal of International Law*, 71, No. 4, 642–73.

Lauterpacht, E. (1990), 'The Turkish Republic of Northern Cyprus — the Status of the two communities in Cyprus', in N.M. Ertekün (ed.), *The Status of the Two Peoples in Cyprus*, Lefkoşa, Public Information Office of TRNC, 10–29.

Leigh, M. (1990), 'The Legal Status in International Law of the Turkish Cypriot and the Greek Cypriot Communities in Cyprus', in N.M. Ertekün (ed.), *The Status of the Two Peoples in Cyprus*, Lefkoşa, Public Information Office of TRNC, 44–58.

Oran, B. (1986), *Türk–Yunan Iliskilerinde Batı Trakya Sorunu* (The Western Thrace Question in Turkish–Greek Relations), Ankara, Mülkiyeliler Birliği Vakfı Yayinlari.

Özkale, L. (1992), *Türkiye'nin Uluslararasi Rekabet Gücü ve AT Üyeliği Sorunu* (Turkey's Power for International Competition and the Question of Turkish membership of the EC), Report, Istanbul, Friedrich Ebert Foundation.

Pazarcı, H. (1982), *La Delimitation du Plateau Continental et les Iles*, Ankara, SBF Yayinlari.

Pazarcı, H. (1986a), 'Has the Demilitarized Status of the Aegean Islands determined by the Lausanne and Paris Treaties Changed?', *Turkish Quarterly Digest*, 7: 29–46.

Pazarcı, H. (1986b), *Doğu Ege Adalarinin Askerden Arindirilmis Statüsü*, (The Demilitarized Status of the Eastern Aegean Islands), Ankara, SBF Yayinlari.

Pazarcı, H. (1986c), 'Lozan Antlaşmasindan 1974'e Kadar Ege'ye Ilişkin Gelişmeler ve Yunanistan'in Ege Politikasi', (Developments Concerning the Aegean from Lausanne to 1974 and the Aegean Policy of Greece), in *Turk–Yunan Ilişkileri* (Turkish–Greek Relations), Ankara.

Psomiades, H.J. (1968), *The Eastern Question: The Last Phase — A Study in Greek–Turkish Diplomacy*, Thessaloniki, Institute for Balkan Studies.

Ronzitti, N. (1982), 'Demilitarization and Neutralization in the Mediterranean', *Milletlerarasi Hukuk ve Milletlerarasi Özel Hukuk Bülteni*, 2, 101–16.

Sander, O. (1990), 'Turkey's Role in NATO: A time for new Perspectives', *NATO Review*, 38, No. 3, 24–8.

Spourdalakis, M. (1988), *The Rise of the Greek Socialist Party*, London and New York, Routledge.

Stavrianos, L.S. (1958), *The Balkans since 1453*, New York, Rhinehart.

Toynbee, A. (1922), *The Western Question in Greece and Turkey*.
TRNC (1985), Three Chapters in Cyprus, Lefkoşa, Government Printing Office.
Valinakis, Y.G. (1991), *Greece and the CFE Negotiations*, Report, Stiftung Wissenschaft und Politik, Ebenhausen, Haus Effenberg.

8
Turkey, the CIS and Eastern Europe

Türkkaya Ataöv

Introduction

The nature of the changes which have occurred in the former Soviet Union, as well as in Eastern, Central and Southeastern Europe should be described as a revolution and not as reforms. The events of 1989 were cataclysmic in spite of some similarities with the unsuccessful reform initiatives of the 1960s.[1] Earlier steps by N.S. Khruschev in the Soviet Union, I. Nagy in Hungary, W. Gomulka in Poland and even A. Dubchek in Czechoslovakia were basically experiments that sought to assimilate new realities into the existing systems. This time, the current political, economic and social order has been overthrown. It is not simply that these societies moved away from one-party control to pluralism, or that they shifted from state-run economies towards market systems or that they ended four decades of isolation; these revolutionary upheavals occurred with great speed and, moreover, simultaneously. The essential basis for statehood in the Soviet Union came to be the individual republics, forcing, in a way, President M.S. Gorbachev to resign because he lost control over the former federal organs. Even in Albania, not automatically connected by the law of linked vessels with the processes which occurred elsewhere, change was set in motion.[2]

One of the two superpowers, the former Soviet Union, lost territories and zones of influence, leaving in its place a fragile 'Commonwealth of Independent States' (CIS), some of which are not only separate and diverse, but also seriously contending with each other — like the Russian Federation and Ukraine — and even fighting out differences with arms in the Caucasus and, to a lesser extent, in Moldova. Not only will Russia's past and sheer size make for an uneasy association, but the republics are preoccupied with their newfound independence. In the meantime, the break-up of the former Soviet Union boosted the membership of the Conference on Security and Cooperation in Europe (CSCE) to 51 and United Nations' membership to 175 with the accession of all the former republics as independent states.

The former Soviet republics and the rejuvenated Eastern European countries have dismantled their obsolete institutions, together with the gendarme-guarding role of the Red Army and its former Warsaw Pact allies. But there is no assurance yet that they have the means to develop adequate substitutes. There are no simple rules of procedure, no reliable precedent. The history of past revolutions belies prophecy. The new distribution of forces in Europe raises a host of economic and political problems and poses questions as to the roles of external actors.[3]

Turkey is one of those external actors. That country gained in stature by virtue of being an element of security in the midst of regions such as the Balkans, the Middle East and the Caucasus, which are beset by troubles. Turkey suddenly cast a longer shadow in all these areas. Having entered this century as a very underdeveloped country, it now puts its signatures to billion dollar projects abroad. It has a great opportunity to exploit its geographical proximity, historical experience, ethnic affiliations and economic potential to create a new atmosphere of cooperation.

Turkey's 'star' is beginning to shine in the changing world balances. Some foreign analysts commented that this country will be a much stronger state in the coming century.[4] With the membership of all the Turkic-speaking republics in the United Nations, there are suggestions of adding Turkish, if all can agree on the dialect spoken in modern Turkey, to the list of official languages of that international organization.[5] The cold war, perhaps unavoidably, had caused Turkish foreign policy to be content with the status quo, moulding the diplomatic cadres in such a way that they remain virtually unaware of the significance of certain global movements, such as non-alignment. The dynamic foreign policy of the previous Atatürk era had given way to a priority of reinforcing Turkey only as a 'Western outpost' facing the Soviet Union. Long described as a 'NATO bulwark', Turkey has now opened up to its big northern neighbour. Utilizing its location, secular tradition and transition to a market economy, it is trying to become a bridge between the West and the former Soviet republics. Although focusing a great deal of attention on the republics with which it has close ethnic, linguistic and religious ties, it is expanding links with Russia, an important trading partner, and all the other countries around the Black Sea. Even its relations with Armenia are rapidly improving.[6]

Continued dependence on the United States cannot be an alternative for Turkey. Some American policies are in harmony with Turkish approaches and some are not. The riparian states of the Black Sea, the new Turkic republics and the Balkans are regions where Turkey hopes to expand economic relations with possibly greater political cooperation at a later date. Such a general policy does not constitute an obstacle to the development of Turkey's relations with the European Community (EC), either.

Consequently, Turkish diplomacy is utilizing new economic priorities in foreign relations. Cabinet members are accompanied by large groups of businessmen, sometimes about a hundred, during official trips abroad. Turkey's diplomatic missions are virtually competing with each other to increase the volume of trade with the countries to which they are accredited. Turkish companies have also become the country's commercial and investment representatives abroad. The old image of the 'warrior Turk' is giving place to the figure of contemporary businessmen.

Hence, Turkey is looking for a special place in the newly forming international and regional balances, which put this country in a most sensitive position on the one hand, and areas of new opportunities on the other. This chapter intends to investigate the strains and opportunities, especially as they relate to Turkey. It is within this framework that Turkey aims at building better relations with Russia, the Black Sea powers and the new regimes in the former Soviet republics and Eastern Europe. Russia is no longer the old military threat to its former adversaries. Although it is still a 'superpower', by virtue of its size, population and nuclear arsenal, the Brezhnev Doctrine is dead, and it no longer has allies. But Turkey, along with many other countries, is worried over the fact that the disintegration of the Soviet system has raised a spectre of its old nuclear warheads being used by various nationalist groups and its redundant scientists selling their skills to irresponsible cliques abroad.

On 16 December 1991, the Turkish government decided to recognize globally, and not based on individual requests, all the republics which had previously comprised the Soviet Union. Azerbaijan had been recognized earlier, and a Turkish consulate had been opened in Baku even before that. The Turkish ambassador to the Lithuanian capital was also accredited to Latvia and Estonia. Elsewhere consulates were opened, and shortly after were elevated to the status of embassies.[7] The decision to recognize all the republics entailed the acceptance of Armenia as a separate independent state. It is not surprising, then, that when the representatives of forty-seven countries and aid organizations met in Washington for a mammoth conference on assistance to the former Soviet Union, Turkey was selected as a forward base, on account of its position, infrastructure facilities and experiences gained during the Kurdish refugee influx from Iraq.

It should also be understandable that Turkey has a special relationship with its 'long-lost cousins' in the Caucasus and Central Asia who follow each other with large delegations in quick succession to Ankara, the capital of the most prominent member of the large Turkic family. Their visits are reciprocated by even larger delegations, the desire to establish closer relations being genuine on both sides. The question is whether Turkey can provide for all the needs of its cousins who are living through the excitement of sudden discovery.

Opportunities are also accompanied by impediments. First, Turkey, as a model of a pluralistic, secular and a modern state, hopes to be the 'beacon of light' for the eastern republics to follow. The present leaders of the latter seem to prefer the Turkish model to those offered by Iran and Saudi Arabia. Second, although the world is now better aware of Turkey's commercial significance as a valve through which the oil of Azerbaijan, the natural gas of Turkmenia and the uranium of Kirghizistan may flow, as much as its continuing strategic importance, emphasized during the Gulf Crisis, the Turks admit that they do not have all the resources to resuscitate single-handedly the economies of the Moslem republics. Turkey is hoping that others will give it a boost in its efforts to develop them. Third, Turkey also looks on with increasing anxiety as the tension between Armenia and Azerbaijan mounts. The prospects of an all-out war between these two estranged Caucasian republics provide nightmares for policy-makers in Ankara. Turkey has been similarly disturbed by the civil war in the former Yugoslavia and the strains in Moldova.

The New Order and security

The Warsaw Pact has been formally dissolved (1 July 1991), with the inevitable consequences that there will be no Soviet troops left on Eastern European soil and that the military functions of NATO are going to be substantially downgraded by disarmament. Although the break-up of the Soviet-led Eastern military bloc produced practical results for Turkey as well, such as the proposed reduction of its army to 350,000 men, it has also created new problems connected with the future of the Western alliance, the compatibility of the armed forces in the newly established CIS, the division of the Black Sea fleet between Russia and Ukraine and the control of the former Soviet nuclear warheads. In addition to these issues directly affecting Turkey's security, there are some frightening events on Turkey's doorsteps such as the armed conflict between Armenia and Azerbaijan that cloud the generally positive picture resulting from the disappearance of the military threat.

NATO is already searching for a new identity following the withering away of the Soviet opposition, once its main source of existence. Wanting to do something to embrace its former enemies, NATO thought up the North Atlantic Cooperation Council (NACC), an East–West forum to debate security issues. But by admitting a number of new states to an ill-defined body like the NACC, the Western countries have taken on a huge number of problems difficult to sort out. So far, Georgia, the scene of a civil war, has been left out, and Armenia and Azerbaijan are virtually at war.

On the other hand, the Russian Federation has not abandoned its attempts to keep the armed forces of the eleven members of the CIS under some form of joint control. It lobbied for retaining a combined conventional army, but three republics (Ukraine, Moldova and Azerbaijan) refused.[8] The other eight drew up plans for a unified command to remain in place for two years, during which they will form their own armies and may or may not join the unified forces.

Ukraine, Moldova and Azerbaijan opted to form their own separate armed forces. While leaving nuclear forces under central control, the Ukrainians seem determined that conventional forces deployed on their territory be under their own command. Ukraine, the second most powerful of the eleven member states, launched its own army when defence ministry staff in Kiev swore an oath of allegiance to the newly independent state. The Ukrainian president also signed decrees appointing himself the commander-in-chief of the national armed forces and stipulating that they are actually the former Soviet units, including the Black Sea fleet with about 300 vessels, later partly claimed by the Russians.

The demise of the Soviet Union left in doubt commitments to scores of treaties, including those on nuclear arms reductions. It also caused serious concerns, shared by Turkey, that nuclear warheads may not be protected with the care shown during the Soviet era. When the Russian Federation, Ukraine and Belarus became (8 December 1991) the three initial parties to the CIS, the Turkish Council of Ministers, in a specific announcement, expected them and the other republics to join the commonwealth to respect the totality of the agreements signed by the Soviet Union. The former Soviet Union and Turkey were both parties to the Conventional Forces in Europe Treaty, prepared within the framework of the CSCE.

The former Soviet Union is believed to have had about 27,000 nuclear weapons. Most of them were within Russia, and some 4,000–5,400 warheads were in some other locations. None of them can now be found on the territory of the former Warsaw Pact allies. Nuclear weapons in the former Soviet Union were kept under tight control. Many people were involved in their launching, and any one of them could break the chain. The prevention of unauthorized use was guaranteed by technical and organizational measures, as well as by reliable safeguarding of munitions and systems for their delivery.

Leaving aside weapons on ships at sea, there were some nuclear warheads in Ukraine, Belarus and Kazakhstan. There were SS-18 intercontinental ballistic missile fields in Kazakhstan (Imeni Gastello, Djengiztobe, Dombarovsky). There were also eighteen SS-19 ICBM silos, again in Kazakhstan (Tyuratam). In Ukraine (Derazhnya, Pervomaisk) were also located 120 missile silos. There were two ICBM bases in Belarus. There were several bomber bases outside the Russian Federation: one in Kazakhstan, eight in Ukraine, four in Belarus and one in Estonia. The bombers stationed there were all capable of carrying nuclear bombs and missiles. The former Soviet Union was encircled with defensive surface-to-air missiles (SAM) that could fire nuclear warheads. There were also short-range nuclear missiles and nuclear artillery in almost every tank, artillery division and motorized unit. There were eighty-six such divisions in the non-Russian republics. Some nuclear weapons have been removed from the Caucausus and the Baltic regions. But to remove them is a long and complicated process.

The former Soviet republics having now become independent, there is concern basically on two issues: (a) the danger of nuclear proliferation and (b) nuclear weapons falling into the 'wrong hands'. The Kazakh, Ukrainian and Belarus leaders announced that they were ready to sign all the treaties on nuclear arms the Soviet Union had signed, and also to get rid of the nuclear arms on their territories. Russian President Boris Yeltsin promised that all Soviet nuclear weapons will be put under strict control and that the other republics with such weapons will join the international Non-Proliferation Treaty. The Kazakh president, Nursultan Nazarbaev, signed a decree permanently closing the test facilities. Their closure was largely the result of years of organizational work by the republic's most influential public body, the Nevada–Semipa-latinsk Movement.

Some serious questions remain in spite of these assurances.[9] Will all non-Russian leaders be equally happy to send to Russia the nuclear arms on their soil? Are their methods of transport and storage adequate? What is the probability of danger from a leak of radioactive plutonium? Even if the warheads are stockpiled on Russian soil, how safe are the storage conditions? Could they be smuggled abroad? What is the risk of defection by very badly paid or unemployed former nuclear experts?

Turkish leadership and opinion-moulding quarters ask these questions especially when there is a possibility that nuclear warheads may fall into the hands of contending parties and of terrorists.[10] In response to some comments in the foreign press that Turkey plans to import nuclear weapons' technology from some of the Turkic republics, the Turkish Ministry of Foreign Affairs denied that the country, having signed and approved the Non-Proliferation Treaty, harboured such plans.[11] Turkey feels concerned at the potential for the proliferation of nuclear weapons following the break up of the Soviet Union.

The Russian market

Turkey, a NATO member, pursued a very cautious and non-provacative policy towards the disintegration of the Soviet Union. Likewise, the Soviet president, M.S. Gorbachev, sent a special representative to Ankara to convey the Russian leader's message to Turkey's President Turgut Özal in appreciation of the latter's stance taken during the abortive coup (August 1991) in Moscow. As a leading Turkish businessman emphasized, the Turkish Republic needed to develop its relations with all the entities within the borders of the former Soviet Union, but especially with the Russian Federation, since that country was an 'untouched giant market'.[12] Consequently, Russian–Turkish economic relations not only developed quantitatively, but their nature was modified beyond recognition. While the Russians expected Turkish capital and know-how, the Turkish press described the opportunity as a 'contractor's paradise'.

The initial step was taken by President Özal, who paid an official visit to the Soviet Union (11–16 March 1991), the first at the presidential level after a twenty-two year interval, on the occasion of the seventieth anniversary of the Soviet–Turkish Treaty of Friendship and Fraternity (16 March 1921). He led a large delegation to the capitals of Russia, Ukraine, Kazakhstan and Azerbaijan, where he signed several agreements. After these, more contacts took place and investments poured in, culminating in a new friendship and cooperation agreement determining the framework of future relations (4 February 1992). It will be normal from now on to hold meetings on the possibilities of improving business with Russia or to open Russian-language courses in the smaller Anatolian cities.

Özal's visit led to a number of agreements, the most important being the Treaty of Friendship, Good-Neighbourliness and Cooperation (12 March

1991). What followed demonstrates the will of the two countries to develop relations in all fields. An important factor contributing to the growing relationship was the complementary character of the two economies. The 1991 treaty, much more all-embracing and pioneering than anything signed before, described the two as friendly states as determined to expand substantially their relations in all possible areas. The parties pledged to maintain their common borders, refrain from the use of force against each other, disallow their territories to be used for similar purposes, to consult at every level at regular intervals and to cooperate against terrorist activities in all their forms.

Another agreement on trade as well as on economic, scientific and technical cooperation, signed the same day, aimed at a sweeping increase in the total trade volume between the two countries reaching $9–10 billion towards the year 2000. It pledged to support the activities of the Soviet and Turkish organizations and companies and their joint venutres in third countries.

The 1991 Soviet–Turkish treaty was the fourth of its kind, after the ones concluded with Germany, Italy and France, in the *perestroika* era. Taken together with the trade agreement, both treaties have political and economic significance basing cooperation on concrete commitments. They show that both sides have the will and the capacity to bring collaboration to an unprecedented level.

Trade relations had already been enlarged with the Natural Gas Agreement (1984), which provided for imports of 120 billion cubic metres of Soviet gas in the next twenty-five years, the amount to be paid for it reaching $700 million per year beginning with 1993. An important source encouraging the increase in trade is the credits given by the Turkish Eximbank. Eximbank supplies Turkish contractors with investment credit to be used in projects in the CIS and gives purchaser credit to Russia (or other republics) to enable them to finance imports. Until the beginning of 1992, it had extended $300 million for exports of consumer goods, another $300 million for investments and $200 million for wheat exports.

Other Turkish banks interested in the radical increase of economic relations with Russia are the Garanti Bank, Interbank and Tekstilbank, which fund some of the credits extended or play a role in loans for financing exports. The former Soviet Tveruniversal Bank, one of the eight banks engaging in foreign trade, and a number of Turkish banks agreed to establish a joint bank to enable closer economic relations.

The new bilateral agreements and the financing of private as well as state banks injected a new dynamism into relations with Russia and created new opportunities for the Turkish entrepreneurs. Already successful in the construction of hotels, hospitals and business centres, Turkish firms have been invited to bid for larger projects. After several individual firms completed the building of housing complexes, tourist centres or health facilities, 'Mir Holding' was formed with the cooperation of four giant companies with exemplary reputations.[13]

A field with possibilities for the Russian firms is the enlargement of plants previously built by the Soviets in Turkey. They include iron and steel

(Iskenderun), aluminium (Seydisehir), an oil refinery (Aliağa), and hydrogen-peroxide factories. Joint investments are planned parallel to the development in trade volume. For instance, the 1,550-metre bridge over the Dardanelles will be realized jointly by Russian and Turkish concerns. Several Russian–Turkish firms have also been established for purposes of joint ventures in their respective territories or in third countries.

Turkism and Islam

The Soviet demise created a 'vacuum' in Central Asia and the Caucasus, where the new republics are experimenting with pluralism, nationalism, religion and the market economy. Turkey considers its present and future role in these areas as a duty and responsibility, as well as an opportunity and a matter of interest. In spite of economic and ideological competition from a number of centres, it is generally acknowledged that Turkey's cultural and historical affinities with the peoples of the region, its democratic and secular features, and its significance as a country with a more-developed economy and technology put it in a favourable position in relation to these lands. The Moslem Turkic republics, on their part, look on Turkey as a fairly advanced romantic model. This view was perhaps reflected in Uzbekistan's decision to hand over its foreign ministry building to Turkey to be used as its embassy.

Only a decade ago, no one could have imagined that Turkey would be so influential in such a vast area (see Figure 8.1). Modern Turkish reached the Chinese border, and the idea of a railway line linking Istanbul with Beijing via Ashkabad, Tashkent and Alma Ata fills all Turkic peoples with emotion. Series of articles on the Turkic world appear in the press,[14] and seminars in remote places invite businessmen to invest in Turkic lands. While 'ministers of Turkic-speaking nations' attend one conference after another, state and private organizations lead campaigns to collect money to aid the Turkic republics.

It is not a surprise that the Central-Asian republics and Azerbaijan sought recognition by Turkey which they felt would lead to international endorsement, and that Turkey was the first to recognize them. Turkey developed good relations with them, without damaging its links with Moscow. It is also natural that Turkey assumed the role of serving as a gateway through which aid, under 'Operation Provide Hope', was channelled to the East. As part of this role, Turkish airports were used in airlift operations, and the Turkish Red Crescent supplied food and medical aid. Further, the second-round of the follow-up meetings, a sequel to the Washington conference (1992) of fifty-four nations to aid the CIS, took place in the Turkish city of Antalya.

The quick and far-reaching *rapprochement* between Turkey and the Moslem Turkic republics might have worried some competing centres in the West as well as in the region. In spite of some feeble tendencies, mainly in unofficial circles, Turkey does not harbour pan-Turkic or pan-Islamic aspirations. When the Turkic peoples had agreed to participate in the CIS, originally founded by Russia, Ukraine and Belarus, their decision had then

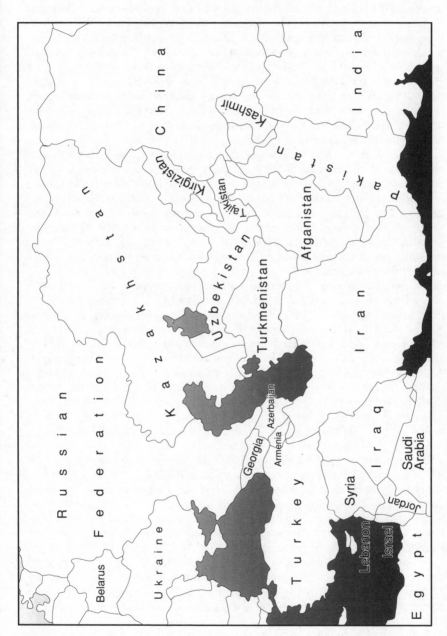

Figure 8.1 Turkey and the republics of the former Soviet Union

calmed Western fears that they would establish their own federation based on Turkic and/or Islamic identity.

It is true that if there is one centre of the Turkic world, this focal point is modern Turkey, and it may be safe to add that for the Turks, 'Turkism' weighs heavier than Islam. The 'Turkish model' is one of a secular, democratic and economically liberal state, which will probably influence the other republics much more than the Iranian, Saudi or even the Pakistani prototypes.[15] The example of Turkey seems at present to be more attractive to a great many Turkic intellectuals, some of whom nevertheless may resent, in future, the frequent references to Turkey as the 'older brother'. Such citations not only bring to mind earlier Russian usage of *starshey brat* (meaning the same), but there are Russian minorities in all these republics, principally in Kazakhstan.

Islam is also on the rise in those regions, presently more as a spiritual phenomenon rather than political. Secular, Sunni and Christian societies are, nevertheless, worried over the future impact of Islamic fundamentalism. It is granted that Islam may be on the rebound throughout the region, evidenced by the construction of mosques and the printing of Korans. But there is also a militant challenge to secular values, hostage-taking or the issuance of death-warrants. Herein may lie a point of convergence of outlook and interests between Ankara and some Western capitals in the so-called 'new world order'.

Iran, which upholds the view of Islamic *umma*, and therefore seems to believe that there should be no boundaries dividing the Moslem communities, sends religious leaders to all the Central-Asian republics and Azerbaijan. It also invites hundreds of young students to Kum, as part of its efforts to introduce fundamentalism. One may assert that Iran and Turkey always had to find the middle way to live side by side as neighbours. According to some commentators, with a lessening of the Russian influence in the Caucasus, a rivalry reminding one of the Ottoman–Persian competition before the nineteenth century, may be in the offing.[16] One may even add that there were differences during the reign of the Shah when both countries were members of the Western-sponsored Baghdad Pact and its successor, the Central Treaty Organization.

Turkey's attempts for a *modus vivendi* were frequently discouraged by Iranian efforts to export religious fundamentalism during the Khomaini era. On account of his overt activities in this respect, a former Iranian ambassador was left with no option but to leave Ankara. The trend changed with the Gulf Crisis, the Kurdish exodus from Iraq, and Iran's search for means to break its isolationism. Iran continues to scorn Turkey's secularism, but *realpolitik* demands better relations. The visit in mid-1991 of Iran's President Hashemi Rafsanjani opened a new chapter in relations often strained in the near past. An accord was even reached on a trans-Turkey natural-gas pipeline from Iran to Europe, later undermined by Turkish seizure of a Greek-Cypriot vessel carrying undeclared arms ostensibly to Iran.[17]

With or without such side strains, Iran seems disturbed by Turkey's secular and cultural influence. So are some other conservative Sunni governments which try to arrest the weight and pressure of Shi'ite Iran. The Moslem Turks of Central Asia are Sunnis, but the Azeri Turks, like the Iranians, are Shi'ites. The Azeris have correct relations with Iran, where millions of their kin live. Many of their leaders, however, have expressed a choice in favour of the 'Turkish model', which considers religion as a private matter for the individual.

A competition connected with Turkism and Islam is ranging around the choice of an alphabet to replace the Cyrillic letters. Iran and Saudi Arabia, which recommend a return to the old Arabic script, are offering free printing presses and other facilities. Turkey suggests the Latin alphabet which suits Turkish phonetics better and is easier to learn. Kazakhstan, with a large Russian minority, seems content with Cyrillic letters. Other Turkic peoples are more open to adopt the Latin script, used by some of them until the Russification campaign of the Stalin era.[18] Turkey showed a willingness to print any number of books the Turkic republics desired, as soon as they determined the draft of their new Latin alphabet.

Support for the Turkic republics

There is no doubt about Turkey's willingness to help the Turkic republics, in terms of utilizing its economic potential and transferring its experience in technology as well as assisting in the field of education. Various forms of support range from planning the establishment of banks to serve this area to a few thousand scholarships for young students, or from the setting up of barter companies to the repairing of historical monuments. The Turkic republics can use almost any form of assistance because they need almost everything, starting with simple bandages and hypodermic needles in the hospitals. Some Turkish analysts suggest that the short-term goal should be to create a transportation and communications system as well as small and medium-sized private enterprises to solve problems pertaining to basic utilities.[19] Others suggest sending retired Turkish diplomats, officers, teachers, academics, bankers, bureaucrats and other volunteers to meet the enormous manpower deficiency in many fields.[20] Although the independent republics have now opted for a market economy, their elites know very little or nothing about its theory or application.

Turkey's Eximbank and the European Bank for Reconstruction and Development (EBRD) are exploring possibilities of aid to the Turkish republics. Turkey has a share in the latter bank. A Turkish Central Asian Bank, with branches in the Turkic republics, is planned to serve the countries of this region.[21] A barrier preventing the building of workable commercial relations with these countries with considerable natural resources is the foreign-exchange bottleneck.

In spite of impracticalities and shortcomings, Turkey initiated a number of economic activities in all those republics. For instance, it was the first to recognize Azerbaijan's declaration of independence and to sponsor its membership in international organizations. Turkey also shipped supplies, at state and private levels, to alleviate the hardships of the people, and negotiated two giant pipeline projects to carry oil and natural gas as well as making investments in telecommunications and cotton factories. Azerbaijan has become home to an oil rush as it opened up its industry to the world for the first time since the 1920s. Baku had gradually slipped down the Soviet government's list of priorities after the Second World War as investment was diverted to Siberia. In charge of its own new oil now, Azerbaijan wants to reverse the trend. The Turkish firm 'Pet Holding' started explorations, while the American firm Bechtel is modernizing refineries. Relations with Armenia having worsened, one problem is how to transport its oil.

According to the agreements signed with Uzbekistan, which assigned Turkey the right to represent Tashkent's interests abroad, the priority areas of cooperation are the production and transportation of agricultural produce, building of light industrial complexes, the search for and extraction of minerals, the manufacture of textile goods, constructing infrastructure for tourism, cooperation in transport and communications and operating food industries.[22] Beating off competition from French, Japanese, Indian and Pakistani rivals, a Turkish firm (Teletaş) signed an agreement with Uzbekistan to develop communications technology. Direct flights began between the capitals of the two countries. Turkey sent the permanent under-secretary of its treasury to Tashkent to advise on the economy.

Turkmenistan specifically asked Turkish businessmen to set up joint companies to exploit the country's natural gas. A Turkish company (BMB), and its local counterpart, agreed on the construction of a natural-gas pipeline eventually to reach Europe via Turkey. Its annual flow capacity will be 15–20 billion cubic metres. Iran has also been trying to persuade the Turkmenian officials to pump their gas to an Iranian gulf terminal shutting Turkey out. The course of the pipeline was important because of transit royalties. Turkey was earning $300 million annually from the Iraqi oil pipelines before they were shut down during the Gulf Crisis. A Turkish firm (Konkur İnşaat) is going to build a tourist complex and a cultural palace in Turkmenistan.

When the Kazakh President N. Nazarbaev came to Turkey to brief the Turkish leaders on his and President Yeltsin's mission to help resolve the Nagorno-Karabagh dispute between Armenia and Azerbaijan, he used this opportunity for enlarged talks on bilateral ties. The two sides agreed to establish or improve waterway, rail and air links to facilitate trade. They established a joint consultation mechanism, while a leading Turkish tele-communications company (Teletaş) began producing electronics and other modern communications equipment in Kazakhstan.

Agreements with Kirgizistan cover almost every field including agriculture, industry, mining, construction, tourism, health, communications and transport. However, Kirgizistan requested urgent food and medical aid from Turkey, which agreed to open credit for the export of 500,000 tons of wheat.

Turkey is not the only country interested in the region. Iran and four former Soviet republics (Azerbaijan, Kazakhstan, Russia and Turkmenistan) formed in 1992 a Caspian Sea cooperation zone, to act independently of the Economic Cooperation Organization founded (1985) by Iran, Pakistan and Turkey. Iran agreed with Azerbaijan to cooperate in oil production and also with Kazakhstan on continuous transportation of goods between the Caspian Sea ports of the two littoral states. The Nakhichevan enclave of Azerbaijan and the eastern Azerbaijan region of Iran signed an economic and cultural agreement, according to which a market will be established on the Jolfa border gate where tradesmen will shop, and there will be an exchange of university students. The Iranian opposition accuses Teheran of increasingly turning to the former Soviet republics (and to China) to get nuclear weapons technology, a charge officially denied.

Among the other contenders, some of the 'lion's share of Azerbaijan's strategic potentials have already gone to high-technology American and French companies. Turkish businessmen, however, are returning with some contracts. A French state-owned firm (Société Nationale Elf Aquitaine) and Kazakhstan signed an agreement to explore oil in an area of 20,000 square kilometres. Turkmenistan opened a representative office in Tokyo.

It is obvious that Turkey cannot provide all the investment and technology requirements of the cash-strapped ailing republics. The Turks hope that some other countries will also help in 'investing in the future'. The United States understands the role which Turkey has selected for itself in the region; the Washington–Ankara axis is breaking out of the traditional parameters of the military sphere. Their new but yet undefined partnership is expected to encompass cooperation in assistance to the peoples of the Central-Asian republics. When Prime Minister Demirel paid a working visit to the United States (early 1992) meeting President Bush, he tried to put across an image of a reliable country sharing common values but also with an increased role in its own region.

While in the United States, Prime Minister Demirel received assurances from President Bush that part of the $24 billion Western aid package for the former Soviet Union would go to the Central-Asian republics. After his return from the United States, Demirel led a 144-person delegation to the Turkic republics, addressing several parliaments, opening Turkish embassies and signing barter-trade accords with all.[23] The Turkish government and the press made 'the plight of the Turks' a national cause.[24] Demirel answered the warm welcomes he received in the capitals of the Turkic republics in a variety of ways, including initiating soft loans to buy wheat and sugar, two scarce commodities in these countries.

In Tashkent Demirel signed eight protocols covering investments, training, road transport, banking, broadcasting and civil aviation. The credit he signed is worth $500 million, the largest Turkey so far accorded the young republics. He also signed nine protocols in Alma Ata on investments, cultural exchange, aviation, transportation, banking, broadcasting, exchange of personnel, encouragement of small and medium-scale industries and a grant of $200 million. Turkmenistan and Kirgizistan will each get $75 million. These facilities will finance Turkish exports and the services of the Turkish contractors. Under this scheme Turkish businessmen will export their products to the Central-Asian republics or will undertake projects there, turning over their claims to anyone of the Turkish banks contributing to the funding. The bank will pay the exporter and will collect the sum either from the Central-Asian importer or from the Eximbank, which has the backing of the Turkish Treasury. The state-owned Ziraat (agricultural) Bank is exploring the idea of a joint venture and plans to open branches in the capitals of the republics. It has already agreed to set up a joint venture with Agro-Industrial Bank, its counterpart in Tashkent which controls two-thirds of Uzbek banking activities.

Turkey submitted to the Central-Asian republics draft constitutions as well as schemes on establishing state apparatus. The start of Turkish television broadcasts to all the Turkic republics was moved up to coincide with Demirel's official visit. The Turkish government rented a satellite channel to make the broadcast possible, reaching about 150 million Turks from the Balkans to Central Asia. Turkish technicians have already built earth stations in the republics for reception. Most of the programmes carry subtitles in Latin script to familiarize the viewers with the characters. It is also hoped that with television broadcasts the differences in dialects will disappear in a short time. Turkey's premier also proposed periodic summits of the Turkic countries, the site alternating between Turkey and a leading city of the Turkic republics.

Some limits to the proposed new relationship should also be clear. As a regional power, Turkey has to conduct its own special brand of foreign policy relative to the area. After having passed through the Baghdad Pact experience, Turkey is reluctant to get bogged down in regional problems and be seen as a springboard for Western powers. Turkey, instead, is seeking the opportunity to develop relations in a mutually advantageous way, including the role it hopes to cut out for itself in the region. It is very important for Turkey to see that the favourable emotions of the Turkic peoples do not become disappointments.

Armenia and Azerbaijan

The Armenian–Azeri disputes not only make Turkey's position difficult but also threaten to turn the Caucasus into a highly inflammable spot in the already violent Middle East. The battle for the control of Nagorno-Karabagh Autonomous Oblast (NKAO)[25] (see Figure 8.2) intensified immediately after the withdrawal of Soviet troops. NKAO, a self-governing region within Azerbaijan, had a population of 168,000 in 1983, the majority of whom were Armenians. In violation of specific treaties regulating borders in the Caucasus but basing their actions on the fact that the majority of the NKAO people are their brethren, the Armenians attacked and occupied almost the whole of the disputed region. Moreover, they sought to link this enclave with Armenia by land through the strategic Lachin town, which also belongs to Azerbaijan. The Azeris report that armed Armenians have unleashed attacks on the autonomous Nakhichevan republic as well, which has about an eleven-kilometre common border with Turkey. Ankara further believes that, according to the treaties of Moscow (16 March 1921) and

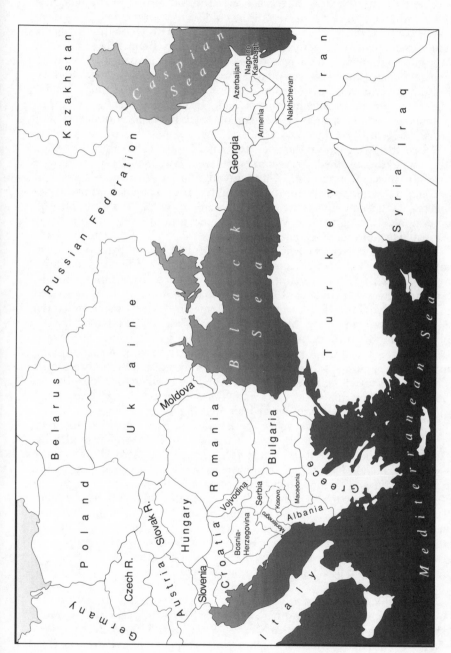

Figure 8.2 Turkey, the Black Sea region and eastern Europe

Kars (13 October 1921), Turkey should have a voice should there be an attempt to change the status of Nakhichevan. In any case, the Armenian attempts to alter borders may cause the eruption of one of the bloodiest ethnic problems since the demise of the cold war.

The conflict which began in 1988 led to the flight of Azeris from Armenia and Armenians from Azerbaijan. The Azeri papers frequently print maps and information about villages wiped out by armed Armenian bands.[26] Armenian newspapers carry similar reports. Although the Russian[27] and the Kazakh governments have tried to defuse the conflict several times, including mediation by Presidents Yeltsin and Nazarbayev, early negotiations foundered when two Azeri helicopters, one carrying negotiators, were shot down, allegedly by Armenian irregulars.

When the Armenian authorities announced (mid-1990) that they were 'disarming' the so-called 'Armenian National Army', some Russian analysts saw no cause for optimism. They argued that the Armenian army had become a 'permanent factor of instability' and 'attracted criminal elements'.[28] The announcement about disarming was a 'widely publicized deception'. Not only were very few of the arms turned in, but some Armenian groups were left entirely intact.

The Armenians, who benefit from a powerful lobby of the diaspora, seem to have stockpiled enough modern weapons to have military superiority over the Azeris. Their arms are reportedly acquired by raiding arsenals, bought from Soviet soldiers or received as part of 'foreign aid' that arrived in packages after the 1988 earthquake in Armenia.[29] There is a view that the Armenians are supported by the 'Christian West' and that they have a powerful lobby abroad, and this may be close to the truth. The Azeris believe that some of the Armenian militants have undergone special training in Lebanese camps and that they are subsequently assisted by mercenaries.[30] The Armenians, who ran over the NKAO and are pushing for a 'corridor' to link it with Armenia proper, seem to have planned to agree to future negotiations, with some strong cards in their hands.

Apart from Nagorno-Karabagh, Nakhichevan, which is an autonomous republic within Azerbaijan, has also become a target of Armenian attacks. While the bulk of the Azeri lands face the southwestern shores of the Caspian Sea, Nakhichevan, situated more to the west, has a common border with Turkey, and Armenian territory separates the two portions of the Republic of Azerbaijan. Although Nakhichevan's common border with Turkey is strikingly absent in some maps of published research,[31] it figures in all reliable sources, and a bridge as well as a railway line connect Turkish and Nakichevan territories. The latter's President G. Aliyev's appeal to Turkey to intervene in case Armenia attempts to alter the status of his autonomous republic demonstrates that Ankara is 'closer' to Nakhichevan than Baku.

Geographical contact with Nakhichevan made it easier for Turkish assistance in food, medicine and other necessities to reach Azeri lands. Demirel and Aliyev signed an agreement (early 1992) for a $100 million Turkish loan as well as for a provision for the construction of a bridge over the river Aras (Araks), air and railway links and measures to bolster investments. A

Nakhichevan–Turkish bank, the first one in the autonomous republic, has also been set up to encourage imports and exports.

Turkey's interest in Nakhichevan, however, goes beyond economic assistance. Turkey believes that, in accordance with the treaties of Moscow and Kars, it should have a say in any change which might occur in the enclave's status. The Soviet–Turkish Treaty, signed in Moscow (1921) and which determines the present border, describes Nakhichevan as an autonomous body under Azerbaijan, on condition that the latter does not relinquish this protection to a third state. Further, the Treaty of Kars, agreed upon seven months later, by Turkey, Armenia, Azerbaijan and Georgia, confirmed the borders and specifically stated that Nakhichevan was an 'autonomous area, defined by enclosure no. 3 appended to the agreement, and protected by Azerbaijan'.[32] Further, any Armenian–Nakhichevan armed clash brings the violence closer to Turkey's border and could also be interpreted as a sign of Armenian expansionism on a new broader scale.

In the recent past, groups of Armenian terrorists have assassinated some of Turkey's diplomats and attacked Turkish and other targets, causing death and bloodshed. It is not only the Yerevan government which has resorted to the use of force in the Caucasus, but sections of the Armenian disapora have persisted with violent methods. For instance, ASALA, an Armenian clandestine organization which had earlier murdered Turkish diplomats and attacked several non-Turkish targets, tried the nihilist method once again when it attempted to assassinate (9 December 1991) Turkey's ambassador in Budapest.

On the other hand, it is in the interest of Armenia, a land-locked country, to cultivate Turkey's friendship and utilize this route to the West. Yerevan indeed needs Turkey as a gateway to the world. Improved relations with Turkey offer Armenia easier access to European markets and the political advantage of ending its regional isolation. Yerevan's Syria-born nationalist leader Levon Ter-Petrosyan, a former dissident and a political prisoner, who won Armenia's first presidential election by a landslide, frequently has seemed to appreciate the strategic location of Turkey which potentially offers an essential lifeline.

Turkey offered the use of its Black Sea port of Trabzon to Armenia, as part of an effort to ease Yerevan's land-locked position. Ankara supported the initiative of a Turkish firm (Alarko), in partnership with Austrian (Rosh Credit) and American (HovSons) companies, to expand the Black Sea port to handle trade between Armenia and the West. Turkey chose to exhibit such goodwill although it has the capacity to encircle Armenia economically and militarily, in association with Azerbaijan. It also harbours concerns about efforts to present the independent Armenian state as a new 'Western enclave modelled on Israel's role' in a region full of potential conflicts.

The Turkic world, on the other hand, is horrified at the armed attacks of the Armenians, the plight of the Azeri refugees and the trampling of existing treaties. Irrespective of eye-witness accounts accompanied by grim photographs in the Turkish press, Ankara is aware that the fuel for hatred provided by the history of the Caucasian peoples may easily lead to a massive human tragedy. Therefore, it has tried to quell Caucasian flames, and has a broad policy agenda, involving maintenance of a sensitive balance in which both Armenia and Azerbaijan have permanent places.

Having ruled out military intervention, Turkey relies on diplomacy to such an extent that some writers described the government's *savoir-faire* as 'the peaceful siege of Armenia'.[33] However, the Armenian officials criticize Turkey for displaying aggressive tendencies towards them by conducting military exercises in eastern Anatolia. Marshal Y. Shaposhnikov, the Chief of the Armed Forces of the Commonwealth of Independent States, was one of the first to point out that these exercises were normal, having been held every year at the same place. Moreover, the military forces taking part were smaller than in previous years.

Since mid-May 1992 Armenia has also been a member of a defence union with Russia and four other Moslem republics, while Azerbijan is not. In case the conflict becomes a general war between the two countries and spills on to Armenian territory, not only will the ability of the Commonwealth of Independent States to mediate be greatly undermined, but arguably, Azerbaijan, or any other country allied with it, may find itself technically at war with Armenia and other signatories of the mutual assistance treaty, including the Moslem Central Asian republics.

Under the circumstances, Ankara has been utilizing its power of persuasion over the conflicting sides as well as all interested parties to convene a conference and create a collective will to end armed clashes. The Armenians, given their supply of arms do not want the issue to become internationalized. Turkey's response has been to uphold the principle of inviolability of frontiers, offer mediation, encourage others to do the same and bring the issue to international forums, such as the United Nations, the CSCE or the NACC.

Guiding the Baku representatives through these international waters, Ankara did not miss any opportunity to improve the chances of peace. It was Turkey that introduced both Armenia and Azerbaijan to the CSCE. The latter passed a resolution in favour of preserving the status of Nagorno-Karabagh. But as the experiences of Cambodia, Lebanon and the former Yugoslavia demonstrate, ceasefires are too easily broken, diplomacy has its own limitations and the CSCE does not have the power to apply sanctions. Consequently, the Yerevan government proceeded on its path and, in violation of CSCE principles, seized land by force. Turkey's application to the United Nations Security Council to send a fact-finding mission to the region and the decision underlining such a need are concrete developments.

The Turkish government finds itself in the middle of domestic pressure for a more effective policy *vis-à-vis* the operations of the Armenians, on the one hand, and the impartiality that it wants in order to retain its influence on both countries and on the international community in genuine efforts to halt bloodshed. Such a balanced official policy does not, however, prevent sections of the Turkish opposition and a part of the press blaming the government for lack of an adequately determined stance, indirectly encouraging the repetition of Armenian assaults. Thousands of fundamentalists took to the streets in Ankara and Istanbul to protest at the killing of the Azeris and radical 'Turkist' circles urged sending warplanes and paratroopers to help restore the legal status quo. Even the moderate opposition accused the government of being a mere spectator, a charge hardly legitimate. Some Azeri leaders have also publicly complained of Turkey's 'passivity'. The critics may have a point when they underline the difference between 'exhibiting strength short of using it' and 'illegitimate use of force'. While the Turkish leadership maintains a restrained approach and also calls on others to refrain from actions that would escalate the tension, its domestic critics assert that it has been unable to regulate and guide events.

The Black Sea Cooperation Scheme

While the eastern shore of Transcaucasia borders the Caspian Sea, its western coasts touch the Black Sea. It is imperative that the riparian states of the Black Sea move towards a new spirit of association. A retired Turkish ambassador was the first to suggest the idea of a 'Black Sea Cooperation Scheme' (BSCS).[34] The Turkish government welcomed the proposal and comments, national or foreign, generally described it as a 'historical recommendation'.[35] The subsequent Ankara, Bucharest, Sofia, Moscow and Istanbul meetings of the Black Sea countries show that there are so far nine participants (Turkey, Bulgaria, Romania, Moldova, Ukraine, Russia, Georgia, Armenia and Azerbaijan); Greece and Yugoslavia were to be invited as founding states. Although Greek papers called it 'the Turks' hallucination of a Black Sea community à la EC,' Athens, which clearly thinks otherwise, applied for membership. The fact that the remnants of the former Soviet Union and Yugoslavia are very much in flux may complicate the evolution of this project. It may not be clear in some instances which political authority will ultimately be responsible for the Black Sea coastal areas. A civil war is going on in Georgia, there is an armed conflict between Armenia and Azerbaijan, and the Tartars seek more voice in the Crimea. Considering the break up of Yugoslavia as well, the number of signatories will be, as a Turkish diplomat put it, 'eleven plus'. Hungary, Albania and, to a lesser extent, the Czech and Slovak Federal Republics have also expressed interest.

Turkey considers Ukraine to be a salient partner in the BSCS. That independent newcomer to the area is the second-most populous (51.4 m.) of the former Soviet republics. Generally believed to be strong in economic potential, Ukraine accounted for about 25 per cent of the Soviet GNP, produced some 21 per cent of all Soviet agricultural output (1989) and possessed a number of well-developed metallurgical and machine-building industries. It is still a vital repository of coal, and its ship-building industry may be an important source of future exports. But it is dependent on Russian fuel, and about 15 per cent of the Donbass coal basin is in Russian territory. Moreover, its labour productivity is low, work discipline is poor, and many factories lack modern equipment. Turkey considered Ukraine's declaration of independence as the immediate result of the irretrievable collapse of the former Soviet Union and its decision to establish its own armed forces as an internal matter of the country. Turkey also welcomed the compromise over the future Black Sea fleet and was warm toward the Ukranian proposal, made during President Leonid Kravchuk's visit to Ankara (May 1992), of demilitarizing the Black Sea. This point, as well as the new dimensions of naval transport, may bring to the fore the need to revise and up-date the Montreux Convention (1936) that governs the regime of the Turkish Straits.

Some Turkish writers also urged the government to give a hand to the Crimean Tartars, whose traditional homeland is now within Ukrainian borders. There are various Tartar groups the overwhelming majority of whom are Sunni Moslems and a small minority (near Kazan) Eastern Orthodox (Kryashen). Their language belongs to the Kipchak division of the Turkic branch of the Uralo-Altaic family. Over 60 per cent of voters in Tartarstan, the biggest of a score of mini-republics within the giant Russian Federation, said in a referendum (1992) that they wanted to turn it into a sovereign state. Those Tartars in the Crimea are Ukrainian citizens, that peninsula having been given as a gift by the former Soviet leader N.S. Khrushchev on the occasion of the 300th anniversary (1954) of Russian–Ukrainian ties. The Crimea is now the centre of electrifying political activity with public meetings, hunger strikes threatened and a variety of publications.[36] The Tartars describe Russian or Ukrainian meddling in the Crimea as a continuation of the war-time (1944) replacement policy. M.A. Kirikmoğlu, a well-known Crimean Tartar dissident and human-rights activist in the former Soviet Union, came to Turkey to seek Ankara's backing for his people to return to their land and also to obtain some aid to alleviate their desperate situation.

Responsive to such pleas, Turkey seeks above all to achieve concrete cooperation. Some initial declarations of the BSCS are decidedly vague and refer to general partnership as a contribution to the Helsinki process and to broad conditions to ensure capital flow, investment and industrial ventures. For Turkey the BSCS declarations mean putting its ties with the former Soviet republics on a multilateral basis. In addition, the overwhelming presence of non-Turkic republics among the signatories supports Turkish assurances that its ties to them are not discriminatory or pan-Turkic.

Since the Black Sea initiative was proposed by Turkey, it offered to provide the funds for the establishment of a coordinating unit in Istanbul as well as 40 per cent of its annual operating costs. Turkey also made preliminary plans for concrete projects, based on the private sector, the state contributing through legal adjustments to assist business. Turkey also supports the idea of a Black Sea Foreign Trade and Investment Bank[37], possibly with a Japanese contribution. The mayor of Ankara initiated the meetings of the mayors from the Black Sea towns to discuss common municipal problems.

Apart from the economic relations of the coastal states, the ecological programmes for the Black Sea and the Danube River are inextricably linked. The 1,776-mile-long Danube empties an area of 320,300 square miles into the Black Sea. The latter is being poisoned by the waters coming from the Danube and the Russian–Ukrainian interior that bring millions of tons of polluting material, including heavy-metal residues.[38] A number of symposia on ecological problems and economic prospects have already taken place, mainly in Turkey. It is envisaged that both the Black Sea and the Danube projects will eventually be funded through a new structure called the Global Environmental Facility (GEF). The Black Sea may recover ecologically if the two environmental projects work out as planned.

Eastern Europe and Turkey

When the extraordinary events of late 1989 transformed the regimes of Eastern Europe, beginning with the pouring of East Berliners into the other half of the city and eventually encompassing even die-hard Albania, Turkish diplomacy also became free from the confines of the cold war era. The contradictory sights of rejoicing on the Berlin Wall, on the one hand, and the sprawling of Nicolae Ceaşescu's body in a barracks yard, on the other, symbolized the co-existence of peaceful change and violence in Eastern Europe and the Balkans. When the annual summit of the seven members of the Warsaw Pact took place in the Soviet capital in mid-1990, only two presidents (Gorbachev and Jaruzelski) had attended the previous one. Even those two soon lost power, and the Warsaw Pact itself was disbanded.

When the whole of Eastern Europe sought, then, a new association and even integration with the world market, Turkey was one of the countries that approached the new regimes with cooperation in various fields. The scope of Turkey's pursuit included pledges of soft loans mainly to be used for buying food and other urgently needed supplies and investments and cooperation even in the military sphere. Ankara wants renewed, good relations with all the countries, from Poland in the north down to Albania in the south. Although some observers claim that an impressive growth in private businesses in Eastern Europe has taken place, offsetting a decline in industrial production, available data do not support such reports. The private sector is expanding, especially in services and trade, but its growth is moderate.

The Turkish leadership is also aware that distant events started casting shadows upon Balkan politics. The Balkans are important for Turkey, not only for strategic reflections and business opportunities but also for the fact that Turkish minorities are scattered all over the peninsula. Even apart from the Turks in Bulgaria, Western Thrace (Greece),[39] the former Yugoslavia, Romania and Moldova, there are more numerous non-Turkish Moslems such as the Bosnians and the majority of the Albanians whose religious affiliation now means much more to them than before (see Figure 8.2). Turkey believes that the agreements, signed at its own initiatives, and regulating military activity in the Balkans, are pioneering security- and confidence-building measures. Turkey signed military cooperation accords with Albania, Bulgaria and Romania some of which were attempts to help reorganize the armies of the former Iron Curtain countries but, at least, to extend ties both on a bilateral and multilateral basis in the Balkans. While Ankara developed closer relations with Romania and Albania, as well as Bosnia-Herzegovina, to counter, in the opinion of some commentators, Greece's new Balkan policy, it nevertheless reacted positively to a proposal on a tripartite dialogue among Bulgaria, Greece and Turkey. In the meantime, Turkey was the second country, after Romania, to recognize the independent republic of Moldova, where the Gagauz, a Christian Turkish minority, lives.

It was new developments in Bulgaria and Yugoslavia, however, that greatly modified Turkey's post-1989 relations with these two countries. Bilateral relations with Bulgaria improved parallel to the acceptance of the rights of the sizable Turkish minority there. The ties between the two states were on the verge of severance in 1989 following Todor Zhivkov's forced assimilation campaign (1984–9) on that minority.[40] Relations showed an upward surge in 1990, nevertheless, beginning with the radical changes in Bulgaria. Although all post-war Bulgarian leaders had offered unconditional support for Soviet policies wherever and whenever it was necessary, Zhivkov's relationship with the former authorities did not heed L.I. Brezhnev's advice on one crucial item, discrimination against the Turkish minority. Zhivkov's assimilation campaign was the most crucial development in a historical process that had reinforced the separateness of the Moslem Turks. The ethnic Turks, the largest of Bulgaria's minorities, were close to 1.5 million, making 10–15 per cent of the total 9 million population. The ethnic Turks were concentrated in the Kerjali region of the south-centre and the Razgrad-Shumen area in the northeast. Bulgaria had conducted several campaigns, including forcing the Turks to migrate (1989) to Turkey, to secure 'ethnic purification' of the country.

The rights of the ethnic Turks began to be restored after Zhivkov's fall. The process, however, was not smooth. The change of regime brought back more than half of the Turks who had sought asylum in the mother country. But their property had been expropriated, sold or lost. Only after several hunger strikes in the Turkish areas did the Bulgarian government approve an indemnity package. However, although the new Bulgarian constitution (1990), the fourth since the country's founding (1879), provides for a pluralistic society including freedom of speech, religion, conscience and the press, it does not refer to the existence of minorities. Bulgarian 'nationalists' tried to break up election rallies organized by the (predominately Turkish) Movement for Rights and Freedoms (MRF), now the third largest political force in the country. Not only the Bulgarian Socialist Party (BSP), the former communists, but also the Union of Democratic Forces (UDF) alienated the MRF (and the movement of Macedonians in Bulgaria). Although the hostility was allegedly on the grounds that no political party ought to be based on ethnic principles, it was probably more of an expression of the racism that had permeated the opposition as well. After all, Zhivkov's anti-Turkish bias had deep roots in the society.

The MRF, initially established to defend the rights of the Turkish minority, won twenty-three seats in the first democratically elected *Narodno Sobranie*, which sat in Veliki Turnovo, the medieval Bulgarian capital. But its leader, Ahmet Doğan, was prevented from taking his seat and delivering his address. The MRF also felt strongly about the teaching of the Turkish language in schools. Turkish had been banned during the assimilation campaign and even before. The new regime at first consented to Turkish lessons as a second language like English but not as a mother tongue. Ethnic Turkish children boycotted classes in 272 schools across the country to press demands for mandatory lessons in their own tongue.

The results of the 1991 elections, which gave neither the BSP, nor the UDF a majority and thereby increased the value of MRF support, strengthened the position of the Turkish minority. Only these three parties passed the 4 per cent threshold. The UDF, until then the major opposition coalitions, won (110 seats) by a narrow margin; the BSP came second (106 seats) and the MRF gained twenty-four seats. The last-mentioned received 7.55 per cent of the votes and raised its electoral support about 2 per cent as compared with the previous election and thus held the balance. With twenty-four parliamentary deputies, more than 1,000 local councillors, 650 village mayors and 20 district mayors, the MRF achieved its best results so far. All of the Turkish, and practically the whole Moslem community, mobilized behind it. Having established itself as the third largest party in the country, the MRF wants to become a non-ethnic political organization.

The fact that the other two parties have now to rely on the smaller Turkish party, and that some large centres like Kerjali have ethnic Turks as mayors, worries some Bulgarians, that is, the extreme right-wingers and some of the socialists. Nevertheless, the minority government formed by the UDF is only the first non-communist cabinet since 1944, and its minister of national defence is the first civilian one since 1934. Moreover, the Bulgarian parliament elected, for the first time, an ethnic Turk as a deputy speaker.

Turkey welcomes Bulgaria's efforts at political and economic reforms as progressive and steady. This development is sometimes marred by the resurgence of ethnocentric nationalism, among a vocal segment of society, directed against the Turks. But the election returns put the latter in a favourable position, while many Bulgarian politicians, who consider anti-Turkish sentiment as a blot on the country's record, are trying to erase it. Hence, Bulgarian prime minister Filip Dimitorv's definition of Bulgarian–Turkish relations as 'excellent'[41] is not much of an overstatement. The trade volume, which was down to $46 million at the end of 1990, stood at $216 million in early 1992. Dimitar Judjev, the first Bulgarian defence minister to visit Turkey since 1917, stated that the perception of a threat from Turkey was 'as dead as the Warsaw Pact'.[42] Moreover, Turkey and Bulgaria signed (6 May 1992) a friendship, cooperation and security treaty[43] which stipulated multidimensional collaboration and confidence-building measures. They pledged to discuss all security problems and solve them without resort to force. The treaty marks the third cooperation accord between the two countries since 1925.

While relations with Bulgaria took a turn for the better, those with Serbia went downhill. Before the Serbian armed attack on the Moslem Bosnians and the ensuing bloodshed, Turkish–Yugoslav relations hardly needed improvement. The two countries were allies in the Balkan Pact (1954), while commercial relations were satisfactory and promised development. Turkey even criticized Germany's decision to recognize the republics of Slovenia and Croatia, basing its judgement on the view that such a move would only hasten Yugoslavia's disintegration and was liable to increase strife. To acknowledge the independence of just two of the republics was also a selective and a poorly judged approach. Ankara, instead, recognized all the republics at a later time, following its own precedent after the dissolution of the Soviet Union.

Bosnia-Herzegovina and Macedonia have sizable Moslem and Turkish minorities. The six million Sunni Moslems of the former Yugoslavia constitute the largest Islamic population west of the Turkish city of Edirne in Eastern Thrace. But not all Yugoslav Moslems are Turks. There are also Slav and Albanian descendants of those who had embraced Islam. Whatever their ethnic background, they are now the third group after the Serbs and the Croats and express an identity distinct from both. Whether Turkish or not, many Yugoslav Moslems show an attachment to Turkey and even consider it a sanctuary in times of crisis. Some Bosnians and Macedonians are of Turkish origin and some are not, but the Moslems of Bosnia identify themselves with the Turks. There are also some Bosnians living in Turkey. Besides, Bosnia-Herzegovina, along with Macedonia, are Ankara's likeliest potential allies in the Balkans.[44] Turkey attributes great importance to the independence and the territorial integrity of Bosnia-Herzegovina, where Moslems constitute 43.7 per cent of the republic's total population and fears that the Serbs and the Croats may divide it.

As Turkey and the world witnessed bloodshed in the former Yugoslavia, a Moslem Bosnian delegation, consisting of high-level representatives of the Democratic Action Party (SDA), came to Ankara in 1992 to elaborate on what they called 'genocide' by the Serbs. They requested Turkey to activate the Council of Europe, the Conference on Security and Cooperation in Europe and the United Nations Security Council to take action. If such measures failed to stop the Serbs, the delegation suggested that Turkey intervene militarily or send them arms and financial aid. Turkey, chose to utilize only diplomacy and tried to interest other countries. The violence, in the meantime, led to a refugee flow to Turkey, where many Bosnian Moslems have relatives.

Turkey also recognised the Republic of Macedonia, where there is a Turkish minority. Greece is strongly against a Macedonian political entity because of its serious concerns over the possible impact of such an entity on its own Macedonian minority, whose existence it constantly denies.[45] Greece, which asserts that the name implies territorial claims on its own northern region, warned Turkey and Bulgaria that recognition of an independent Macedonia would harm stability in the Balkans and relations with Athens. Turkey simultaneously extended recognition to the four former Yugoslav republics, including Macedonia.

Turkey's relations with Romania should not be overlooked, since Ankara is willing to open credits to boost efforts to build a market economy there and is also interested in Moldova (Pridnestrovskaya Respublika) and its Christian Turkish minority. A new cooperation accord, the first since the 1989 revolution but reviving a pre-communist-era treaty (1933), provides the legal framework for relations with Romania. Turkish support can only partly help overcome the country's isolation on account of lack of capital. With respect to Moldova, Turkey recognized it and signed a bilateral accord to establish embassy-level diplomatic ties. There is now renewed Turkish interest in the Gagauz, or the Christianized Turks, living mostly in Moldova and the adjacent territories,[46] especially since they have declared their own republic (1990). Having their own aspirations,[47] the Gagauz requested Latin alphabet textbooks from Turkey, the right to attend Turkish universities, and financial help and assistance from Ankara to build an airfield near Chaderlung.

Conclusions

The end of the cold war and the radical changes in the former Soviet Union and Eastern Europe are two of the developments that will dominate the international scene for the remainder of the twentieth century. They will have massive consequences, both in terms of their handicaps in the short run and potential benefits in the long term. What are generally called 'reforms' have little chance of success if the economies remain dismal and if the new regimes are associated with a general drop in living standards, unbreachable inequality, mounting ethnic tensions and war. Although previously almost unlimited funds were appropriated for armaments, for subsidizing right-wing dictators and supporting anti-communist guerrillas, no large-scale aid is forthcoming from the West.

A general war, in which Turkey would also be involved, was unlikely even before 1989 or 1985, and Europe was the least likely place for a military conflict between the superpowers. Russia is now concerned with modernizing and strengthening its economy, which necessarily entails drastic military cuts. This new development makes Russia increasingly less dangerous for Turkey and creates the opportunity for that country to increase its presence and influence in Central Asia and the Caucasus. Although the Turkic-speaking Moslem peoples have emerged with a new individuality from the Adriatic to the Sea of China, thus putting the Ankara government in a different light in the eyes of the world, there are no racial or expansionist messages in Turkey's initiatives. Turkey rejects the concept of any change in borders, either in the form of enlargement or shrinkage.

The government and the people of Turkey feel a sense of responsibility, on the other hand, toward other Turkic peoples, irrespective of the regimes they may eventually choose. The Turks frequently refer to a moral obligation to respond to countries with which it has ties of blood, language and faith. It is only natural for Turkey to mobilize its own resources and also encourage some Western investments to be channelled into the Turkic republics, where the Turkish representatives preach the messages of democracy, secularism and the peaceful solution of disputes. Authoritarianism, militant Islam and ethnic tensions may, nevertheless, threaten havoc if the switch to a new economic model fails to produce signs of recovery. Feeling that it is racing against time, Turkey has launched a programme of diplomatic, economic and technical assistance. It has promised up to $1.2 million for the five Turkic republics, 10,000 scholarships, and has already helped them to join the CSCE and set up banks. It will now seek their inclusion in the International Monetary Fund and the General Agreement on Tariffs and Trade. It will try to put them on the developing countries' list of the OECD.

However, Ankara pursues balanced policies toward the Russian Federation, the other non-Turkic republics and Iran. It pays special attention to expanding ties with the western states of the CIS as well as with its ethnic cousins in the south. Within the framework of the new order, they all constantly invite Turkish businessmen to make investments in their countries.

The new order also faces violence between Armenia and Azerbajan as well as in Bosnia, both of which have significance for Turkey. Bulgaria, with which Turkey had a serious dispute over the treatment of its Turkish minority but which is now the first country in Eastern Europe to hold a second round of free elections since the change, is a comparatively peaceful island in the generally unstable Balkan peninsula. The Turkish-dominated Movement for Rights and Freedoms sticks firmly to the line of calmness in the face of provocation, and is thus a stabilizing factor in Bulgarian politics. Turkey and Bulgaria have also agreed to reduce and withdraw their troops along the border, and not to hold any major manoeuvres within fifteen kilometres of the same.

As far as the violent ethnic tensions are concerned, Turkey prefers to follow a cautious policy. It repeatedly emphasizes the importance of diplomatic efforts to bring about a lasting ceasefire between the warring parties and secure a negotiated peace. Playing down the alternative of adventurous courses, Turkey encourages the third parties to adopt an impartial approach to armed conflicts and makes efforts in various forums to restore peace.

Notes

1. Arvind Gupta, 'Similarities Between the Soviet Union's Present Efforts at Socio-Economic Reforms and the Czechoslovak Reforms of the Sixties,' *Strategic Analysis*, New Delhi, XXII, 2, January 1990, 1025–36.
2. Janusz Ziolkowski, 'The Roots, Branches and Blossoms of Solidarnośc,' *Spring in Winter: the 1989 Revolutions*, Gwyn Prins (ed.), Manchester, Manchester University Press, 1990, 40.
3. Radovan Vukadinović, 'External Actors and the Changes in Eastern Europe,' *Review of International Affairs*, Belgrade, XL, 950, 5 November 1989, 1–4.
4. For instance: Annie Kriegel in *Le Figaro* as quoted by M. Perlman in *Milliyet*, October 1991.
5. Interview with Professor Ilber Ortaylı in *Cumhuriyet*, 27 January 1992.
6. Ercan Vuralkan, 'What Kind of Foreign Policy?' *Turkish Daily News*, Ankara, 3 December 1991.
7. *Resmî Gazete*, Ankara, 23 Subat 1992. Azerbaijan was recognized earlier by the out-going Motherland Party government. The new elected government on the other hand, preferred a package recognition making no differentiation among the republics of the CIS.
8. V. Miheev, 'Yadernaya Knopka . . . Prava Cheloveke . . . Rynochnaya Stihiya,' *Izvestiya*, 23 December 1991; V. Litovkin, 'Armya gotova podchinitsa presiden-

tom: Presidenty ptayutsa dogovoritsa me jdu soboy,' *Izvestiya*, 31 December 1991.
9. N. Yelistratov, 'RSFSR bolshe nyet; Yest' Rossiya; Yadernaya derjava,' *Izvestiya*, 25 December 1991.
10. International Terrorism: the Nuclear Dimension,' *Terrorism*, 84, 1986, 351–78.
11. *Milliyet*, 9 January 1992.
12. Güntekin Köksal, the president of Pet Holding, in the *Turkish Daily News*, 7 November 1990.
13. Türkkaya Ataöv, 'Mir in Russia,' *Turkish Daily News*, 26 February 1992.
14. For instance: *Cumhuriyet*, 15–21 December 1991. Several government offices and private publishers brought out sizable volumes of bibliographies and handbooks on the Turkic peoples: T.C. Basbakanlik, Devlet Arşivleri Genel Müdürlüğü, *Türkiye Dişindaki Türkler Biblioyografyasi*, Vols I–II, Ankara, 1992; Türk Kültürünü Araştirma Enstitüsü, *Türk Dünyasi El Kitabi*, Vols I–III, Ankara, 1992; T.C., Kültür Bakanliği, *Karšilaštirmali Türk Lehçeleri Sözlüğü*, Ankara, 1991.
15. Artun Ünsal's interview with Professor Bernard Lewis in *Hürriyet*, 13 November 1991.
16. For instance: Stefanos Yerasimos, 'Bölgesel Güç Olma Zorunluluğu,' *Cumhuriyet*, 19 February 1992; *Al-Majalla*, 22–26 November 1991.
17. *Briefing*, Ankara, 881 (23 March 1992), 16.
18. Bill N. Şimşir, *Azerbaycan'da Türk Alfabesi: Tarihçe*, Ankara, Atatürk Kültür, Dil ve Tarih Yüksek Kurumu, 1991.
19. For instance: Muammer Tekeoğlu, 'Orta Asya ve Ekonomik Iliskiler,' *Milliyet*, 14 March 1992.
20. Ilter Turan, 'Türk Cumhuriyetlerine Gönüllü Uzmanlik,' *Cumhuriyet*, 20 February 1992.
21. *Para*, 10, 8–14 March 1992, 17–18.
22. For the text of the agreement: *Resmî Gazete*, 21 February 1992.
23. Demirel dropped Tajikistan from his itinerary while news came that President Nabiyev had fled Dushanbe.
24. For instance: Ilnur Çevik, 'Turks of Asia, a National Cause,' *Turkish Daily News*, 2 May 1992.
25. 'Dağlik Karabağ' in Turkish, the first word meaning 'mountainous' and the second 'the black orchard.'
26. For instance: *Seher*, Baku, 4 April 1992. An avalanche of refugees, running away or expelled, overloaded both countries' capacity to cope.
27. Earlier in January 1990, the Soviet army had stormed Baku, with tanks and troops, causing the death of hundreds of Azeris, thereby alienating Azerbaijan's public opinion from the Russians as well as the previous regime. For documents on that intervention see: *Chyorny Yanvar'-Baku-1990*, Baku, Azerneshr, 1990.
28. For instance: Marina Shakina, 'The End of the National Army?' *New Times*, Moscow, 38 1990, 24–5.
29. A similar earthquake in Central Asia only a few weeks later brought virtually no response from the West.
30. Ismet Gaibov and Azad Sharifov, *Armenian Terrorism*, Baku, Azerbaijan Publishing House, 1992.
31. Christopher J. Walker (ed.), *Armenia and Karabagh*, London, Minority Rights Publications, 1991, 6 and 60.
32. Kamuran Gürün, *The Armenian File*, London, K. Rustem and Bro., Weidenfeld and Nicolson, 1985, 265–6.

33. For instance: Yalçın Dogan, 'Ermenistan'a Barıs Kuşatması,' *Milliyet*, 14 March 1992.
34. Sükrü Elekdağ, 'Karadeniz Isbirliği ve Refah Bölgesi,,' *Cumhuriyet*, 20 February 1990.
35. For instance: Oktay Eksi in *Hürriyet*, 4 February 1992.
36. *Emel*, Ankara, 186 September–October 1991, 1–3.
37. Sükrü Elekdağ, 'Karadeniz Ekonomik İşbirliği,' *Cumhuriyet*, 7 November 1991; *Sükrü Elekdağ*, Karadeniz Bankasi,' *ibid.*, 8 November 1991.
38. Celâl Ertuğ, 'Karadeniz ve Ekolojik İşbirliği,' *Cumhuriyet*, 23 February 1992.
39. An important Turkish source: Baskin Oran, *Türk-Yunan Iliskilerinde Bati Trakya Sorunu*, 2. B., Ankara, Bilgi, 1991.
40. Türkkaya Ataöv, *The Inquisition of the 1980s: the Turks of Bulgaria*, Washington, DC, EAFORD, 1990.
41. *Turkish Daily News*, 4 May 1992.
42. Turkish papers, 13 March 1992.
43. It is called 'The Treaty of Friendship, Good-Neighborliness, Cooperation and Security', signed by the two prime ministers in Ankara.
44. See: Hadi Uluengin in *Hürriyet*, 21 April 1992.
45. Türkkaya Ataöv, 'The Ethnic Minorities in Greece,' *A.Ü. Siyassal Bilgiler Fakültesi Dergisi*, 463–4 December 1991, 15–33.
46. Harun Güngör and Mustafa Argunsah, *Gagauz Türkleri*, Ankara, Kültür Bakanliği, 1991; Abdülmecit Doğru and Ismail Kaynak, *Gagauz Türklerinin Sözlügü*, Ankara, Kültür Bakanlığı, 1991.
47. For Gagauz documents on their own aspirations in Moldova: *Materialy*, Kompat, 1990.

9
Islam in Turkey

Feride Acar

Introduction

Any discussion of Turkey's conceivable place in Europe includes, openly or between the lines, the question of how the religion of the overwhelming majority of Turkish citizens, Islam, would fit in with that position. The question is raised primarily because, in the last two decades, Islam — a little known and little-cared about foreign religion of distant peoples — has come to acquire a new proximity and new radical and violent connotations in the Western mind. This new proximity was symbolized in all major Western European countries by the presence of large numbers of Muslim Turkish migrant workers, identifiable through their unfamiliar language, dress and not always 'acceptable' social habits. The new radical and violent connotation of Islam, on the other hand, was promoted by such mass-media images as the anti-Westernism of Khomeini's Iran, the terrorism of Lebanon or of Libyan guerrillas, and the intolerance of the anti-Salman Rushdie campaign. Often such perceptions have led to a view of Islam and Muslim peoples as a relatively homogeneous group that share important social, cultural and political — if not economic — characteristics. They are assumed to stem from their religious identity.

It is not my objective here to discuss the falsity of such perceptions or to elaborate on the extent of the genuinely broad variations existing within the so-called 'Islamic world'. However, it should be pointed out that, even if for purposes of taxonomy, the label 'Islamic' was applied to the group of societies in which Turkey is demographically included, it would be necessary to place her in a category by herself. As a society where 99 per cent of the population are believers of Islam, and a rather radical version of state secularism has been institutionalized for the last seventy years with all its social, political, cultural and international implications, Turkey's case *sui generis* demands special attention.

The following discussion aims to shed some light on the role of Islam in contemporary Turkish society, through an analysis of the nature of the different Muslim population groups and their politics. The background aim of the exercise is to assess the impact of Islam on Turkey's integration with Europe.

State and religion in Turkey

Some trends in a strained relationship

As distinct from other Muslim political systems, the presence of a strong state legitimized primarily on non-religious, social and political grounds has been a critical factor colouring the heritage of the modern Turkish state (see for example, Mardin, 1983, Toprak, 1988; Sunar and Toprak, 1983; Kazancıgil, 1991).

In different periods and circumstances in Ottoman–Turkish history, many diverse groups of elites have been known to share the common attitude of placing the state above religion. The otherwise quite varied ideologies of anti-clericalism, statist-reformism, 'Jacobin-Kemalism', secular-positivism, Westernism or leftism purported by the various segments of ruling intelligencia have all prioritized the state over religion. Consequently, the Ottoman–Turkish experience has historically demonstrated a noticable inclination away from the ideal of a society organized exclusively on religious principles and run by a purely theological state. Although the Sultan-Caliph was, in name, both political and spiritual leader of his subjects, his religious leadership was always overshadowed by his political and military identity.

The radical secularism of the reforms made after the declaration of the Republic, formally separating religious and state affairs, have appeared against this background. They reinforced these long-existing tendencies in consequence of both the ideological preferences and the pragmatic, political considerations of the Kemalist elite at the time.

The vigour of prioritizing state over religion has somewhat subsided over the years (its peak being the years of single-party domination in the 1930s and 1940s). But occasional 'outbursts of secularism' by military and civilian elites against what were commonly referred to as 'reactionary' forces in society have taken place throughout the post-1950 multiparty era. In other words, throughout history so long as the social 'centre' controlled the state and religion was relegated to the 'periphery' (Mardin, 1973; Heper, 1980), despite some concessions and compromises, the backbone of the traditional (im)balance between state and religion was maintained.

Obviously, this was not achieved by repression or state coercion alone. The intricate relationships between the economy, the political institutions, the education system, the mass media and the state bureaucracy functioned to support this structure for some time. It is for this reason that the seemingly sudden appearance of Islamist movements and cadres in the central political arena, and in the decision-making and controlling positions of the state in the Turkey of the 1970s and 1980s attracted attention and caused apprehension. In the international atmosphere of post-Khomeini-Iran, this sometimes led to exaggerated fears in the popular media.

In fact, so far as Islamist forces were concerned, these were indeed decades exhibiting clear signs of Islamist ascendance. In much of the 1980s Islamic revivalism was the most active social and political movement in Turkey. Many indications of this rising tide could be discerned in society. Since the 1970s Islamists had started to develop an increasingly more observable presence in intellectual and political life. There was the establishment of political parties such as, first, the short-lived National Order Party (NOP) and later, the National Salvation Party (NSP) — overtly espousing Islamist views, despite existing constitutional and legal limitations. The opening of large numbers of Imam Hatip Schools throughout the country (Akşit, 1991) was another obvious sign of such development.[1]

In the ensuing decade, Islamist literature gained a larger share of the reader's market than ever before in Turkey. Islamists, easily recognizable by dress, style of life etc, emerged in unprecedented numbers among those urban, highly educated, professional or bureaucratic groups and politicians that traditionally made up the 'centre' of Turkish society. Islamist demands came to be expressed in overt activism of various sorts: the demonstrations and sit-ins of Islamist young women in the universities on the head-scarf issue; mass-media supported campaigns for segregated public transportation; street demonstrations against constitutional court decisions and state actions; and incidents of terrorism. Practices such as the establishment of no-interest banks and financial institutions were legalized and state supported, while educational policies such as establishing obligatory religious education in public schools or spreading Koran courses to the countryside were put into action.

Transition to the multi-party sytem in 1946 and the forceful emergence of the Democrat Party (DP) on the scene of Turkish politics from the 1950s are often mentioned in association with the early, albeit limited, movement of Islamist forces into the 'centre'. But the social and political transformations of the 1970s and 1980s largely illustrated what appeared to be an unprecedented advent of Islamists in the secular republic.

International developments, such as the Islamic Revolution in Iran, parallel and/or resulting Islamization efforts in some Arab countries — Afghanistan and Pakistan — and the overall climate of the glorification of Islam no doubt facilitated this advent. Specific political events within Turkey were also partly responsible for the rise of Islamist movements in the 1980s. Among these were the experiences of the violence-ridden late 1970s, when extremist youth groups of leftist and rightist views engaged in active civil-war-like combat, thereby creating a strong societal demand for peace. Also important was the 12 September 1980 *coup d'état*, which put into action a series of policies that, in effect, overstepped the pragmatic intentions of the military regime and evolved into tolerant and concessional state attitudes towards the Islamists (Şaylan, 1987).

Structural explanations also suggest that, in Turkey, the rise of Islamists in contemporary times is a gradual process which has benefited from the very facilities provided by the secularizing and democratizing reforms of the polity, the structural transformation of the economy and the cultural void created in the process in earlier eras (Mardin, 1989a; Sayarı, 1979). The Islamist groups' acquisition of legitimacy and their incorporation into the ranks of the elite by the late 1970s and 1980s are thus related to their ability to re-introduce Islam as an alternative ideology. As a corollary of this line of analysis, Islamist revivalist developments may be perceived as indications of the forces of the 'periphery' emerging in the 'centre', and thus as signs of consolidation of pluralist democracy. It is this last line of argument that perhaps deserves special attention with reference to the latter part of the 1980s.

Since the mid-1980s some indications of a significant change in the nature of the relationship between religion and state can be discerned in Turkish society (Sunar and Sayarı, 1986). In other words, the direction of the main axis of interaction between Islamists and secular forces has begun to shift from open antagonism and confrontation to toleration. This change is primarily exemplified in the secular camps' discourse on Islamists. At present, the conventional conception of Islam and secularism as polar opposites, incompatible with one another, shows signs of giving way to the alternative conception of coexistence of the two ideologies and their supporters in the institutional framework of a pluralist democracy and/or civil society.

Such a shift in the attitudes and discourse of the secular groups reflects the change in the nature of the basic debate in post-1980s Turkish society. Currently, the fundamental debate is on the question of the 'consolidation of pluralist democracy/civil society' rather than on any one specific dimension as independence, progress, development, equality, internal peace etc. In the past, the fundamental axis on which society's choice was exercised had been one or the other of these values. This often reflected a prioritizing attitude in favour of the arguments of the 'centre', at the expense of the alternative values supported by 'peripheral' groups. Since the mid-1980s the central issue on the agenda of Turkish politics has increasingly become the consolidation of pluralist democracy/civil society; political discourse, in general, has reflected this. This is, by definition, an inclusionary discourse developed around an issue of method rather than an exclusionary one of specific content as nationalism, radical secularism, progressivism or the other popular 'isms' of earlier eras had been.

Initially, the so-called 'civil society advocates' emerged among the intellectual elite of academics and journalists basically opposing the militaristic state of the early 1980s. Later, however, such discourse spread to wider segments of society. Today, it would not be inaccurate to state that a popularized version has become the ascending political ideology, shared alike by the leadership of mass political parties on the left and right, as well as by those subscribing to a wide array of 'new' social movements such as environmentalism, feminism, peace and ethnic identity. This transformation was obviously also influenced by the global political changes of the late 1980s.

In the contemporary scene some Islamists also exhibit signs of joining this bandwagon. The concentration of debates in the Islamist press on issues of pluralism and Islam and the affinity of some Islamist publications to the language and terminology of liberal democracy bear witness to this fact (Acar, 1991a; Güneş-Ayata, 1991).

However, the extent of this apparent 'sharing of concerns' should not be blown out of proportion. The creation and use of a more inclusionary ideological framework in the exercise of politics in contemporary Turkey is still primarily confined to the world-view and political discourse of the secular groups. In the recent past, notions and principles of pluralist democracy/civil society have acquired increasing popularity and found expression in such socially powerful and legitimizing agents within the secular bloc as political party programmes, leader outlooks[2] and popular media sources.

In the Islamist camp, despite the above-mentioned tendency of some circles to join the bandwagon, as far as the more established groups with large support bases are concerned, such overt liberalization often appears to be tactical, marginal and/or sporadic. The election-time propaganda appeals of the Welfare Party (WP)[3] and the ideas of a few Muslim intellectuals, whose communication is, by definition, more directed to secular audiences than Islamists, appear to reflect loyalty to pluralist principles or commitment to strengthening civil society institutions. Yet, in the publications of Islamic orders (*tarikats*), and other religious groups, distinct signs of a changing outlook or discourse seriously purporting pluralist democracy/ civil society are still difficult to find (Ayata, 1991; Güneş-Ayata, 1991; Acar, 1991a).

To the extent that these publications reflect the intracommunal communication of the Islamists, relative absence of such liberalization in these circles is significant. The Islamic orders or quasi orders continue to constitute the backbone of the Islamist movement in Turkey with respect to funding capacity, centralized organization, large recruitment base and political power potential. Therefore, the extent of their reluctance to identify with the ascending discourse of pluralist democracy/civil society defines them as authoritarian, patriarchal loci of opposition. As such, they have been identified as constituting a fertile and receptive ground for undemocratic politics and totalitarian rule (Güneş-Ayata, 1991).

The development of a pluralist, democratic consciousness — the rise of an inclusionary ideology of peaceful coexistence of different groups — is a positive sign of social and political development in the scale of contemporary world values. The position of Islamists and the relationship between them and others on this dimension is thus a critical aspect of Turkey's chances of integration with Europe and Europe's evaluation of the identity of contemporary Turkey. Thus in order to shed light on present and future political dynamics, within Turkey and between Europe and Turkey, analysis of the historical and structural forces related to the nature of Islam and Islamist groups in Turkish society is needed. The nature and composition of the Islamist groups in society, the changes that can be discerned in their world-views and/or relationships with others over time, as well as the differences and similarities that exist among them, need therefore to be reviewed.

Islam in contemporary Turkish society

Nominal Muslims and the pious majority

As in other societies, but perhaps more so in Turkey, the Islamic contingent is rarely the monolithic entity it is sometimes made to appear. Not only is the 'so-called 99 per cent' Muslim population of the country divided between Sunni and Alevi sects[4] but, sociologically and politically, an even more significant line of division separates the ordinary nominal and/or devout Muslim majority (not to mention differences among them) from a minority mobilized for the Islamist cause.

An extensive discussion of the specific historical factors explaining this phenomenon largely falls beyond the scope of this chapter. Suffice it to say that the essentially non-theological character of the traditions inherited from the Ottoman Empire, the absence of a colonized past thereby depriving Turkish Islam of the opportunity for developing into a potent protest ideology or linking itself to the coat-tails of rising nationalism (as it did in some Arab societies) lie behind the present picture.

With the establishment of the Turkish Republic, the cultural dichotomy of conservative Islamic communitarian values versus the progressivist Westernizing secular world-view (also partly inherited from the Ottoman past, but much legitimized and reinforced by the new regime) has come to be established in Turkey. Thus, on the surface, religious conservatism and secular nationalism have emerged as polar extremes.

The latter cultural ethos promoted by the elite of the Republic emphasized nationhood, rationality and science, modernization and secularism of a rather radical sort. In fact, Republican reforms in Turkey aimed at making what is often referred to as 'separation of state and religion'. More accurately, this could be called 'control of religion by the state' in affairs pertaining to the public sphere. Thus, Republican reforms of secularization attempted to eradicate religious influence from political, legal, educational and social spheres through a series of radical steps such as the abolition of the Caliphate, the disestablishment of Islamic law courts, the unification of all educational institutions under secular state control, and the declaration of all Sufi orders and religious fraternaties to be illegal (Lewis, 1968).

However, Republican ideology, despite the radical break it achieved from the previously dominant values and institutions of the Ottoman legacy, did on another plane share more commonalities with it than first meets the eye. This new world-view and its political expression also did not promote individualism and individual rights vis-à-vis the group, an orientation that only since the mid-1980s has come to be overtly promoted and popularly supported in Turkey. On the contrary, it emphasized communitarianism, but substituting 'nation' for the 'community of believers' as the object of unconditional allegiance and loyalty. This has meant that for many Islam was effectively replaced by an alternative communitarian ideology of nationalism–patriotism as a basis of social organization and political culture. It also meant that the legacy of authoritarian tradition from the Ottoman past was further reinforced by part of the nationalist ethos.

At the same time, another part of this same ideology introduced, in society, the seeds of democracy by publicly promoting democratic institutions (Özbudun, 1988) and the secular notion of the sovereignity of the people.

Second, the success of the secularizing reforms in the early years of the Republic effectively set in motion a process that has made religion, for many in contemporary Turkish society, a private matter concerning only the conscience of the individual. Republican secularism, by concentrating almost exclusively on the question of liberating the affairs of the state from religion's influence, in effect relegated Islam to the private sphere, an area with which it basically did not interfere. Thus, the new state's social policies did not take on an aggressive mission of neutralizing Islam at the individual level.[5] A personalized, individualized and rather peculiarly secularized Islam was created for the consumption of the citizens of the Republic in the privacy of their homes.

As a result, for Turkish people religion came to represent an array of beliefs and practices that ranges from the almost nominal subscription of the Westernized urban elite (whose practice of Islam is more or less confined to exchange of social niceties in the mosque-yard during a funeral) to the fasting, praying, Hadj-going, deep personal piousness of the masses. While the feasibility and/or validity of such Turkish Islam may be debatable on the ecclesiastical front, its sociological reality is undeniable as exemplified in the rather humourous but highly expressive utterance 'Thank God we are secular' (Tapper and Tapper, 1987).

For the majority of Turkish people who may exhibit different degrees of piousness, Islam today is far from being an effective regulator of social, political or economic life. As one observer of the Turkish scene has put it, 'two generations of Turks have grown up who find no difficulty in being simultaneously citizens of a secular republic and Muslims in varying degrees of devoutness' (Lewis, 1988: 267). Any analysis of the role of Islam in Turkish society at the present or in the future needs to attribute significance to this sociological fact.

Political parties, Sufi orders and other Islamists: the activist minority

A different side of the picture created by the relegation of Islam to the private sphere is expressed in the view 'religion however, survived in the family and the small community life not only as the culture of the people but taking (eventually) the form of a diffuse ideology that reflected dissatisfaction with the elite values and institutions imported from the West' (Ayata, forthcoming). Today, those who are mobilized by this type of ideology or world-view, and who aspire to shape personal, social and political life according to the dictates of Islam, may be termed the Islamist contingent in Turkish society.

Analysts indicate that since the 1950s Islamist appeals have found greatest expression and support within the ranks of the lower- and middle-class 'bazaar groups' (Mardin, 1989b; Saribay, 1985a) in small towns or provincial cities in Turkey. However, it has also been argued that the rising tide of Islamism in the 1970s and 1980s was based on a change in the traditional social-class bases of Islamist forces. The support of 'the nascent moyen bourgeoisie' has been pointed out as a major socio-economic factor that largely lay behind such development. A product of the national market developed after the 1950s, this group of merchants, businessmen and industrialists of medium-size operations in the labour-intensive sectors is concentrated in the small-industry zones of all the Turkish cities. It is argued that they have combined in their world-outlook the piety of the small-town traditional 'bazaar' community and the more nationally defined attitudes of a modern bourgeoisie resulting from their integration with the market (Ayata, forthcoming).

This economic location of the Islamist forces, and the active role they have played in the political life of the 1970s, has also paved the way for the emergence of, in the following years, some Islamists within the ranks of the bourgeoisie. They are privileged with regard to access to state-distributed resources and credit through their Islamic connections among the increasing number of bureaucrats and government officials. The Islamist contingent has benefited from state patronage and has taken part in joint investments with international Islamic capital. Observers have pointed out that a good part of the rising Islamist movement in the 1980s was financially backed by this segment of the Islamist population (Ayata, forthcoming; Ahmad, 1991; Yeşilada, 1988).

Thus, in the last two decades, a change can be traced from the closed, small-community, traditional, homogeneous sociological base to a noticably more open, national-scale, modern and heterogenous base of Islamist forces in Turkish society. Such change has meant that today, while members of the Islamist contingent in Turkey share a basic commitment to elevate Islam to the position of being the fundamental political and social regulator in society, serious fragmentation exists among them. Such fragmentation has several axes that at times, crosscut, and at other times, overlap with one another.

With regard to their organizational bases, Islamist groups can be categorized as Islamist political parties (National Salvation Party (NSP) of the 1970s and the Welfare Party (WP) of 1980s); traditional and neo-traditional Sufi orders (tarikats) or quasi-orders (the most important of which are the Nakşibendi, the Kadiri, the Rufai, the Süleymanci, the Nurcu); and other groups. Significant variations in tradition, outlook and style exist among and within each one of these types of Islamist organizations. Islamists in different political parties, followers of different orders, or members of various radical Islamist groups often conflict or compete with one another on matters of ideology, strategy and tactics. The contents of the tremendous number of publications they have been issuing indicate both the severity of the competition going on within the Islamist contingent and the active struggle they are engaged in with the secular world. (Çakır, 1990; Güneş-Ayata, 1991; Acar, 1991a; Ayata 1991; Meeker, 1991) Among the topics of disagreement, perceptions of and relations with the West are central. While all are overtly anti-Western, differences exist between groups in the intensity and nature of their opposition to and repudiation of the West.

Above and beyond organizational and intra-organizational divisions, the Islamist contingent is divided on the basis of ideology. Cultural versus political Islam (Göle, 1991) define alternative paradigms neither of which is internally homogenous. In this sense, while party Islam is obviously political and activist, by the very fact of being systemic it is less radical than the Islamist ideology purported by some of the other organizations or intellectuals. In fact, Islamist criticism and ideological appeal generating from the annals of the Welfare Party fall within an essentially modernist and systemic line. This is despite the party's rhetorical opposition to Turkey's alliance with the West and her affinity with things Western — ranging from interest-based banking to membership in the EC to feminism. Accordingly, the WP, trying to increase its share of votes in the 1991 election campaign, adopted a propaganda platform in which worsening income distribution, corruption in government and general moral decline in society were especially stressed. These are not issues that exclusively appeal to religious voters.

In Turkey, major loci of organized Islamist groups are the Sufi orders. While information on the numbers involved in different orders or their combined total are not possible to obtain, their significance as very powerful pressure groups in society is well-known. Much of Sufi Islam in Turkey is also predominantly political.

The dominant features of traditionalist or neo-traditionalist Sufi Islam, (Sheppard, 1987), as it is most visibly represented by the Nakşibendi in Turkey, are emphases on ascetism, respect for the hierarchical structure of the order, loyalty to the sheikh, radical rejection of Western values and culture, and strict adherence to an all-encompassing, detailed Islamic behaviour code. (Güneş-Ayata 1991; Acar, 1991a; Ayata, 1991) The Nakşibendi have conventionally engaged in a strategy of trying to conquer the state apparatus through penetration and have, in fact, often been successful in this (Mardin, 1991). In the Ottoman Empire they did not develop a tradition of 'questioning the legitimacy or the integrity of the Ottoman Sultanic position' (Mardin, 1991:134) or opposing the existing state[6] but, rather, a strategy of conquering the state via infiltration to use it for Islamic ends has been their choice. Consequently, they have concentrated a good part of their efforts, despite the essential character of Sufism, on raising proper cadres who would gain and use power for the elevation of Islamic principles in society.

Such a strategy is also-reflected in the current behaviour of the Nakşibendi in Turkey. The 'this-worldliness' of the Nakşibendi has been critical in securing the order's power position in politics. The flexibility the order has shown in matters such as setting its agenda according to the successes and failures of the secular regime in Turkey (Mardin, 1991), and its making selective use of issues and arguments on the basis of the sociological realities and experiences of Turkish society (Acar, 1991a) reflect the highly adaptive and political nature of the order's identity.

While leaders of the Nakşibendi order have always been in direct touch with politics in Turkey, since the 1980s they have increasingly provided electoral support for several political parties and/or personally engaged in efforts to establish their own political parties. The affiliation of Mr Erbakan, leader of all three of the Islamist political parties (NOP, NSP and WP) with the sheiks of the most prominent branch of the Nakşibendi order and the political bargaining that had secured for him, at critical points, the endorsement of the order's leader is common knowledge (Çakir, 1990; 36–9). By the same token, the support provided by the Nakşibendi order to the Motherland Party (MP) at its inception, and during the post-1980 interim period of Mr Erbakan and company's forced absence from the political scene, is also well known.

Thus, the largest Sufi order in Turkey, the Nakşibendi, has not only been active politically but has, at different times, also overlapped with one or another political party, securing for itself a distinct space and bases of legitimation in the national political arena. In the recent past, such overlapping of the Nakşibendi order and political parties has taken place through the order establishing and/or supporting Islamist political parties and/or constituting prominent Islamist wings in the secular political parties of the right in Turkey.

Similar phenomena can also be observed in the case of the connection between the Democrat Party (DP), the Justice Party (JP), the True Path Party (TPP) line and the followers of the Nur movement.

The Nurcu, a neo-traditionalist Islamist movement of the Republican era, with roots in the Nakşibendi tradition, have been known to stress 'belief' more than proper conduct. Dwelling on the need for strengthening belief among Muslims in Turkey, followers of the Nur movement aim to create a conservative, non-Western, non-secular, Islam-shaped moral order simultaneously with an advanced, science and technology-based material order. Observers have indicated that in the Nurcu world outlook science and religion, scientific investigation and being a devout Muslim are so closely integrated that the former are viewed as divinely ordained activities (Mardin, 1982; Mardin, 1989b).

Political reflections of this world outlook have been an association of the Nurcu with, first, the Democrat Party (DP), the original parliamentary representative of the commercial, agricultural and professional new groups of the 'periphery' in Turkish politics in the 1950s. It later became associated with its political successors, the Justice Party (JP) and the True Path Party (TPP). All of these parties have opposed the bureaucratic/military tradition of the 'centre' and have been responsible for widespread development of party patronage and clientelistic relations in society (Özbudun, 1981; Sayarı, 1975; Sunar and Sayari, 1986). This tradition in Turkish politics has often articulated a discourse based on a perception of being victimized by the 'centre'. As champions of populist appeals, they have voiced the call for the restoration of 'national will', which they often conceived in terms of a simplified majority democracy. Opposition to 'state will' or 'bureaucratic will' has been their basic rhetoric (see, for example Karpat, 1959; Özbudun, 1987; Eroğul, 1970; Saribay, 1991; Acar 1991b; Ahmad, 1992)

The organized support of such religious groups as the Nurcu community has acted as both a supplier of ideology at the intellectual level and a mobilizer of 'bloc voting' at the electoral level for these political parties at different times. In fact, at specific periods in the recent past, the relationship between the Nurcu groups and these parties has become observably closer. One such instance is in the post-1983 period, when the TPP went through difficult times on account of its inability to compete effectively with the then new Motherland Party (MP), which was also partially dependent on the support of the rival Nakşibendi order. Reliance on the support and mobilization potential of the Nurcu community at that point was obvious in the close relationship the party's leadership then enjoyed with this Islamist community (Acar, 1991b).

Such association however, should be evaluated in proper pespective. In the 1980s, the centre–right parties developed close associations with different Islamist groups. Yet, this proximity has not reached the point of a successful takeover of these parties' world outlook, leadership or organization exclusively by the Islamists. These political parties, despite short-term and basically tactical fluctuations, remained 'catch — all' parties within whose ranks and leaderships the Islamist contingent was represented sometimes as a wing, and at other times, in blended fashion. In the 1980s, unlike earlier eras, such representation took the form of direct representation of the Islamist groups in the various levels of party organization rather than being an indirect relationship, via conventional pressure group/political party interaction (Ayata, forthcoming). This may have accounted for the more vocal expressions of, and the increased legitimacy accorded to, the Islamists' views and demands in society. But such direct participation of Islamist groups in national politics against and alongside secular groups, often within the structure of the same party, has also contributed to the elaboration of the already present heterogeneity of Turkish Islam. In other words, the theological, philosophical and ritualistic fragmentation that existed within the Islamist contingent in Turkey was further elaborated by the superimposition on it of divisions along political party lines developed in the competitive politics of a parliamentary democracy.

The theory of pluralist democracy argues that crosscutting religious and political affiliations produce 'strange bed fellows' who negotiate, bargain and/or cooperate with one another. In the process, they moved away from non-compromising, extremist stands to mutually tolerant attitudes and moderation. The dynamics of the relationship between some religious orders and centre–right political parties in the recent history of Turkish politics often indicate a partial confirmation of this argument. While the Islamist rhetoric and ritual of the groups that take part in the arena of competetive politics remain strong, such behaviour and language gradually becomes part of a routine political message and looses its religious connotation.

For instance, attendance at the 'cuma' prayer in a mosque or even fullfilling the Hadj obligation — if one's socio-economic status is suitable — often function as symbols of belonging to a political community in much the same manner as carrying party flags, banners or other insignia of ordinary political movements. In this context, the WP leaders' habitual call for a 'just order' to be established in Turkey, or representatives of the religious wings of MP or TPP demanding the strengthening of 'morality' and criticizing 'materialism' in society are, more often than not, code words for reiterating party and movement identification and re-establishing ingroup–outgroup boundaries. By the same token, women wearing the headscarf and a long loose coat often denote membership in a subculture and a political community, the relative strength of which in society is demonstrable by their numbers.

In fact, the centrality of the 'headscarf dispute' on the political agenda, and the processes that lie behind it, are indicative of the political rather than spiritual nature of the issue. The Islamist groups campaigned for women university students and public employees to be allowed to wear 'Islamic dress' while they attended higher-education institutions (or worked in public offices), a practice the Constitutional Court has ruled unconstitutional in the secular state. The campaign was adopted largely owing to the fact that Islamists' claims here were expected to receive — as indeed they did — wider support in different parts of society. On the one hand, the Islamist position on women's role and dress could be presented in such a manner that it is difficult to separate it from the merely traditional stand on these matters. Islamists' values regarding women are often indistinguishable from the dominant patriarchal, male-chauvenist norms of Turkish society. On the other hand, the Islamist demand for 'freedom to dress as one wishes', often justified on democratic principles and human-rights arguments, is obviously compatible with the liberal, pluralistic values of many among the elite intellectual groups. Consequently, more than anything else, the headscarf issue was a politically promising rallying point. It effectively functioned as a symbol of movement identity/loyalty; a launching pad for support from outside groups and a platform on which coalitions between political forces of very different and often contradictory worldviews could be formed. Through its selective use and emphasis, the Islamist contingent has demonstrated it is operating within and taking advantage of the norms of democratic politics.

To what extent such proficiency also signals a general willingness by the Islamic opposition to function within the rules of contemporary pluralist democracy is still not clear though. Many signs of the systemic nature of Islamist opposition in Turkey may be discerned, particularly with respect to the traditional conservative Islamist groups that are politically active through the mechanisms of religious parties or have merged with secular establishment political parties. But there is also ground to think that such visible behaviour may be tactical or simply defensive stands by these Islamists groups and individuals. In this context, there needs to be recognized the presence of radical and/or revolutionary Islamist groups that overtly deny the legitimacy of secular democracy (Kazancigil, 1991) and altogether refuse to take part in the politics of the existing system, aiming for its total destruction through either 'political' or 'cultural' revolution.

In Turkish society, militant Islamist groups and organizations who are engaged in aggressive, political activism against the secular state, its institutions and the values and attitudes it advocates are relatively insignificant with regard to their support bases. To the extent they use violence or practise terrorism, these groups appear to face negative reaction not only from non-Islamist sectors of society but also from conventional party and traditional order Islamists alike. In fact, the systemic nature of party Islam is clearly demonstrated in its relationship with some radical and extremist Islamist groups.

For instance, the Welfare Party does have a rather strong support base among the Kurdish population in southeastern Turkey. But in the face of the recent Kurdish challenge to the Turkish state, the mainstream Islamist position, in line with its tradition of refraining from open conflict with the state, has made a point of distancing itself from the Kurdish separatist movement. While some radical Islamist forces of marginal stature have made attempts to gain ground on this issue the WP—which in recent election campaigns has been engaged in a distinct attempt to project a less 'exclusively religious' image and to appeal to non-Islamist groups—has been at pains to distance itself from the Kurdish ethnic identity. The party has refrained from taking any stand other than the conventional 'unitary state', 'national unity' platform in its election campaigns in the southeastern provinces where both radical Kurdish separatist forces and marginal militant Islamist groups were challenging its support (Çakir, 1992).

Radical Islamist intellectual groups and individuals, also quite marginal in terms of their current power base, are none the less visible and articulate in contemporary literary and intellectual circles in Turkey. Today, many Islamist intellectuals engage in rather open dialogue with the secular contingent through the ways and means of academic, political or social interaction such as participation in panel discussions or conferences and the publication of journals and books of quasi-academic nature. Often they utilize the theories and terminology of the secular academe familar to non-Islamist audiences and readers.

Yet, through such shared terminology or communication exchange with the non-Islamists, some very radical discourse on the fundamental irreconcilability of Islam and modernity is often articulated by these intellectuals and consumed by educated youth, particularly in the universities. Potential mobilizing power and the future role of such intellectual elite-based radical Islamist ideology need to be carefully evaluated.[7]

Many Islamist intellectuals often have rather cool relationships with traditional Islamist organizations and groups, (for example, orders) (Güneş-Ayata, 1991; Meeker, 1991). This means that intellectual Islamists, who are dissociated from Islamic orders, have little mass support and consequently less direct political salience in contemporary Turkey where traditional and neo-traditional Sufi orders continue to constitute important power bases of Islamist parties and/or wings of centre–right parties. Such dissociation also accounts for the fact that the traditional Islamist groups are, to a large extent, deprived of intellectual leadership of competitive calibre. The future impact of radical Islamist intellectual discourse on Turkish society will be commensurate with the development of the absorptive capacity of pluralist democratic institutions and the responsiveness of economic measures in the country so far as the needs of the Islamist contingent and the socio-economic strata they represent are concerned. International developments can be expected to influence this picture, too.

The fragmented nature of the Islamist contingent in Turkey, indicated by the variation in their organizational bases and ideological orientations and strategies, is further complicated by the fact that Turkish Islamists in political parties, Sufi orders or intellectual groups are all products of the Turkish experiment with secularism and democracy. Their very being thus reveals an acknowledgement of the secular world and the non-Islamist, nominally Muslim and/or devout majority in this society. Changes in the social, economic and political factors defining the relative position of different classes and groups and the nature of the relationships among them influence the fate of the Islamist movement in Turkish society. In this context, existing sociological and political reality attributes a critical role to the actions and reactions of non-Islamist forces in society.

In the latter part of the 1980s in Turkey, when the ascending discourse of the 'centre' was increasingly formed around a commitment to the ideal of pluralist democracy/civil society, one also observed a partial re-emergence of a unified secularist bloc largely motivated and facilitated by an apprehension or fear of rising Islamic fundamentalism. This development is noteworthy. There was an increasing awareness of the need to maintain a 'countervailing power' against Islamists. This was put into operation not only by the old-guard secularists but also by representatives of those movements pushing hard for the development of pluralist democracy/civil society in Turkey. Changes can be observed in: the discourse of the feminists and women's groups, from earlier quasi-alliance with Islamists in the name of opposing the status quo, to confrontation over the issue of patriarchal domination; in the activities and speeches of some key figures of the metropolitan bourgeoisie who abandoned their conventional strategy of ignoring religious identity and contributed to the formation of associations and civil society organizations in defence of secularist principles; and the over-sensitive treatment of the news of Islamist activities by the influential national press. These all indicate the presence of such a tendency.

Having to exist within a secular state and a polity, alongside the reality of influential non-Islamist forces in society, it is inevitable that the Islamist movement in Turkey interacts with and responds to such development.

Some concluding remarks

Islamists: signs of diversity or uniformity?

Despite their fundamental ideological commitment to the creation of the ideal Islamic society and its state, for the time being most Turkish Islamists continue to reflect a reluctant acceptance of coexistence with the institutions and values of the secular establishment. The boundaries of such reluctant acceptance have never been rigid and have always demonstrated a sensitivity to external forces and a capacity to adapt themselves to surrounding national and international conditions. The changes in the nature of the Islamist movement in Turkey should be evaluated in this light.

In this context developments external to Turkey will, no doubt, also influence the Turkish scene and the Islamists' position in it. Developments in and relations with neighbouring Iran have special salience here. This country's efforts to export the Islamic revolution to secular Turkey, the presence of which was perceived by hard-liners there as a concrete negation of the Islamist ideal, may be expected to decline in consequence of Iran's so-called moderation. Conversely, however, the opening up of 'new frontiers' in the Central Asian Turkic and Muslim republics can be expected to produce new confrontations and competition between Iran and Turkey. The relative strength of the Islamist movements in Turkey is likely to experience gains or loses according to the dynamics of the respective world-views in these regions.

In the recent past, the Turkish state's anti-Saddam position in the Gulf War, and its close alliance with the Western bloc, has also influenced its relationships with Saudi Arabia and Western countries, both having indirect impacts on the Islamist movement at home. It has been speculated that the decline in the number and circulation of Islamist periodicals and journals since the Gulf War has been due to the decrease in the financial support supplied by the Saudi and Gulf State sources to the Islamists in Turkey. While such claims are almost impossible to prove, the position of the Islamist contingent in Turkey with regard to the Gulf War and Turkey's position in it have been interesting. Beyond a vague discourse on the 'regretable nature of a war amongst fellow Muslims', protest at the Turkish state's unabashedly pro-Western policy was hardly as strong as one would expect given the Islamist groups' normal rhetoric on anti-Westernism. Such restraint could be read as another reflection of the crosscutting loyalties experienced by political Islam in Turkey on the national and international levels.

Observers have also attributed the rise of Islamist movements in Turkey in the 1970s and 1980s partly to the public's feeling of resentment and humiliation resulting from the Turks' repudiation by Western Europe (Weiker, 1985). In this context, alliance with the Western bloc in the framework of the Gulf War may be seen as having influenced the national political climate, in the short run, to create a less favourable foundation for Islamist appeals.

The presence of a durable climate of supportive, positive relations with Europe, however, can only be expected to develop on the basis of universally shared principles and values. The ascending ideology of the present decade in Turkey is shaped by pluralist democracy/civil society values and incorporates secular and Islamist contingents in peaceful coexistence. Therefore Islam in Turkey should not be expected to exert a negative force on Turkey's democratization potential and her integration chances with Europe.

The institutional structure of a secular state, the sociological reality of significant non-Islamist population groups, and a working competitive democracy have been important contributions to the outcome in the Turkish case. Developments in recent political and social history indicate that, within this framework, Islamist forces conventionally regarded as elements of anti-democratic, authoritarian tendencies that work to distance Turkey from contemporary Western values and institutions may paradoxically function as (willing or unwilling) agents of democratization, visible signs of pluralism and important components of civil society.

By managing to create a distinct space for themselves in the political arena, dominated almost exclusively by secularist actors in the early years of the Turkish republic, the Islamists in recent years became one of the many visible political movements defining a modern pluralist polity. The recent appearance of alternative dynamics on the national political scene (that is ethnic and Turkic identity questions), and the fact that Islamist groups and views have not so far emerged as representatives or champions of any one of these new vital concerns of Turkish politics may further point to Islamist movements' future identity as non-revolutionary, systemic loci of opposition. However, to what extent this appearance is paralleled by a genuine commitment of the major Islamist forces in society to the principles and norms of pluralist democracy is equally critical. Both the future of the Islamist contingent in Turkey and — more importantly — that of Turkish democracy's attempt to succeed in moving from statist authoritarianism to civil society-based pluralism (Kazancigil, 1991) will be highly influenced by this.

In this chapter, factors such as the fragmented nature of the Islamist contingent, the unique socio-cultural presence of large secular Muslim population groups, the functioning of a political democracy, and an ascending commitment to the ideology of pluralist democracy/civil society by secular groups in the 'centre' were discussed as contributing to the present nature of the Islamist movement in Turkey. These observations may provide bases to evaluate the Turkish Islamist groups at present, as signs of social and cultural diversity and political pluralism more than as likely bases of a serious non-democratic, totalitarian movement arising to impose uniformity on society. The way things stand at the outset of 1990s, there is sufficient cause to be found in political and social developments in Turkey to indicate that Turkey's membership of the 'democratic community of Europe' will hardly be deterred by Islam or Islamists in this society.

However, it should not be overlooked that the economic conditions of the country, particularly the danger of deteriorating income distribution (fuelled by the high rates of inflation and unemployment) remain as non-negligible forces. They have the potential for creating socio-economic circumstances where closer and exclusive ties between the Islamist opposition and poor population groups may be established, providing Islamist forces with the strong power to mobilize economic as well as social protest. International developments concerning relations between Muslim and non-Muslim populations, within Europe and its environs, may also present threats for reversing existing tendencies, for polarizing and sharpening Islamists' identity and relative power position in Turkey.

Notes

1 The National Order Party was established in 1970 by Mr N. Erbakan, an independent deputy from Konya. After its banning in 1972, on the ruling of the Constitutional Court, Erbakan and his associates established the National Salvation Party commonly known to espouse similar religious views. The NSP, however, was formed on legally more secure grounds. From the general elections of 1973, when it recieved 12 per cent of the votes nationally, it became firmly established in the Turkish political scene (Saribay, 1985b; Toprak, 1981). In the following years the NSP, playing a key role in the much fragmented composition of parliamentary politics in Turkey, was the unchanging junior coalition partner in governments formed first by Mr Ecevit, the leader of the social-democratic Republican People's Party (RPP) and then twice by Mr Demirel, the leader of the centre-right Justice Party (JP). The latter two coalition governments, which also included the ultra-right Nationalist Action Party (NAP), were popularly known as the Nationalist Front. They provided the NSP with an unprecedented base of social and political legitimation as well as possibilities of political patronage to its supporters and activists through state-controlled economic and bureaucratic resources. Large-scale recruitment from the Islamist population groups to the ranks of the state bureaucracy, and noticable increases in the numbers of second-level religious educational institutions (Imam Hatip Schools) alongside the secular educational institutions of the Republic emerged as hallmarks of the Islamist advance in Turkey during the 1970s.

2 For an illustration of the political views and religious stand taken by the centre-right TPP, and its leader Mr Demirel, during the 1980s, see Acar (1991b).

3 The Welfare Party is the Islamist political party established in 1983 when the three-year ban on political activity imposed by the military junta in 1980 was lifted and a return to parliamentary politics started in Turkey. It was formed as the heir-apparent of the former NSP abolished by the junta. The WP developed on the more or less same religious political platform and was based on similar cadres. Mr Erbakan, the leader of the two former Islamist parties, NOP and NSP, officially became the chairman of the WP in 1987 after the legal ban on his political activities — along with other former leaders of other parties — was lifted through a national referendum, and court proceedings on his allegedly improper activities as leader of NSP ended with his acquital. The party received 7 per cent of votes nationally in 1987, while elections held in 1991, revealed 16.7 per cent support for the joint ticket of the alliance established by WP and the ultra-right Nationalist Work Party. The alliance, formed prior to the national elections, has since been dissolved.

4 The Alevi are an Anatolian Turkish sect, a variant of Shia, which claims approximately 20 per cent of the population in Turkey. Having lived with the Sunni majority in peaceful co-existence throught the Republican era, the Alevi, religiously less conservative than the Sunni Muslims, have generally been staunch supporters of republican secularism, as well as the statist social-democratic tradition of RPP and SPP. In the latter part of 1970s, some incidents of Alevi–Sunni conflict erupted in violent form in a few central Anatolian provinces. The 1980s has witnessed an increased awareness and demand for recognition of Alevi religious and cultural identity.

5 Similar treatment by the state can be observed with respect to patriarchal family norms and traditional gender roles in Turkey, too. In the Turkish Republic, traditional, patriarchal norms pertaining to gender roles were also allowed to continue and flourish in the family context simultaneously, as the state took very radical actions and created a politico-legal order based on the equality of men and women pertaining almost exclusively to the public sphere (Kağitcibaşi, 1990; Acar, 1991a; Acar, forthcoming).

6 It has, however, been pointed out that as 'Kemalist Turkey became more secularized the bonds of Islamic identity and solidarity . . . [of] other ethnic groups to the state loosened' and at least one ethnic, nationalist rebellion of the times the Shaykh Said revolt of 1925, made use of the symbols and organizational framework of the Nakşibendi order (Ahmad, 1991).

7 For a summary and analysis of the views of some prominent Islamist intellectuals see; M. Meeker (1991); B. Toprak (1987) and N. Göle (1991).

References

Acar, Feride (1991a), 'Women in the Ideology of Islamic Revivalism in Turkey: Three Islamic Women's Journals' in R. Tapper (ed.), *Islam in Modern Turkey: Religion, Politics and Literature in a Secular State*, London, I. B. Tauris and Co. Ltd., 280–303.

Acar, Feride (1991b), 'True Path Party' in M. Heper and J. M. Landau (eds), *Political Parties and Democracy in Turkey*, London, I. B. Tauris and Co. Ltd., 188–201.

Acar, Feride (forthcoming), 'The Gold Bracelet Syndrome: Culture, Social Change and Women in Turkish Universities' in S. Lie and L. Malik (eds) *Women in Higher Education*, London, Kogan Page, (forthcoming).

Ahmad, Feroz (1991), 'Politics and Islam in Modern Turkey', *Middle Eastern Studies*, 27/1, 3–22.

Akşit, Bahattin (1991), 'Islamic Education in Turkey: Medrese Reform in Late Ottoman Times and Imam-Hatip Schools in the Republic' in R. Tapper (ed.), *Islam in Modern Turkey, Religion, Politics and Literature in a Secular State*, London, I. B. Tauris and Co. Ltd., 145–170.

Ayata, Sencer (1991), 'Traditional Sufi Orders on the Periphery: Kadiri and Nakşibendi Islam in Konya and Trabzon' in R. Tapper (ed.), *Islam in Modern Turkey: Religion, Politics and Literature in a Secular State*, London, I. B. Tauris and Co. Ltd., 223–53.

Ayata, Sencer, (forthcoming), 'The Rise of Islamic Fundamentalism and the Institutional Framework' in A. Eralp. M. Tunay and B. Yeşilada (eds), *Socio-economic and Political Transformations in Turkey in the 1980's*, New York, Praeger.

Çakır, Ruşen (1990), *Ayet ve Slogan: Turkiye'de Islami Oluşumlar*, Istanbul, Metis Yay.

Çakır, Ruşen (1992), 'Islamcıların Gündemini de PKK belirliyor' *Birikim* 33 January, 27–31.

Eroğul, Cem (1970), *Demokrat Parti*, Ankara, SBF Yayınları.

Göle, Nilüfer (1991), *Modern Mahrem*, Istanbul, Metis Yay.

Güneş-Ayata, Ayşe (1990), 'Class and Clientelism in Republican Peoples Party' in Sirman Nukhet and Andrew Finkle (eds), *Turkish State, Turkish Society*, London, Routledge, 159–183.

Güneş-Ayata, Ayşe (1991), 'Pluralism Versus Authoritarianism: Political Ideas in

Two Islamic Publications' in R. Tapper (ed.), *Islam in Modern Turkey: Religion, Politics and Literature in a Secular State*, London, I. B. Tauris and Co. Ltd., 254–79.

Heper, Metin (1980), 'Center-Periphery in the Ottoman Empire with Special Reference to the Nineteenth Century' *International Political Science Review*, 1, 81–105.

Karpat, Kemal (1959) *Turkey's Politics: The Transition to a multi-party system*, Princeton, NJ, Princeton University Press.

Kazancıgil, Ali (1991), 'Democracy in Muslim Lands: Turkey in Comparative Perspective', *International Journal of Social Sciences*, 43, 343–60.

Kağıtçıbaşı, Çiğdem (1982), 'Introduction' in Çiğdem Kağıtçıbaşı (ed.), *Sex Roles, Family and Community in Turkey*, Bloomington, Indiana University Press.

Kağıtçıbaşı, Çiğdem (1990), 'Women's Intra-Family Status, Education and Employment in Turkey' in *Proceedings of the Conference Improving Employment Prospects for Women in a Changing Society*, Ankara, Turkish Employment Organization and OECD, 107–21.

Lewis, Bernard, (1968), *The Emergence of Modern Turkey*, Oxford, Oxford University Press.

Lewis, Geoffrey (1988), 'The Present State of the Turkish Republic' *Asian Affairs*, 75/3, 261–72.

Mardin, Şerif (1973), 'Center-Periphery Relations: A Key to Turkish Politics', *Daedalus*, 102, 169–90.

Mardin Şerif (1982), 'Bediuzzaman Said Nursi (1873–1960) The Shaping of a Vocation' in F. Davis (ed.), *Religious Organization and Religious Experience*, London, Academic Press.

Mardin, Şerif (1983), 'Religion and Politics in Modern Turkey', in James P. Piscatori (ed.), *Islam in the Political Process*, Cambridge, Cambridge University Press, 138–59.

Mardin, Şerif (1989a), 'Culture and Religion Towards the Year 2000' in *Turkey in the Year 2000*, Turkish Political Science Association, Ankara, Sevinç Matbaası, 163–86.

Mardin, Şerif (1989b), *Religion and Social Charge in Modern Turkey: The Case of Bediuzzaman Said Nursi*, New York, State University of New York Press.

Mardin, Şerif, (1991), 'The Nakşibendi Order in Turkish History' in R. Tapper (ed.), *Islam in Modern Turkey: Religion, Politics and Literature in a Secular State*, London, I. B. Tauris and Co. Ltd., 121–42.

Meeker, Michael (1991), 'The New Muslim Intellecturals in the Republic of Turkey' in R. Tapper (ed.), *Islam in Modern Turkey: Religion, Politics and Literature in a Secular State*, London, I. B. Tauris and Co. Ltd., 189–219.

Özbudun, Ergun (1981), 'Turkey: The Politics of Clientelism' in S. N. Eisenstadt and R. Lemarchand (eds), *Political Clientelism, Patronage and Development*, Beverly Hills, Sage.

Özbudun, Ergun (1987), 'Turkey' in E. Özbudun and M. Weiner (eds), *Competitive Elections in Developing Countries*, Durham, Duke University Press.

Özbudun, Ergun (1988), 'Turkey: Crisis, Interruptions and Requibriations' in L. Diamond, J. L. Linz and S. M. Lipset (eds), *Democracy in Developing Countries, Vol. 3 Asia*, Boulder, Lynne Rienner, 187–229.

Saribay, Ali Yaşar (1985a), 'Türkiye'de Siyasal Modernleşme ve Islam', *Toplum ve Bilim*, 29–30.

Saribay, Ali Yaşar (1985b), *Türkiye'de Modernleşme, Din ve Parti Politikası: MSP Örnek Olayı*, Istanbul, Alan Yayıncılık.

Saribay, Ali Yaşar (1991), 'The Democratic Party, 1946–1960' in M. Heper and

J. Landau (eds), *Political Parties and Democracy in Turkey*, London, I. B. Tauris and Co. Ltd., 119–33.

Sayarı Binnaz (1979), 'Türkiye'de Dinin Denetim Islevi' *A. Ü. Siyasal Bilgiler Fakültesi Dergisi*, **33**, (1–2), 173–85.

Sayarı, Sabri (1975) 'Some notes on the beginning of Mass Political Participation in Turkey' in E. D. Akarlı with G. Ben-Dor (eds), *Political Participation in Turkey: Historical Background and Present Problems*, Istanbul, Boğazici University Publishers.

Şaylan Gencay (1987), *Islamiyet ve Siyaset Türkiye Örneği*, Ankara, V. Yayınları.

Sheppard, William E. (1987), 'Islam and Ideology: Towards a Typology', *International Journal of Middle Eastern Studies*, **19**, 307–36.

Sunar, Ilkay and Binnaz Toprak (1983), 'Islam in Politics: The Case of Turkey', *Government and Opposition*, **18**, 421–41.

Sunar, Ilkay and Sabri Sayarı (1986). 'Democracy in Turkey, Problems with Prospects' in G. O'Donnell, P. C. Schmitter and L. Whitehead (eds), *Transitions From Authoritarian Rule: Southern Europe*, Baltimore and London, The Johns Hopkins University Press, 165–86.

Tapper, Richard and Nancy Tapper (1987), '"Thank God We're Secular!"', Aspects of Fundamentalism in a Turkish Town' in L. Capan (ed.), *Aspects of Religious Fundamentalism*, London, MacMillan, 51–78.

Toprak, Binnaz (1981), *Islam and Political Development in Turkey*, Leiden, Brill.

Toprak, Binnaz (1987), 'Islamic Intellectuals of the 1980's in Turkey', *Current Turkish Thought*, **62**, Istanbul, Redhouse Yayınevi.

Toprak, Binnaz (1988), 'The State, Politics and Religion in Turkey' in M. Heper and A. Evin (eds), *State, Democracy and the Military: Turkey in the 1980's*, Berlin and New York, de Gruyter.

Weiker, Walter F. (1985), 'Turkey, Middle East and Islam' *Middle East Review*, Spring, 27–32.

Yeşilda, Birol (1987), 'New Political Parties and the Problems of Development in Turkey', *New Perspectives on Turkey*, **1**, 35–51.

Conclusions

10
Conclusions: looking to the future

C. Balkir and A. Williams

Writing in mid-1992 the future of Europe itself looks very uncertain, let alone that of Turkey's relationships with Europe. The seemingly inevitable shift towards political union has at least been deflected by the result of the Danish referendum on the Maastricht agreement. There is also a long and growing list of applicants for membership, and decisions will have to be taken about these in the near future. The most that can be ventured at this stage, therefore, is to suggest that there are four hypothetical models for the future of international institutional arrangements within Europe. These are: first, the transformation of the European Economic Space (EFTA and the EC) into an enlarged Community, but probably excluding Iceland and possibly excluding Norway; second, the addition of some Central and Eastern European countries to this former group — these are most likely to be Poland, Hungary and Czechoslovakia (as a whole, or parts of); third, the additional inclusion of most of the other Eastern European countries and of some of the former Soviet republics, most likely the Baltic states, and perhaps Russia, Byelorussia and Ukraine; and fourth, the inclusion of some of the southern and eastern republics of the former Soviet Union.

Which, if any, of these futures lies in store for Europe is a matter of speculation and it is difficult to suggest any firm predictions. Here it is necessary only to note some of the implications for Turkey. Arguably, the larger the Community then the greater the diversity and the easier it will be to accommodate Turkey with its, partly, differentiated economic, social and political structures. It can also be hypothesised that the larger the Community, the more likely it is that 'widening rather than deepening' will be applied to EC institutions, and that there will be greater scope to accept member states with more variable features. Against this, it can be argued that the larger the Community then the more likely there is to be 'queue shuffling'; the early 1990s have already demonstrated that the appearance of potential new members, such as Poland, has the effect of relegating serious consideration of the Turkish application. There is also the argument that the larger the Community the more likely it is to include proportionally more countries making demands on structural-assistance funds. This would have implications for any additional members.

Turkey's acceptance as a full member of the EC will not depend solely on external conditions. Also important will be domestic economic, political and social circumstances. The 1990 Commission opinion on the 1987 application charted out some of the critical issues. These include sustaining high growth rates during the 1990s so that there is some convergence towards EC GDP levels in absolute and per capita terms. There is also a question about Turkey's ability to move to greater economic openness, and in particular its commitment to completing the customs union by 1996. There are doubts as to whether many sectors are sufficiently competitive to withstand the economic shock that this may entail. Equally, however, there are some Turkish sectors — notably textiles and clothing — which would stand to benefit from greater mutual opening of trade between Turkey and the EC.

There are grave structural problems to be overcome if the Turkish economy is to converge with those of the EC. While the precise outcome of the economic and monetary union programme agreed at Maastricht is in doubt, there seems little question but that economic pressures will lead to some form of increased monetary co-ordination in the EC. With an inflation rate of 71 per cent at the end of 1991, a debt service ratio of 28 per cent, a foreign-debt burden of around $43 billion, and a massive budget deficit, the challenges for Turkey are enormous (*Financial Times*, 21 May 1991). Moreover, they can only be seriously tackled by also facing up to highly sensitive issues of taxation reform, reduced state support for inefficient nationalised industries, and delays in much needed infrastructural developments. Any government — even one with a massive parliamentary majority — would find it politically difficult to impose the painful adjustments demanded by such a programme.

There are also political issues on the agenda. Twelve years after the 1980 military intervention, Turkish democracy seems more securely set on the pathway to a relatively stable pluralist democracy. Thus far the political system has proven robust enough to accommodate the 1991 electoral victory of the True Path Party and the return to power of Mr Demirel. It has also accommodated the division of power between Mr Demirel as prime minister and Mr Özal as president. Moreover, the Demirel government has instigated important constitutional reforms, improvements in human rights and police practices, and has at least sought a negotiated political solution to the Kurdish question. There is no doubt that EC leaders will be looking for convergence in terms of these indicators as well as in terms of economic ones. The Kurdish issues may prove the most intransigent given popular sentiment in this ethnic group and in Turkish society at large. Yet, this is likely to be an issue of increasing concern to the EC, not least because of the tragic experience of the former Yugoslavia which has led the Community to take a firmer line on the rights of ethnic groups. Finally, there is the issue of accepting a country where Islam is the creed of the majority into a

Community which is overwhelmingly Christian in culture. While the Commission opinion studiously avoided bringing this issue into the open, there are plenty of populist politicians in the member states who are keen to do so. Acar's chapter in this volume makes it clear that Islam is a diverse culture, and Turkey has proven that a secular state where the majority adhere to the Islamic faith is practicable. But despite these objective facts, the Turkish membership does face the obstacle of northern European xenophobia.

The third element in the equation which will determine the outcome of the Turkish application is the domestic political situation in the member states. The Community is not a monolithic political body, or even a federal body. Rather it is still, in most respects, based on intergovernmentalism. There are already varying shades of enthusiasm among the member states for the Turkish application: these range from the modest encouragement of the British government to the hostility of the Greek government. The key player, however, is probably Germany. In the early 1990s events in Germany probably moved against Turkey; among these were the higher than anticipated costs of unification, the rise of the new right, and hostility to growing numbers of refugees which spilled over to reinforce existing antagonisms to Turkish immigrants. The Turkish application is therefore best described as being in the balance, at least in terms of medium-term acceptance.

While the issue of Turkish membership is an important question for the 1990s, it is not the only feature of Turkey–Europe relations. Turkey is surrounded by obstacles and opportunities in Eastern and Central Europe, in the former Soviet republics, and in the Middle East. New political relationships can be formed in Europe outside of the EC and, indeed, outside of Europe. In a sense these have lessened the imperative for full membership of the EC. There are attractive alternative roles available such as being a regional power or the principal ally of the United States or the EC in relation to the surrounding region. A number of Turkish politicians, including Mr Demirel, have been discussing these alternatives in recent years. However, there is one virtual certainty to be faced. The world economy has been crystalising around three poles: Japan Incorporated, the United States-dominated Americas, and the Single Market European Economy. Other poles may be added in future depending on developments in the former Soviet Union and China. The EC is the only pole to which, realistically, Turkey can gravitate. Therefore, while the question of Turkey's relationship with Europe may change in form and strength, it is unlikely to go away. It is vital to the future of both Turkey and Europe.

Index